HOOSIERS
ON THE HOME FRONT

★ ★ ★

HOOSIERS
ON THE HOME FRONT

★ ★ ★

EDITED BY

DAWN BAKKEN

INDIANA UNIVERSITY PRESS

This book is a publication of

Indiana University Press
Office of Scholarly Publishing
Herman B Wells Library 350
1320 East 10th Street
Bloomington, Indiana 47405 USA

iupress.org

Manufactured in the United States of America

First printing 2022

Library of Congress Cataloging-in-Publication Data

Names: Bakken, Dawn E., editor.
Title: Hoosiers on the home front / edited by Dawn Bakken.
Other titles: Indiana magazine of history.
Description: Bloomington, Indiana : Indiana University Press, [2022]
Identifiers: LCCN 2022011608 (print) | LCCN 2022011609 (ebook) | ISBN 9780253063458 (hardback) | ISBN 9780253063465 (paperback) | ISBN 9780253063472 (ebook)
Subjects: LCSH: Indiana—History, Military. | Indiana—History—Civil War, 1861-1865. | World War, 1939-1945—Indiana.
Classification: LCC F526 .H65 2022 (print) | LCC F526 (ebook) | DDC 355.009772—dc23/eng/20220328
LC record available at https://lccn.loc.gov/2022011608
LC ebook record available at https://lccn.loc.gov/2022011609

CONTENTS

HOOSIERS
ON THE HOME FRONT

★ ★ ★

Introduction

DAWN BAKKEN, EDITOR

THE FIRST ISSUE OF THE *INDIANA MAGAZINE OF HISTORY* (*IMH*) appeared in print in 1905. The *IMH*, a peer-reviewed journal sponsored by the Indiana University (IU) Department of History, is one of the oldest continuously published state history journals and now operates as part of IUScholarWorks. The journal publishes articles by academic scholars and independent researchers; its archive is also filled with original diaries, memoirs, and letters. Many of the articles and the primary source documents treat the subject of Hoosiers on the battlefront—from territorial days to the twentieth century—and their loved ones back home.[1]

This collection showcases eleven *IMH* articles on the Indiana home front. Readers will meet, among others, Joshua Jones of the Nineteenth Indiana Volunteer Infantry and his wife, Celia; Attia Porter, a young resident of Corydon, Indiana, writing to her cousin about Morgan's Raid; Civil War and World War I veterans who came into conflict over the Indianapolis 500 and Memorial Day observances; Virginia Mayberry, a wife and mother on the World War II home front; and university students and professors—including antiwar activist Howard Zinn and conservative writer R. Emmett Tyrrell Jr.—clashing over the Vietnam War.

Wars are fought on the home front as well as the battlefront. Spouses, family, friends, and communities are called on to sacrifice and persevere in the face of a changed reality. Individuals and societies seek to understand the meaning and purpose of the conflict; they often disagree over what constitutes patriotism and loyalty to one's country in a time of war; in the aftermath of war, they look for ways to honor and commemorate their loved ones.

The Civil War was a test of endurance and loyalty for both men and women. Newspapers, sermons, poems, and songs affirmed that, as J. Matthew Gallman puts it, "patriotic women sacrificed and suffered."[2] Women's duty was to give up their men to fight for the Union and then to support them. Women helped run family farms and businesses, managed money and collected debts, and raised children. They rolled bandages and formed societies to raise funds for the care of wounded soldiers. Women waited for news of their loved ones, carried in letters that might take weeks to reach them.[3]

In July 1861, twenty-three-year-old Joshua Jones enlisted in the Nineteenth Indiana Volunteer Infantry. Two years before his enlistment, he had married Celia Gibson; the couple settled on a farm near Muncie, and their son, George, was born in June 1860. Joshua began writing to his wife in August 1861, as his regiment trained for battle. Celia preserved his letters and handed them down through her family, but her letters to her husband did not survive. Nevertheless, a picture of Celia's life emerges from Joshua's words.[4]

Families on the home front longed for any news. Joshua, like so many other soldiers, tried to share some part of his experiences but hesitated to share too much of the horrors of war. He wrote in September 1862, after the Second Battle of Bull Run, of how he had been forced to listen for incoming cannon balls and shells, "fall[ing] down when they bursted to keep from getting killed." But he added, "I would not had you or Mother to of known Just my situation for nothing in the world while you was going about the house or in your bed asleep."

Many of the letters Celia received dealt primarily with family and business. Like other rural women, Celia took on responsibility for running the farm and finding workers in the absence of her husband's labor. Joshua tasked Celia with dealing wisely with the money he sent home, paying the family's debts, and transacting business. He also sent instruction on how to raise their son: "I want our little boy to be learned to do as he is told and be mannerly to evry body. I do not want to See a bad little boy like Some Children when I Come home."

Joshua's letters reveal that the couple loved each other deeply and longed for the day when he would return home to family life. Celia must have written to Joshua about the pain it caused her to see people around her who seemed unaffected by the war: "You spoke of your feelings when Seeing others Sporting around home. . . . Often do I think of the hapy days when I Could Sit down to Breakfast with you . . . and laugh while we was eating and talking to each other as hapy as too kings. My dear I can See now that we lived as pleasant a life as any too on earth."

In late September 1862, Celia received a letter from one of Joshua's commanding officers. Written just after the campaign at Antietam, it gave her the news no wife wanted to hear: her husband had been shot and his leg amputated. Lt. George W. Green conveyed Joshua's reassurance that he was recovering and Celia might "expect him home some time this fall." Celia must have written back immediately, but her letter never reached her husband. One of the last two letters she preserved came from regimental surgeon J. N. Green: "I deeply regret to iform you that your husband is no more."

Celia and her son continued to live in the Muncie area after Joshua's death. She married again in 1903, at the age of sixty-five, and after losing her second husband in 1929, she lived with her son, George, and his family.

Life on the Civil War home front brought a different kind of challenge for many Indiana families. Political discord was rife in the Hoosier state well before Republican governor Oliver P. Morton, a staunch supporter of President Abraham Lincoln and the war effort, put out his first call for recruits. Hoosier Democrats believed in the Union, but many felt that the best way to preserve it was to allow Southerners to keep their slaves and maintain their way of life. Democrats railed against Lincoln's declaration of war and the draft, his Emancipation Proclamation, and the curtailment of civil liberties by the governor and military commanders. Some formed secret societies, such as the Knights of the Golden Circle, who attempted to foment rebellion against the state government.[5] Others were no less vocal about their opposition but confined their dissent to letters published in sympathetic newspapers and heated discussions among friends and family members.

Members of the staunchly Democratic Demaree family—twelve siblings and their spouses—lived in Johnson County, Indiana, and in the neighboring state of Kentucky, corresponding frequently on everyday matters, such as the weather and crops as well as politics and the war. Many Hoosiers had relatives in Kentucky, a Union state that in various ways stood as an uneasy border between the North and the Confederacy. For Indiana Democrats opposed to Morton's and Lincoln's conduct of the war, family ties between the two states often made for difficult politics.[6]

A series of family letters survive, all written to George Whitefield Demaree, a Kentucky Democrat who held strong sympathies with the South and supported states' rights and slavery. In 1856, as western territories struggled over allowing slavery in their soon-to-be states, the family shared news of a Kansas relative who had "voted the proslavery ticket" in the new territory. William Shuck, the husband of George's sister Susan, also told George about the victory of Democrat Ashbel Willard over Republican Oliver P. Morton in Indiana's gubernatorial election: "We beat the [b]lack republicans abolitionis Negro Steal[e]rs."

Eight years later, in October 1864, Peter Demaree wrote to George about the presidential campaign, predicting Lincoln's reelection and declaring that "the Sun of American liberty is a bout Seting never to Raise a gain." Like many fellow Democrats, the Demarees also opposed the federal draft, instituted after the Enrollment Act of 1863. As J. Matthew Gallman notes, Republicans and War Democrats who supported the draft viewed it as an opportunity for draftees to show their bravery and their loyalty to the Union.[7] In stark contrast, the Demarees viewed the draft as a violation of states' rights and individual liberty, and they proudly told Kentucky relatives that the family had pitched in to help thirty men in their township avoid the draft by paying substitutes.

In a letter written after the Union victory in 1865, Shuck expressed the family's sympathy for defeated Southerners: "There case is deploreabel in the extreme. ef they could be allowed to return home in peace & follow there daily occupation with there slaves around them they would be doing wel."

There is no indication in the Demaree letters that anyone joined the Knights of the Golden Circle or a similar society, but at least one member of the Kentucky branch of the family took an active role opposing Lincoln. Brother Samuel joined the Confederate army and, before he was captured and imprisoned, rode with John Hunt Morgan through Kentucky into Indiana and Ohio. Morgan's Raid was the only major incursion of Confederate troops into Indiana, and perhaps because of that fact, it still looms large in the state's history.

On the night of July 7, 1863, Morgan and about twenty-five hundred Confederate cavalry crossed the river from Kentucky and began their raid through the towns and farms of southern Indiana. They stole food and horses as they rode through the countryside. On July 9, they overpowered the state militia defending Corydon and took possession of the town, pillaging stores for money and goods and demanding cash in return for not burning shops, mills, and homes. As Morgan moved into Ohio, Union troops followed, sometimes creating rumors among terrified civilians that another Confederate attack was imminent. Middleton Robertson was a Jefferson County farm boy in 1863 but vividly recalled many decades later "something that happened a few days after Morgan had gone out of the state. Some men came along, riding fast and furious past my Uncle's place, pausing just long enough to tell us that the Confederate leader, General Forrest, had destroyed Paris [Kentucky] by fire and was coming our way, burning buildings and killing men." The troops turned out to be Union soldiers, but Northern troops commandeered supplies as well, in addition to taking the few horses that farmers had managed to hide from the Confederates.[8]

In the wake of the raiders, Simeon Wolfe, the editor of the *Corydon Weekly Democrat*, reported that "a vast amount of damage by horse-stealing and other plundering has been done which it is impossible for us to detail at the present time." Town residents wrote to their friends and relatives about the battle. Young Attia Porter informed her cousin Private John C. Andrews that "we have had rather exciting times in Indiana." At first, her letter made light of recent events—"the battle raged violently for *thirty* minutes, just think of it!"—but then Attia admitted that the July day had been "the awfullest day I ever passed in my life" because of rumors (untrue) that had reached the family of her father being shot by the Confederates.[9]

Five days after Morgan and his men left Corydon, Wolfe estimated "the loss to our citizens at the least at $100,000." It would not be until 1867, two years after the end of the war, that some final reckoning of Hoosier losses took place. The state General Assembly formed a commission to investigate the claims of southern Indiana citizens related to their losses—to both Confederate and Union forces—during Morgan's Raid. Stephen Rockenbach has studied the 468 claims, totaling more than $86,000, filed by Harrison County residents with the commission. He discovered a tortuous history that continued for two decades through the state legislature and the federal quartermasters' office, exemplified by the 1869 session of the Indiana Senate, where lawmakers argued as to whether Morgan should be referred to as a general or as a marauder, disputed the state's responsibility to pay damages committed by federal troops, and ended the session with no funds allocated.[10]

The shadow of the Civil War loomed over Indiana, and the nation, for many decades and in many ways. Caroline Janney writes that "veterans worked tirelessly to assure that the Union memory would neither be forgotten nor eclipsed by that of their former foes. Too many lives had been lost for them to do otherwise."[11]

In 1866, a group of Union veterans formed the Grand Army of the Republic (GAR), an organization dedicated to ensuring lasting memory of soldiers' sacrifice for the Union and to advocating on behalf of veterans. The most enduring legacy of the GAR was Memorial Day, which set aside May 31 every year as a day of remembrance and solemn commemoration.

By the 1880s, every northern city and town conducted Decoration Day ceremonies on May 31. Bands played, politicians offered speeches, and children placed flowers on soldiers' graves. The GAR issued manuals suggesting appropriate rituals for the solemn day. Then in 1911, on a newly built automobile racetrack on the western outskirts of Indianapolis, Memorial Day in Indiana changed. From its inaugural year, the Indianapolis 500 was a massive success. The 1913 race drew a crowd of one hundred thousand spectators—and the race was scheduled to take place every year on May 31. Members of the GAR were outraged at what they viewed as sacrilege. Controversy continued for years; letters to the editor in local newspapers argued vociferously for and against this new kind of Memorial Day celebration. In 1923, the state General Assembly passed the Moorhead Memorial Day bill, which would have prohibited all commercial sports events on the day. However, as Nicholas Sacco discovered, when the GAR sought support for the bill from World War I veterans—members of the new American Legion—they found considerable opposition instead. Members of sixteen Legion posts from central Indiana signed a letter published in the *Indianapolis News,* stating that Indiana residents did not need "legislative direction in their private observance of Memorial Day." Governor Warren McCray vetoed the legislation, and the Indianapolis 500 continued to be run on Memorial Day.[12]

Definitions of patriotism and loyalty are frequently contested in the midst of wars and in their wake. When the United States entered World War I, many people began to look differently at their German American neighbors. Propaganda was painting German forces as slavering, murderous beasts; any promotion of the German language and German culture became suspect.

Indiana had seen widespread German immigration since before the Civil War, but in the decades following the war, Germans came to comprise a significant percentage of the state's immigrant population.[13] Indianapolis was among the Hoosier cities boasting a large and active German American community: the 1910 census recorded that almost half of the residents of foreign birth or parentage were German American. The city's Männerchor was nationally known; the Indianapolis Turnverein served as one of the city's largest athletic and social clubs. City residents had their choice of several German-language newspapers, and the public school system offered a wide selection of courses on German language and culture from elementary grades through high school.

Then in 1917, the United States entered into the war in Europe. Fidelity to the German language and German culture looked, to many Americans, like loyalty to the enemy. Paul Ramsey has traced the progression of anti-German sentiment through the Indianapolis schools from 1917 to 1919.[14] In 1917, the Indiana State Teachers' Association affirmed "the old ideals of American life and patriotism" while simultaneously decrying "the German rulers" who had "filled our lands with spies." In January 1918, the school board abolished the teaching of German in elementary schools; by early 1919, two separate bills in the state legislature effectively ended the teaching of German in the city's schools for the duration of the war.

Only two decades after the end of World War I, the United States watched another war spread across Europe. Virginia Trickey was a journalism student at IU when she and her sorority sisters heard about the Munich Pact on the day their sorority rush began.[15] Virginia graduated in 1941 and went to work writing for the company newsletter at L. S. Ayres department store in Indianapolis. She volunteered at the local United Service Organizations (USO) when the United States entered the war and took the civil service exam in hopes of joining the Women's Auxiliary Army Corps. Virginia had met Joseph Mayberry while working at Ayres, and by spring 1942, the two were considering marriage. Joe was drafted into the army; Virginia gave up her civil service appointment to the War Department in Washington, DC; and the couple married in August, Virginia wearing "a new gingham suit" she bought at Ayres. They lived briefly in a tiny apartment in Indianapolis, Virginia working in a defense plant. Then Joe headed for officer training in Maryland, and a pregnant Virginia returned home to live with her parents.

After Joe finished his training, Virginia Mayberry became one of the tens of thousands of wives who followed their husbands from one posting to another, back and forth across the country. As Emily Yellin notes, the women were often referred to, somewhat disparagingly, as "camp followers."[16] But, as Mayberry's memoir reveals, women made substantial sacrifices to keep their families together. The first years of the Mayberrys' marriage involved a series of moves, as far east as Cincinnati and as far west as Great Falls, Montana.[17] The couple struggled to find decent housing and often moved at least once within a town to find better accommodations. "In three and one-half years of marriage we had made twelve moves," Virginia stated matter-of-factly. She traveled with her baby (later with two children) on trains and buses to catch up to her husband as he was transferred from post to post. Forty years after the couple returned to Indiana and settled down in peacetime, Virginia remembered her time as a "draftee's wife" not for its frustrations and difficulties but as "an adventure."

The home front of World War II America looked very different for Japanese Americans. Prejudice against Japanese Americans flared in the aftermath of Pearl Harbor. In February 1942, President Franklin D. Roosevelt issued Executive Order 9066, authorizing the War Department to forcibly relocate Japanese residents, regardless of their citizenship status, to detention camps.

Thousands of young Japanese Americans found themselves expelled from or unable to gain admittance to most universities and colleges, particularly those in the West. Many applied to midwestern and eastern institutions, hoping to continue their education. A few midwestern universities and colleges decided to admit Japanese Americans, but as Eric Langowski has discovered, IU was one of the institutions that denied admission to Japanese Americans during World War II.[18]

When IU began receiving applications from Japanese American students in 1942, university administrators turned to the board of trustees for a definitive admissions policy, and in their May 9, 1942, meeting, the board took up the question. Trustees and university president Herman B Wells discussed practical issues: Would admitting more out-of-state students affect in-state admissions? Would the presence of Japanese Americans on campus cause tensions? Then the board president, Ora Wildermuth, set a different defining issue for the discussion: whether Japanese Americans were capable of loyalty to the United States. He expressed his opinion, shared by other trustees, that Japanese Americans could not be trusted: "I can't believe that any Japanese, no matter where he was born, is anything but a Japanese." As the trustees discussed whether the admissions ban should apply to Indiana residents of Japanese descent, Wildermuth added that he feared "that any Jap would get into subversive activity whenever he would have a chance."[19] Wells concluded the discussion with his opinion that admitting any Japanese Americans might lead to tensions and potential "disturbances" on campus. The board of trustees voted unanimously to deny admission to Japanese Americans.

The admissions ban remained in place at IU until honorably discharged Japanese American veterans began to apply to universities across the country, including IU. The board lifted the ban on honorably discharged Japanese Americans in December 1944; they lifted the ban on all Japanese Americans in September 1945. Not until fall 1946 did Japanese American students return to Bloomington.

By the mid-1960s, as the Vietnam War dragged on and Americans saw a war televised to their homes each night on the news, the country fractured over support of or opposition to the war. College campuses were often centers of protest, even in the conservative Hoosier state.[20]

In Bloomington, students and faculty at IU sharply divided over support for the war. In fall 1967, antiwar student groups were planning an October 30 protest over the university's allowing Dow Chemical (the makers of napalm) to recruit on campus. Then the Convocations Committee announced that they had invited Secretary of State Dean Rusk to speak at the university auditorium on October 30. In response to faculty and student objections to that invitation, the committee invited historian and antiwar activist Howard Zinn to speak on campus later in the semester.

Zinn had published *Vietnam: The Logic of Withdrawal* in March and had become one of the most outspoken and well-known opponents of the war. Alex Lichtenstein has transcribed a portion of his previously unpublished speech, written as a direct response to Rusk.[21] After detailing his objections to the war and the government's conduct of it, Zinn spoke about the concepts of loyalty and patriotism: "I think we owe loyalty to our fellow Americans, who are in danger of being killed by the incompetence of the government. . . . Patriotism isn't blind support of the government, and it's not blind allegiance to the flag. It's support for the people of the country, and for the principles that the nation is supposed to stand for. And therefore, patriotism may require opposing the government at certain times."

Photographs of the crowd that met Dean Rusk's visit to IU show some students holding signs that read "Stop the War" and others carrying signs calling for "Victory in Vietnam." Opposition to the war was widespread, but it was by no means the majority stance on campus. Conservative Republican groups drew widespread support from students and faculty who believed in President Richard Nixon and the policies of his administration. Based on newspaper accounts and university records, as well as interviews, Jason Lantzer has discovered that "the other side of campus" contributed a number of important leaders to the national conservative movement.[22]

Student organizations, including the IU chapter of Young Americans for Freedom and the Conservative League and its Student Committee for Victory in Vietnam, promoted conservative representation in student government and advocated for support of the war and US troops and against the spread of communism. IU graduates who went on to play important national roles in the conservative movement of the 1970s and beyond included Tom Huston, who became an associate counsel in the Nixon administration; Phil Crane, who served Illinois in the US House of Representatives from 1969 to 2004; Paul Helmke, who served three terms as mayor of Fort Wayne, Indiana; and R. Emmett Tyrrell Jr., an IU graduate who in 1967 began a small local publication titled *The Alternative*. The publication grew into the nationally influential *American Spectator* and moved its headquarters to Washington, DC, during the administration of President Ronald Reagan.[23]

NOTES

1. See also Dawn E. Bakken, ed., *Fighting Hoosiers: Indiana in Two World Wars* (Indiana University Press, 2021).

2. J. Matthew Gallman, *Defining Duty in the Civil War: Personal Choice, Popular Culture, and the Union Home Front* (Chapel Hill, NC, 2015), chapter 6.

3. On women's lives during the Civil War, see, for example, Judith Giesberg, *Army at Home: Women and the Civil War on the Northern Home Front* (Chapel Hill, NC, 2009). On the Indiana home front, see Richard F. Nation and Stephen E. Towne, eds., *Indiana's War: The Civil War in Documents* (Athens, OH, 2009), 87–103; Nicole Etcheson, *A Generation at War: The Civil War in a Northern Community* (Lawrence, KS, 2011).

4. Ralph Berwanger, ed., "'Absent So Long from Those I Love': The Civil War Letters of Joshua Jones," *Indiana Magazine of History* 88 (September 1992).

5. On Indiana Democrats and politics during the Civil War, see, for example, A. James Fuller, *Oliver P. Morton and the Politics of the Civil War and Reconstruction* (Kent, OH, 2017); Thomas E. Rodgers, "Copperheads or a Respectable Minority: Current Approaches to the Study of Civil-War Era Democrats," *Indiana Magazine of History* 109 (June 2013); Stephen E. Towne, "The Persistent Nullifier: The Life of Civil War Conspirator Lambdin P. Milligan," *Indiana Magazine of History* 109 (December 2013).

6. William Eidson and Vincent Akers, eds., "Democratic Attitudes in Johnson County during the Civil War Era: A Look at the Demaree Papers," *Indiana Magazine of History* 70 (March 1974).

7. Gallman, *Defining Duty in the Civil War,* chapter 5.

8. Middleton Robertson, ed., "Recollections of Morgan's Raid," *Indiana Magazine of History* 34 (June 1938).

9. Arville Funk, ed., "The Battle of Corydon," *Indiana Magazine of History* 54 (June 1958).

10. Stephen Rockenbach, "'This is Just Hope of Ultimate Payment': The Indiana Morgan's Raid Claims Commission and Harrison County, Indiana," *Indiana Magazine of History* 109 (March 2013).

11. Caroline E. Janney, *Remembering the Civil War: Reunion and the Limits of Reconciliation* (Chapel Hill, NC, 2013), 104.

12. Nicholas Sacco, "The Grand Army of the Republic, the Indianapolis 500, and the Struggle for Memorial Day in Indiana, 1868–1923," *Indiana Magazine of History* 111 (December 2015).

13. Giles R. Hoyt, "Germans," in *Peopling Indiana: The Ethnic Experience,* eds. Robert M. Taylor Jr. and Connie A. McBirney (Indianapolis, IN, 1996), 146–81.

14. Paul Ramsey, "The War against German American Culture: The Removal of German Language Instruction from the Indianapolis Schools, 1917–1919," *Indiana Magazine of History* 98 (December 2002).

15. Virginia Mayberry, "Draftee's Wife: A Memoir of World War II," *Indiana Magazine of History* 79 (December 1983). Virginia edited two other articles that appeared in the *IMH*. Joseph died in 2001, Virginia in 2003.

16. Emily Yellin, *Our Mothers' War: American Women at Home and at the Front During World War II* (New York, 2004), 16–19.

17. Joseph Mayberry served his years in the army in the United States.

18. Eric Langowski, "Education Denied: Indiana University's Japanese American Ban, 1942 to 1945," *Indiana Magazine of History* 115 (June 2019).

19. In 2007, after a letter from Wildermuth clearly stating his white supremacist views came to light, a movement began on the IU Bloomington campus to remove Wildermuth's name from the university's intramural center. The building was renamed in 2018.

20. See, for example, Elizabeth A. Belser, "What's That Sound? Political Action and the New Left at Purdue University" (MA thesis, Indiana University Bloomington, 2017); Margaret Fosmoe, "Fifteen Minutes, 50 Years Later: Members of the 'Notre Dame Ten' Recall Campus Events of the Vietnam War Era," *Notre Dame Magazine* (Winter 2019–20).

21. Alex Lichtenstein, ed., "'Patriotism May Require Opposing the Government at Certain Times': Howard Zinn's Antiwar Speech at Indiana University, December 1, 1967," *Indiana Magazine of History* 110 (June 2014).

22. Jason Lantzer, "The Other Side of Campus: Indiana University's Student Right and the Rise of National Conservativism," *Indiana Magazine of History* 101 (June 2005).

23. The *American Spectator* is now published online at https://spectator.org.

1

"absent So long from those I love"

The Civil War Letters of Joshua Jones

EDITED BY EUGENE H. BERWANGER

JOSHUA JONES SERVED IN THE 19th Indiana Volunteer Infantry Regiment from his enlistment on July 29, 1861, until his death on September 30, 1862.[1] His regiment was part of the Iron Brigade, one of the most outstanding military units in the Civil War. The brigade consisted of the 2nd, 6th, and 7th Wisconsin regiments; the 24th Michigan; and the Indiana 19th. Until 1863 it was the only unit on the eastern front to be composed solely of troops from the Old Northwest. Created as part of a military reorganization on the eastern front in October, 1861, the brigade remained undistinguished until the Battle of South Mountain (September 14, 1862) when General Joseph Hooker used the word "iron" to describe its valor.[2] The Iron Brigade continued to serve with distinction through the Battle of Gettysburg, in which it lost two-thirds of its men. In the following months the brigade was strengthened with units from the eastern states. Losing its character as a western division, the Iron Brigade continued, but as Mark M. Boatner explains, "it never recovered its former punch."[3]

Much of what is known about enlisted men in the Iron Brigade comes from Wisconsin and Michigan sources. In his definitive study of the brigade, Alan T. Nolan relied heavily on manuscript sources from those two states. He lists only three manuscript collections for Indiana, and among them, only one, a diary, was kept by an enlisted man.[4] Joshua Jones's letters home during his brief military career are a valuable addition to what is known about the life of the common soldier in the Iron Brigade, especially those who served in the 19th Indiana.

Aside from his letters, and his service and pension records, little is known about Jones. He was born in 1838 and may have lived his childhood and adolescence as a farm lad near Muncie, Indiana. On March 20, 1859, at the age of twenty-one, he married Celia Gibson, whom he had known for ten years. Their only child, George (Eddy) Edgerlie Jones, was born on June 3, 1860.[5] What impelled Jones to leave his young wife and child for military service is unknown. He may well have been swept up in the wave of patriotism that spread throughout the North following the Confederate attack on Fort Sumter in April, 1861. Urged on by Indiana's Governor Oliver P. Morton, volunteers from throughout the Hoosier state responded favorably to President Abraham Lincoln's call for troops. Large numbers of them congregated at the state fairgrounds in Indianapolis to be organized into regiments and assigned to duty. In July, 1861, young men, most from central Indiana towns such as Muncie, Winchester, Franklin, Spencer, and Indianapolis, were mustered for a three-year tour of duty into the 19th Indiana Volunteer Regiment under the command of Solomon Meredith. A Republican and friend of Lincoln, Meredith had strong antislavery leanings,[6] but if he influenced his men's thinking about abolitionism, it is not evident in Jones's letters. Jones never mentions slavery or any contact with blacks, although it seems likely he would have encountered slaves or free blacks in the Washington, D. C./Virginia area.

The letters clearly indicate the hardships of war. Jones was committed to the Union cause and hoped for an early Union victory. As the fighting became more intense and camp life less stationary, however, some pessimism began to creep in. Guard duty, unappealing food, and marching in cold, wet weather lessened his zeal for military life. By 1862 Jones was mentioning the possibility of death more frequently, all the while hoping for a leave of absence that would give him temporary relief from soldiering and a chance to see Celia and George again.

The letters also indicate that Jones was more contemplative than the average enlisted man. Bell I. Wiley, in his study of the Union soldier, reports that most enlisted men spent their free time gambling, drinking, or seeking other pleasures and that they frequently went into debt to engage in such entertainments.[7] Perhaps because of his religious beliefs (although he does not dwell on the topic) or because he saw the war as a means of profiting personally, Jones did not partake in such activities. Indeed, he seemed to have taken advantage of those who did. He loaned money at interest and sent his earnings home; he also sold personal items that others might want and appeared especially pleased when he made a profit. That this was a conscious effort on his part is demonstrated in his statement to Celia that "Some is Smart and Some aint. . . ."

Jones's correspondence indicates that he had some formal schooling or at least private instruction. Although his letters, compared to those written by his company commander and his surgeon, have deficiencies in grammar, punctuation, and spelling, they are superior to many—perhaps most—of those of his contemporaries.

Jones's letters, for the most part, were written to his wife, Celia. Following his death she continued to live in the Muncie area until the Great Depression of the 1930s. She married again, at sixty-five years of age, to John L. Driscoll in 1903, and became a widow for the second time in 1929. Her last years were spent in the home of her son and daughter-in-law, George and Mary Jones of Muncie. During her widowhood and second marriage she saved Jones's Civil War letters and passed them on to her son and grandchildren.[8]

Camp Morton Indianapolis[9]
Aug the 1th 1861

Dear Wife & little Boy & friends

I take my pen in hand to let you know that I am well hoping this will find you all the Same.

Well Celia we got our uniform yesterday & we are going to get our guns tomorrow & we leave here a Saturday [illegible word] for Washington City I will Send my Clothes to the Depo in Care of Garret Gibson[10]

if I can get my likness I will Send it too. I Cannot Come home any more untill the war is over if I live I will be at home when the war is over & if it falls to my lot to fall in Battle it will be in defence of my Country tell all that take themSelves to be my friends that I bid them farewell for my life is not Insured I dont know that I Shall ever have the pleasure of meeting you all any more or not but if I dont you must all take Care of your Selvs while I am exposed to the Enemy who are trying to distroy our government I look for nothing but hardships Exposed to bad weather poor grub & long marches & dodging bulets and Sords & bayonets we may Come through Muncie but I dont know whether we will or not

I will write when we get in Camp I guess I have wrote all for the time So farewell friends and Relations yours till Death

Joshua Jones

Washington City
Camp Calarama[11]
Aug the 19th 1861

Mr. J. W. Abrell[12]

Sir I take my pen in hand to Write you a few lines to let you know that I am well at present hoping these few lines may find you all in good health We are Encamped on the North Side of the Potomac River on mount Calarama in view of Washington City and Elexandria we Can See the Ships on the Hudson bay[13] we can hear the Secession Cannons evry morning very plain This is a wet morning it has Rained evry day but three Since we have been hear I Seen the Battle ground of Arlington hights[14] the timber is all Cut to Smash with Bullets it is all pine and Cedar and loral on the mountains in the valeys it is porsimmon and Tamberac and Spruce Trees I want you to write and tell me whether George and Wm Ross has gone yet or not I would like to See George in Ranks here Runing up and down the mountanes I Rather think it makes aman look up for the ground to be out all night on a Scout and come in in the morning and Eat a little dry bread and cold meat then Rap up in a wet blanket and lay down on the Side of the hill with your feet against a rock to keep you from Sliding down the mountain and a Rock for a pillow if you want one the other night when we was a Sleep in our tents the Alarm was raised that the Rebells was coming it was just like a lot of Seard hogs Runing over one another and falling down Some got Stuck with Bayonetts while others got bumped with guns on the heads.

there is Sevral boys here that would just as Soon be at home. We will [be] Called in to Action in 2 or 3 weeks then the fun commences I have wrote all that I can this time you must write just as Soon as you get this and tell me all the good news

So No more at present Yours with Respect

Joshua Jones

Washington City Fort Smith[15]
Sept the 12th 1861

Dear Companion

I am well this morning and hope this will find you the Same I Received your letter and was glad to hear from you, but you did not write all that I wanted to know well now I Can tell what many others Cannot night before last while I was on gard our pickets was attacted I was on the Reserve we was rallied and the Bullets fell like hale around us

yesterday about 3 oclock we marched 4 miles towards Farfax Courthouse there we was fired on by the Rebells the [brim ?] Shells flew and the Cannon Balls whistled and the dirt flew all around us they are just now barying one of our Regiment the report Sais that the Rebells lost one hundred and our Side Six and 7 wounded I did not get a Shot we was in the Rear of the brigade[16] next Sunday we are going to have another trial at them I seen what I never seen before if I live through the next Battle I think I am all right now Celia go to Patrick Carnickles[17] I Sent twenty dollars there for you keep this till I Come home I think we will be all rite when I get back the hardest time I ever Saw has ben in the last too days I cannot tell you half but keep your Spirits up

I am bound to raise or fall nothing Bothers me but my little family that I left be hind

write Soon
Farewell

Joshua Jones

E Street Hospital
Washington City D C
October the 5th 1861

Dear Companion

I will have to Say to you that I am not well[18] the Second day (Sept 14th) after I wrote your last letter (Sept 12th) I was taken Sick I was taken with a Chill and fever and it Run in to the Tifoid fever I never was So Sick in my life but I am geting better I can Set up in bed and write a little at a time I am very weak and poor it has Cut me down very fast I laid in my tent a little too long I got Cold on my lungs I have a bad Cough

I am well taken Care of here I am in a good ward and have a good attendent ward No 27 You must not let my being Sick discourage you for I think I will get along now if I dont get a backset my Side hurts me more now than it ever did before I would like to hear from home mighty well I have not had a letter for a long time but there may be Some letters at the Camp for me

I Suppose you got that money that I Sent to you keep that money it is better than gold it is worth 3 cts on the dollar at Indianapolis and in kansas and Nebrasca it is 7 cts on a dollar it will be payday again the 2nd day of November then I will Send about 25 dollars

I dont want you to forget me I want you to Remember where I am and what I Come here for

John and Rebecca [Abrell] I want you to Remember that I am not out of Reach of letters yet I guess the old man does not Care where I am or what becomes of me I have never got a word from him yet he appears to [be] very distant to me I dont know why it I dont think I ever done him any harm in my life that I know of

I would like to See you all being Sick makes me think of a great many things that I would not think of if I was well I am geting very tired of Staying in bed so long I hope I can walk out in a few day in to the hall I must Stop writing I am So weak and tired you must all write to me

Joshua Jones

Well Celia I cant write much this time[19] I am too feeble to Sit up long at a time I do not know when I will get away from here but you may Direct your letters the [same] as before and I will Send for them if I Stay here long oh how I would like to See little George but it is no use to think about it

Write often your husband till Death

Joshua Jones

From a poor Soldier to his wife and little Boy good by

Loved ones at home
Ever of thee I am fondly dreaming[20]
Thy gentle voice my Spirit can Cheer
Thou wer the Star that mildly beaming
Shone ore my path when all was dark and dreary
Still in my heart thy form I cherish
Every kind thought like a bird flies to thee
Then never till life and memory perish
Can I for get how dear thou art to me
Morn noon and night where ear I may be
Fondly I am dreaming of thee.

Ever of thee when Sad and lonely
Wandering afar my Soul joys to dwell
And then I feel I love thee only
All Seems to fade before affections Spell
years have not chilled the love I cherish
True as the Stars hath my heart been to thee
Never till life and memory perish
Can I for get how dear thou art to me
I am ever fondly thinking of thee.

1851 sheet music of the popular English ballad "Ever of Thee I'm Fondly Dreaming." *Courtesy Boston Public Library, Digital Commonwealth.*

Oct 12th 1861
Washington City
Headquarters Camp Fort Craig[21]
Regt. 19th Co. E

Dear beloved

Wife I take my pen in hand to let you know that I am geting better Since this morning I got your letter   I was So glad to hear from you   I have got out of the hospital but I am very weak but I think I will get along now   I hope this will find my dear in good health and little boy also   well Celia you Said you got that money all Safe   our Regiment moved while I was Sick   we are on Arlington hights 1 mile from long Bridge a Cross the Patomac South of Washington garding Fort Craig   well Darling   about them feathers   I think if you Can get them for 30 cts a pound you had better buy 25 or 30 pounds if you can get new feathers   what do you think   I have to lay my oilcloth down and lay on that   my bones are geting Calloused   Celia I would give my intrest in this war to See you and our little boy   I have often wanted to See you but never So bad as I do now   I would not take a thousand dollars for your picture but I got it wet   I laid out allnight in the rain   the case is alittle Spoiled but the pretty girl is there yet   that is all I care for   we will have a Sweet time when I get home but when that will be I do not know   there is some talk of us going to Hatras Inlet on the North Carolina Coast a long ways from here.[22]

Celia I Sent my boots with my clothes but not my hat   I expect that kigers folks got them for Vols but I dont know whether they did or not   I dont want to loose them   Sam Pruitt paid me that too dollars   be Sure to pay Haines for that wheat[23]   I dont know what else to write   I have wrote evry week to you   I love to write to them I love So Dearly

Nomore at present my Sweet little wife
Remember who loves you above all others
Your husband till Death

Joshua Jones

Write to me Soon as you get this

State of Virginia
Fort Craig
Nov the 7th 1861

Dearly beloved and ever Remembered Wife

I take the pleasure of writing to you to let you know that I am well at present

hoping this may find you in good health.

your kind letter of the 20th of Oct Come duly to hand you Spoke of your feelings when Seeing others Sporting around home Well my dear Celia Can you imagine the feelings of the one who loves you so dear when he thinks of a quiet home and a tender loving wife and little Sweet boy often do I think of the hapy days when I Could Sit down to Breakfast with you and See the little boy Stick his head up in the Bead and laugh while we was eating and talking to each other as hapy as too kings my dear I can See now that we lived as pleasant a life as any too on earth. oh Shall it ever be my most hapy lot to meet my beloved wife and little boy once more; if it is the will of Almighty god that I Shall I will promise mySelf never to leave them again to be Compelled to Stay any length of time untill I am Stricken down by the hand of death.

but dear I have a narrow path to travail while this Rebellion lasts oh Could I take my Super with you this night and have a long talk with you it would be one of the greatest pleasures that ever I enjoyed oh may the time Speedily Come when Rebellion will [be] put down and peace Restored once more for I think that I Shall never Return untill the Stars and Stripes is floting over all the States in the union god forbid that any other flag Should ever wave.

I want our little boy to be learned to do as he is told and be manerly to evry body I do not want to See a bad little boy like Some Children when I Come home. Well Celia I am going to Send you thirty dollars for you to take Care of you will find it at the Bank in Muncie

You need not Send any Clothing to me.

I got a letter from Pery Ross yesterday here is a Ring in Remem-berence of your husband you must Save all that you Can for I will be So glad to see that my dear is trying to help me I want to have the good of my hardships when I get home.

give my love and best Respects to the old folks and Susan also write Soon and a good long letter

nomore at present but Remaines your husband till Death

Joshua Jones

Sweet Wife good By

Arlington Hights
November the 12th 1861

Dearest little Wife

I Received your letter or Johns Rather last night I had just wrote a letter to you a day or too a go

I have just Come off gard I had a hard night of it I Stood at the magazine 4 hours and upon the parapet 4 hours to gard the Canons the magazine is what the Canon balls and Cartriages is kept in it Rained Some and the wind blew pretty Cool it was dark and I Could hardly See to keep on the parapet wall it is only 6 feet wide Well my Sweet little wife you wanted to know if I had [nocked ?] any more apples Since I was at paps or not I have not it takes money to nock them here a good apple Sells for 5 cts here and you know that I am too Stingy to pay that my little Sweet I thought that I Seen more pleasure that time with you than ever I Seen in all my life without you

I often think of the Sweet times we have had togather I do beleave that we love each other the best of any too in the world. You Said you got that Ring I Sent you well I am going to Send another well it is in the other letter of the 7th of November you Said you had Sold the [dog?] that was Right

tell me if you have paid David Haines you will find thirty dollars at the Bank for you I drawed 26 and mad Some making Rings and Some washing Close for the boys I dont Spend much I want to have a big pile when I get home write good long litters when you write take that paper to the Bank and get gold for it keep in good heart and Save all that you Can and it will be all Right when I get home I am well and in good Spirits. I look a head to a better day I have not much to write this time. I feel Sleepy and bad to day I will write more the next time No More at Present I Ever Remain your Husband Till Death.

Joshua Jones

Arling[ton] Hights
Fort Craig Via
Nov. the 24th 1861

Dear and loving little wife

I Can inform you that I am Enjoying a Reasonable portion of health and it is my greatest wishes that this will find my loving wife and Sweet little boy in the Same State of health. I Received your loving letter and was glad to hear from you when I Seen your hair and little Georges I Could not help Sheding tears I never had Such feelings in my life it was almost like meeting with my lover. The hapiest day of my life is to come that will be when I Can take my loving wife by the hand and lay my arms around her and kiss her sweet lips That is the Day I am longing to See you know how well I used to like to have holt of your little hand I can almost feel it now you know I like to feel it too my Celia and the good times we used to have and that we will have when we See each other again is all my [Studies ?] but that day is not known when we will meet but here is a consolation the longer I have to Stay the more money aint that So Celia can you dout that I love you when I have Risked my life in this Rebellion and put up with all of the hardships of Soldiering just to make a Raise for the Comfort of my little family you know that it must be horrible to my mind to have to be absent So long from those I love So well besides the exposure and hardships I have to bear with who is doing mor for their family or Country than your little boy

The grandest Review that ever was known your boy was at it was helt between Munsons hill and Baleys Crossroads on the 20th of Nov 1861 Seventy thousand troops 104 Canon 17 batteries you will See the account of it in the papers it was a grand Site.[24]

well Celia if you put the money in the Bank it will draw 6 per cent interest although I am willing for you to keep it but evry dollar is one when a man gets it by the hardest put it in the Bank if you want to.

tell me if you got them feathers I will have to Stop it is time for dressparad here is my heart and Some of my hair.

give my best Respects to your father and Mother tell them I want them to write often

No more at present I ever Remain your husband till Death

Joshua Jones

Write Soon

Arlington Hights Fort
Craig Via.
Dec. the 18th 1861

Dear Parents

I again Embrace the present oportunity of addressing you. the truth Compelles me to Confess that I am not atall well, but this goes hoping to find you all Enjoying good health and a pleasant life we have just got in from picket gard where we was very much exposed to danger and the Inclemency of the weather both night and day for five days we was on the out posts within one and a quarter [miles] of the Rebell pickets I was not well when I Started and I am Still no better the picket line is about ten miles west of here and we left Camp at eleven oclock and marched out there with our knapsacks on with a heavy lode in them and haversacks full of mule meat and dry hard bread and a canteen full of water and our Cartriage boxes on with 40 Rounds of Cartriges in them which Contains a long ball weighing one ounce and an ounce of powder we got there about sundown very tired and warm and I was put on a post with two other men where the Rebells generally passed they killed one of the Wisconsin boys there three days before that. there we Sit in the cold all night with gun in hand watching for them and listening for them to fire at us but I did not see a Rebell or hear a gun fire but the boys down along the line on the Right wing Said they heard a Shot or too but Some of them if they hear a brush crack it sounds like thunder to them. the next day our Company Crossed the line and went forageing we went in to an orcherd and got Corn where the union troops never went in and all got out alive we got too loads of Corn foder and all there was too Rebell Cavalrymen passed in Site of us but they went off double quick. this trip is the cause of my having a bad cold hard Cough and Sore lungs which is very unpleasant. I Received aletter from Celia to day Stating that you was all well which I am always glad to hear this is a hard life to live but I can bear it all if I can here of you all being well but if I Should hear of Celia or the little boy being Sick or if She was dissatisfied any way or misused and I have to Stay here and could not come to take care of her I would have the most miserable life to live of any human on earth because I hope the day is coming when I can have a little quiet home with her once more and Enjoy the peace and pleasure around our own peaceable fire Side I want you all to write to me for it is cheering to

Read a letter from you and the pleasure that a Soldier Enjoys otherwise are few and far between.

I will close for the present by asking you to answer Soon

I ever Remain yours untill Death

Joshua Jones

let Celia Read this letter

19th Regt. Co. E
Camp Craig
Jan 8 1862

Dear Celia

I take my pen in hand to write you a few lines to let you know that I am well, and hope these few lines may find my dear Wife and little boy in the very best of health. Well Celia as there is not any thing of Importance going on in Camp I will have nothing new to tell you you wanted me to Send you a present well I dont know what to Send but when I go to the City I will try to get you Something I am going to Send my little George a picture of Col. Ellsworth who was killed at Elexandria while taking down a Rebell flag[25] if you Cant read this writing I will get Some body to write for me but however. Celia I will not Send any money home this time but look out next payday for Sixty dollars I bought a watch for twelve dollars and a half and Sold it to Isaac Branson for Eighteen and a half next payday[26] Some is Smart and Some aint Smart

well Celia I will tell you what I have been thinking a bout I think if pork is only worth $2.50 cts per hundred you had better buy about two hundred pounds and Salt it down it will be a good thing for us for pork will be high next Summer but do as you think best I would like to know what has become of my Corn

you may Sell my watch if you can get ten dollars for it and if you Cant you may Send it to me and I will Sell it and Send you the Cash I heard that Vol Kiger was maried I guess you will get that money of him yet you Said you had bad luck So had I = I got your likeness Case Spoiled So we are even aint we duck.

I will Close my letter by Remaining your admirer and husband till Death

Joshua Jones

Write Soon good by

Arlington
Fort Craig Virginia
Feb the 6th 1862

Ever dear and beloved Celia

your letter Come to hand last night and found me well and glad to hear from you but Sorrow to hear that Eddy was not well but I hope when this Comes to hand it will find my little Sweets both in good health. you Said that Mat had been Saying Something about our money well Celia you know that I would Rather that you would have our money than any body else for it belongs to you and me and we are just the Same as one you done just Right with the money and So we are Satisfied it is no body elses bisness I told you to do as you pleased with the money just a purpos to See what kind of a wife I had to contrive and I find out that I have got just as good Industrious and prudend a women as any man and it makes me love you dearly to think that you are doing all that you can to make us comfortable after I get home as many of a women would have Spent evry cent of that money while her husband was Risking his life for it besides the hardships he had to under go.

I can Say that I have Sent as much money home as any other man in this Company there is men here that has got wives at home that is needy and they are Spending their money for whiskey and geting drunk and buying all other foolery that does not profit them one cent. I dont buy any thing but paper or Something to Send to you not even an apple or pies or Cakes for they Sell them awful high.

I have Sold my watch for 15 dollars and the fiddle for 5 if they come. I can Send 75 or 80 dollars next time I am going to make all I can.

well darling about you going to See Martha I have nothing to Say you can do as you please with your own money about them pies and Cakes and other thing I think they would be So good it has been So long that I have had to live on hard dry bread and it light bread too or hard Crackers and a little fat rotten cold pork Sevral of the boys have got boxes of provision Sent to them one woman come and brought her man Some provisions I can get any thing that you are a mind to Send but dear I havent got but a little money not any more than will pay the express on the fiddle and watch I loaned it all out but you can pay the express there and get a Receipt for the box if you want to but I hate to ask you to Send it and pay the expence [for shipping it] both for it is too much you can use your pleasure about Sending it I Sent a numberell [an umbrella] to Haineses Store by a man that was here after a Soldier that died is [it] was Directed to Garrett Gibson I want you to get it and keep it here is your miniture but you must be Sure to Send Eddys and yours back and take good care of this one you Spoke about me having to lay on my oilcloth you cant help that and if them that talks about it dont like it let them lump it. I think I will be at home in the Sumer or fall you need not be uneasy for I love you and I know you are pretty and virtuous too and I dont want a better woman than my little Celia. I have not got the watch yet you Said that picture looked natural I thought it was a poor picture I will have another one taken if I have a chance and send it to you / look on the other Sheet I will Close my letter on this I am out of paper[27] here is a kiss for aint it Sweet it ought to be I have Saved it long anough I dont know what to tell you only that you are pretty and Sweet and a good loving kind little wife and would like to See you and hug and kiss on them Sweet lips kiss Eddy for me and tell him to be a good little boy till pap comes home again

No more this time
your Ever loving husband
Write Soon,

Joshua Jones

Camp near Elexandria Va
April the 2nd 1862

Dear and Ever Remembered Wife

I take my pen in hand this morning to answer your kind letter which I Received lastnight and to let you know that I am well and hope these few lines may find my Celia and little Eddy in the Same State of health.

Well Celia we are not gone yet but we are looking to go evry day there is So many troops to Ship that it takes a good while to all get on the Steamers but it will not be long till we will get on for our division goes on board next we are just laying here in the laurel brush Ready to go any time[28] Well Dear we got our pay a day or too a go and I Sent 55 dollars to the Bank on deposit Cap Wilson Said he would make them give me 6 per cent Intrust So I Sent it there in Stead of Sending it to Pary[29] I did not get all that was coming to me or I could Sent more I will Send 50 dollars next time I got them postage Stamps and was glad to get them but I did not get the picturs I do wish you would Send them I will Send mine and then I do want yours I got the watch and fiddle I got 5 dollars for the fidle and twelve for the watch next pay day I Save all of the money that I get to Send home to keep my pretty Sweet wife and little boy and my Self when I get home keep in good Spirits Dear for they cant kill me I am coming home if any bod[y] does then we will have a good time the balance of our lives I think your father and John [mite?] write to [me] oftener if they thought any thing of me but it is all Right I will Remember them while I am fighting to Save their as well as my own Country I will Close for this time by asking you to answer Soon and Send them pictures write good long letters and tell all of the news that you can think of. your Ever loving husband

Joshua Jones

when this you see
Remember me though
many miles a part we be

good by Celia

here is the picture of your ugly husband who is in the army

this is a Laurel leaf

Via
Camp Near Fredricksburg
April 28th 1862

Well my Dear Celia

I will write you a few lines to let you know that I am geting along as well as could be expected although I am not very well but it is my hearts Desire that this may find you well and Enjoying life pleasant I can get along if I can hear of you and the little boy being well, for you are the main dependence for pleasure and Satisfaction the longer I Stay a way the more I think of you and the better I love you I am geting tired of this way of living it is So hard and disagreeable I am not well half of my time any more it Raines So much and we have to lay on the cold and wet ground and nothing that I like to eat we was 5 days with 2 days Rations and 4 of them days we was marching hard Crackers and old tuff beef and no Salt and we had to Roast it on the fire I got a letter from Pary last night he Said Some of the friends did not like it because I talked of Sending my money to him I want you to tell me who it is if you know I think it would be Safer in their house because it is not So apt to get burnt up you may give that Certificate to Pary then if any thing Should hapen you will not be to blame it is not because I think that you cant take care of it but I dont want you to be to blame if any thing Should hapen that the certificate was lost I will Send 50 or 55 dollars more in 2 or 3 weeks and I will let Pary go to the Bank and get the Certificate let me know how much money John Abrell got and who he give for Security you may look for me home this Sumer or fall you may dry apples and get evry thing that you can I am coming home on a furlow if the war is not over but I think the war will Soon be over then I will be the hapyest man in the world when I can be with my Sweet wife and little boy but live in hops and do all you can for our future Comfort and pleasure I will have to Stop for this time Write Soon give me all of the Satisfaction you can about evry thing

Ever Yours Respectfully
Joshua Jones
to Celia

Fredericksburg Va
June 26th 1862

Dear Companion

I take my pen in hand to Inform you that I Received your letter of the 16th Stating that you was all well it found me in good health & Enjoying my Self well as it had Rained all night & when I got up this morning I was Surrounded by water & in my nest the water was about two inches deep & I am not dry yet. it Stormed tremendous hard it has Swept away the Rail Road a gain.[30] There has been 3 men drowned Since we come here but none of our Regt but Thomas Gilbert tried to cut his throat[31] you Said that you got that money & my likeness also. I dont know whether I will Send any money home this pay day or not for our year is up the 29th of July & we have to pay for all of the clothes that we drawn over the amount of $42 but I will not have but little to pay if any but I think I can make a Speculation a trading.

you Said that you had planted garden Stuff & was going to make apple butter & fix things all Right that is Right you will never loose any thing by it for I am coming home on a furlough this winter if we are not discharged Cap sayes he will get me a furlough if it can be had at all. I think Mat has made a wild Shot if he knows when he is well off he had better keep out of the army for it not a place for pleasure nor a field for play unless he wants to play with lead balls & Sometimes they throw them pretty hard & they Rattle a Round like hail

tell mother that I will Send her a present just as Soon as I can get one that is worth Sending tell her that if She will keep in as good Spirits as I am all will be Right.

I cant get home this summer but I will come next winter I think I am going to join the artillery if I can get off from Cap Wilson. here is a paper for you to Read & a card as a token of my love for you I wish you would Send me a Muncie paper you can Send it as I did this. I Sent you two more pictures how do you think they look & who do you think they look like keep in good heart I think I will get to kiss your Sweet lips again Someday.

well I must bring my letter to a close I am on Poliece to day corporal of the Poliece Squad. kiss Eddy a time or too for me oh how I would like to See him & his mother.

No More but Remaines your Most Affectionate Husband

Joshua Jones Cpl[32]

Fredericksburg
Stafford co Virginia
July 15th 1862

My Dear Wife

I am once more permitted to drop you a few lines in answer to your kind comunication of the 5th and 8th which come to hand a few minets ago & was Read with great pleasure   to hear from home once more & to hear that you was all well & in good Spirits for that is Really the only & greatest pleasure that I Enjoy.

Dear Celia if you only knew what a great pleasure & Satisfaction it is to me to Read a letter from your hand you would Surely feel more Interested in writing to me   I began to think that I was Entirely forgotten by my only nearest & dearest friend for it was So long before I got a letter from her. you said that you had put up Some currents & was going to put up Some cherries & had your quilt about half out   you are Some[thing]   I always knew that you was a Smart girl but I did not like to Say So.

I often think about the Evening that Eliza Jane called me to the house & you was on the bed crying & I talked So hard to you   I feel Sorrow for it & hope you will forgive me for it

I did not do it because I did not care but because I thought it the better way to get you Reconsiled   you know that I think more of you than any thing Else on Earth for we could have So much fun & Satisfaction with Eachother Runing a Round & taging & catching Eachother & fondling over Eachother So loving. you must have your picture taken Just as nice as you can So it will look pleasing & Sweet & Send it to me.

My Dear wife you must Ever Remember the one that loves you So dear

you Said that you was at the forth [July 4]   I was too but I was laying in my tent all day Sick & almost Smothered to death it was So warm   I was thinking about you all day & wandering where you was & what you was doing.

We have had a pretty good time while we have been here but we are under marching orders now & will leave here Soon for Richmond or Gordensville.[33] I think the fight at Richmond will End the war if they will Stand & fight & not Evacuate but I fear that we are going to have to fight England & if we do I have no hopes of Ever getting home but if not I think that you may look for me this winter.[34] you Said that you got them pictures I got Eddys picture he is a pretty little boy he takes that after his pretty Mother & his Smartness too but his [Sponkeyness ?] he takes after his old father.

there has Sevral died here this week it is So hot one man fell out of the Ranks yesterday at dress parade he was Sun Struck he had not been well for a few days tell John that I have wrote him too letters Since he has wrote to me. tell the old folks that I Received their Respects but can not give a letter in Return for compliments tell them to write oh how I would like to See my Celia & our little boy you must write when you feel like it but if I did I would write all of the time I will have to Close for this time asking you to write without delay I will Ever Remain your affectionate & Loving husband until Death

Joshua Jones

farewell Celia Eddy good by

when this you See
Remember me
though many miles
a part we bee

Cedar Mountain
Culpepper Co Va
Aug 18th 1862

My Dear Companion

it is again that I am permitted to drop you a few lines to let you know that I am well & hope these few lines may Reach & find you well & in good Spirits. You must Excuse me for not writing Sooner for we have been marching for the last two weeks we made a Reconoitering about two weeks ago out toward Richmond & got in a Skirmish with the Rebels and for a while the case looked a little Billious but we got back by loosing Several prisoners[35] they [Confederates] had us cut off Entirely at one time & they dashed around among us pretty lively for a while When we got back to Camp we got orders to march the next morning at 4 oclock to Reinforce Banks So we did not get much Rest[36] we did not get here in time to get into the fight[37] we are now laying at the foot of Cedar mountain on the Edge of the Battle ground I was all over the Battle ground yesterday there is plenty of the Rebells that is barried So Shallow that their hands & feet is Sticking out & Some places there is So many in one hole & since they have Swelled their Shoulders or hips are above the ground & the maggots are all over them it creates a dreadful Smell there is plenty of peaces of arms legs & all parts of men Scatered over the fields I Seen lots of hair & blood & bloody clothes with bulet holes in them & dead horses any amount of them our men is baried alittle better they are baried in trenches there is two trenches about 30 Rods long & there they are layed Side by Side our loss is Said to be over one thousand the Bomb Shells & bulets is laying thick all over our Camp two men was killed yesterday by leting a Shell fall & it Exploded it was a percusion Shell I Can not tell half in a letter but you will See the account in the papers the battle was between Slaughter mountain & Cedar mountain Tell Parys that I have wrote to them last I would like to know how Johns is geting along & whether they are Still trying the Serve the lord & how people Seem to like the drafting in general you used to Say that there was no danger of being drafted what do you think now. what I Say comes true Sometimes.[38]

Bart Harter is not dead yet he is too [illegible] ornery[39] I will Send you five dollars in this letter I did not get all that was coming to me this pay day & want to Send home anough next time to make out two hundred dollars I loned out Some on Intrest till next pay day

tell Mother to keep in good Spirits tell all of the friend to write if they [illegible] like it all of the boys gets more letters than I do. now my Dear Celia I want you to write me if no body Else does for I love you more than all the world & I am content when I can hear from you I dreamed of huging and kissing you all night last night oh how [happy] I was but how bad I did feel this morning.

I must close write Soon

oh how [I] love & want to See my Dear Celia good bye Celia from your [lover ?]

Joshua Jones cpl

Fort Warren Virginia[40]
Sept 6th 1862

My Dear Wife

I am truly thankful that I am granted the privilege once more of Informing you that I am Still a live & well & Sincerely hope these few lines may find you all well & Enjoying your Selves well. Celia this is one privilege more then I Ever Expected to Enjoy but thanks to the almighty I have come out alive. the Bombardment comenced at the Rappahnnock [River] on the 21st of August & it lasted 3 days at that point we was under the fire three days & nights there then we marched to Gainesville & was Shelled all of the way there & on the Evening of the 28th one mile north of Gainesville we had an Engagement with the Enemy which lasted till after dark[41] it was there that I feared that I would End my days the man on my left was Shot down & both of the men to my Right was Shot Jacob Miller was wounded & fell at my feet & his gun hit me on the Shoulder as he fell[42] I got one ball hole in my hat & one through the left Side of my Coat we lost 260 that night on the 30th near the old Bull Run Battle ground we had an other Engagement which lasted till the Evening of the 31st our losses is Said to be Seventeen thousand the dead & wounded lay So thick that we could not help Steping on them when we was changing our position on the field our Regiment come very near all being taken prisoners they did get Several I can tell you all about it when I get home we will not have to fight any more for a while for our corps is ordered back to Washington to rest & Recruit up & protect the capi[tal] you need not be uneasy now I think I will get home Safe our flag is all Shot to peaces John Harter & Bart was not in the fight[43] they are both cowards we have been under fire altogether 9 days. Cap got your letter to day I wrote you a letter from Slaughters mountain about the 18th of Aug & Sent five dollars in it I have not had a letter for a long time I am going to quit writing I have not heard from your father nor John Abrell nor Pary nor any body Else for two or three months Can it be possible that they have all forgotten me I Sometimes do not care if I am killed only for your Sake I often thought of you during this Battle & thought if you only knew that I was on the Battle field part of the time fighting & part of time Standing watching & listening at the canon balls & Brim Shells So I could dodge them or fall down when they bursted to keep from geting killed I would not had you or Mother to of known Just my Situation for nothing in the world. while you was going about the house or in your bed aSleep I was Either laying on the Battle field in the Raine or Seting up anodding it Rained three days you have no Idea what we have to go through tell Neps that old John has got a Bulet in his neck our Major was killed[44] the Adjutants horse was Shot from under him[45] I will close on the other Sheet[46]

View toward Antietam Creek from Gen. George McClellan's camp, September 18, 1862. *Courtesy Library of Congress, Prints and Photographs Division.*

On the Battle field of Tietam Creek Md
Sept. 25th 1862.

Mrs. Jones:

By the request of your husband I write to let you know of his whereabouts and condition. Doubtless ere this reaches you you will have seen or heard through the Papers of the misfortune with which he met in the battle of the 17th of this month. But for the purpose of giving you a more satisfactory account of the matter he desires me to write and tell you to some extent the particulars as they really are. Then to commence I will say that as our Reg't. was making a charge on the rebels—and when they had got within the rebel lines—he was struck by a musket ball, taking effect in right leg—just above the ancle—breaking and literally shivering the bone to attoms. being too severely wounded to get back off of the field himself and the rebels were in too strong numbers at this point—, our Regiment had to fall back a short distance—leaving the dead and wounded in the hands of the rebels—. They took him back into their lines where he remained without any attention being paid to his wound from Wednesday morning—the time when he was wounded—until Friday afternoon when the rebels evaccuated their position. At this time our boys went over and found him and brought him back but his wound was so sore by this time that he could not bear to be hauled in the ambulance—so they carried him to the Hospital on a stretcher—for such purposes—a distance of three or four miles—where he now is and his wound is receiving proper attention. his leg had to [be] amputated—, in consequence of the bone being so badly shivered. they had to take it off about two thirds or three fourths of the way up between the ancle and the knee—just about the place that the garter fastens. He is getting along as well as could be expected under the circumstances. He says to tell Perry Ross—and your Father—that he received their letters—but that they need *not* expect him to answer them soon—as he is not able to write to any one now. He says that you may expect him home some time this fall—so soon as he is able to come. he will not be any longer able for the service—and will be discharged. I hardly know how to tell you the best way to direct letters to him but think that the safest and surest way is to direct them as heretofore, and I will use my best endeavors to have them forwarded to him at the earliest opportunity. However if you think best you might try one directing in this manner, Joshua Jones Co. E. 19th Reg't Ind. Vol. In Hospital at Keedysville, Washington Co. Md[47] But as the Hospital is not a permanent one—and liable to be mooved at any time—think the former the surest way—.

I presume that it will be some time yet before he will be able to write himself—and it will doubtless be a gratification to you to hear how he is getting along—. I will therefore take it upon myself to inform you from time to time as I may be able to hear—, how he is progressing. Trusting that you may bear this sad intelligence with becoming fortitude, and in a manner worthy the wife of so brave and patriotic a husband, remembering that though he must suffer much pain and forever the loss of his limb—, yet his life has been spared and that you will soon have the gratification of again seeing and enjoying his presence—that though his loss is a severe one—yet the reflection that the sacrifice was made in so noble a cause will in part compensate for the inconvenience and he will bear through life a living testimony of his devotion for his country and her institutions.

With regards

I am very Respectfully

Geo. W. Greene[48]
Lieut Co. "E" 19th Ind. Vol.

Sharpsburg Md Oct 8/62

Mrs. Joshua Jones

Dear Madam

Your letter to your husband directed to my care bearing date Oct 1st came to hand today In reply I deeply regret to iform you that your husband is no more, that he passed from this life Sept. 30th. You have doubtless received this melancholy intelligence ere this, as a friend of his was here several days before his death when all hope of his recovery was gone His leg was amputated below the knee by Dr Obensole of this regiment several days before I saw him (the 20th of Sept I believe) and while I was sick in Washington[49] I just saw him about 7 days before his death Since the amputation up to that time the leg had been doing well, but on my first examination I discovered a small gangrenous or mortified spot which extended rappidly in spite of all our efforts to arrest it It is known as hospital gangrene which once started is difficult to arrest He received every possible attention & kindness that could be bestowed on anyone away from home His sufferings were not very great

I was ordered to another post before his death I think he died the following day Henry Marsh of Muncie was Set apart especily to wait on him[50]

His remains were decently buried in a cemetry near by & a board placue at his head with his name & regt egraved upon it With expressions of deepest sympathy for you in this heavy affiiction and the hope that God will give you strength to bear up with Christian fortitude and resignation I am your most sincere friend and obt Servant

J N Green[51]
Asst Surg 19th Ind Vols.

Sharpsburg Md
Oct 8th 1862

Dear Madam

Dr Green wrote the enclosed letter which he was not going to send as I had writen to My Father of the death of your kind, noble and brave husband. the Drs and I found Joshua at a barn (where he had been taken by the secesh) his wounds had not recd any attentions until we came he was then taken to Keedysville on a litter (he had been put in an ambulance but he could not be hauled so they carried [him] there (3 or 4 miles) where his foot was amputated and did well for a while but mortification set in when he sunk rapidly. I was sent with the Regt after the Battle but afterwards orderd to Keedysville as soon as I came he was glad to see me and wanted me to see to him which I did with the other nurses and a lady from Boston who was very kind to the boys. (she came to wait on the soldiers voluntarily) he received *good* attention after he was found. A day or so before he died I was talking to him of his relations he said he wanted me to write to you but not then, when he got better, but he [was] getting worse I spoke to the lady nurse and she and I went in and told him that the Drs had given him up and if he wanted to send any word to you I would write it. he said for "you to take the best care of your seffe and child that you could." "Selia you know I have done the best I could for you". "I am prepared to die". he was in hopes that he would get well until I told him he was going to die. he passed away very quietly not haveing but little pain. Capt Wilson had a coffin made for him costing $6.00. and a head board was placed up for him in the grave yard. Capt Wilson speaks very highly of him as a soldier both on the Battle field and camp I always saw him at his post where ever it was. My sincere prayr is that God may bless you with the consolations which alone come from him and his protection in your bereavement that you may meet togeather arround the throne. You can learn of the date of my Father as I sent a letter to him stateing his death. Remaining your Friend I subscribe my selfe

H. C. Marsh

EUGENE H. BERWANGER was Professor of History at Colorado State University, Fort Collins, Colorado. This article originally appeared in volume 88, September 1992.

NOTES

1. [William H. H. Terrell], *Report of the Adjutant General of the State of Indiana* (8 vols., Indianapolis, 1866–1869), IV, 398.

2. Alan T. Nolan, *The Iron Brigade: A Military History* (Ann Arbor, Mich., 1961), 3–28, 130.

3. Mark M. Boatner III, *The Civil War Dictionary* (New York, 1959), 428.

4. See Nolan, *Iron Brigade*, especially 386.

5. Joshua Jones files in "Service Records of Volunteer Soldiers who served in Organizations of the State of Indiana," Record Group 94 (National Archives, Washington, D. C.); and "Pension Records of Volunteer Soldiers who served in Organizations of the State of Indiana," *ibid.*

6. Roy P. Basler, *The Collected Works of Abraham Lincoln* (9 vols., New Brunswick, N. J., 1953–1955), IV, 196. See also Nolan, *Iron Brigade*, 20–21.

7. Bell I. Wiley, *The Life of Billy Yank: The Common Soldier of the Union* (Garden City, N. Y., 1971), 247–75.

8. The Joshua Jones letters are presently the property of Ralph Becker of Fort Collins, Colorado. Mr. Becker's wife is the great-granddaughter of Joshua Jones. "Declaration for a Remarried Widow's Pension, February 11, 1929," in Jones file, "Pension Records of Volunteer Soldiers who served in Organizations of the State of Indiana."

9. Given the conditions under which they were written, Joshua Jones's letters are amazingly legible and easily read. As was true of many of his contemporaries, however, Jones infrequently used any marks of punctuation, including periods at the end of sentences, and frequently failed to capitalize the first word of a sentence. In addition, he used capital letters for many words, particularly those beginning with *s*, *c*, and *y*, that are not generally capitalized. To make for easier reading double spaces have been used to indicate sentence breaks in this transcription. Although every effort was made to determine Jones's intent, arbitrary decisions concerning capitalization and paragraphing were sometimes unavoidable. Location of headings, greetings, and closings has been standardized to correspond to modern usage. Words, dates, and abbreviations that were inserted above the line have been brought down to the line. Jones often drew hearts or flourishes at the end of his letters, frequently including the name of the person to whom the letter was written as well as his own. His and his wife's names were often connected in some way. These flourishes have been omitted. Words or phrases inserted in the margins have been placed at the end of the relevant letter

after Jones's signature. Explanatory words or phrases have been placed in brackets; words that are unclear but for which an attempted transcription has been made have been followed by a question mark and enclosed in brackets; illegible words have been so designated in brackets.

10. In all probability Garrett Gibson, an early pioneer in Delaware County, was Jones's father-in-law.

11. Camp Kalorama was a temporary facility on Kalorama Heights, where a government hospital for communicable diseases was located. Today the Kalorama Heights triangle is bordered by Massachusetts and Connecticut avenues and the Rock Creek and Potomac Parkway; it is bisected by Kalorama Road. Margaret Leech, *Reveille in Washington, 1860–1865* (New York, 1941), 205.

12. According to Ralph Becker, whose wife is a great-granddaughter of Joshua Jones, John W. Abrell was Jones's brother-in-law. At the close of this letter Jones—as was his wont—wrote the names of those to whom the letter was sent, J. W. Abrell and Rebecca Abrell, presumably John's wife.

13. The reference here is unclear. Jones may have meant that portion of the Potomac River just to the east of present-day Theodore Roosevelt Island. It is wide enough to allow ocean going vessels access to the city, and Jones would have been able to see it from his location on Kalorama Heights.

14. Undoubtedly Jones means Arlington Mills, where a clash took place between Union and Confederate forces on June 1, 1861. Arlington Mills is located between Arlington and Alexandria, Virginia. E. B. Long, *The Civil War Day by Day: An Almanac, 1861–1865* (New York, 1971), 81.

15. There was no Fort Smith in the Washington, D. C., area; however, the reference in this letter to the fighting around Lewinsville implies that "Fort Smith" may have been a bivouac located on the Smith farm, about two miles east of Lewinsville. Jones refers throughout his letters to "camps" that were probably only temporary bivouacs. He and comrades undoubtedly named these areas, but they never had any formal designation as camps. For locations see George B. Davis, Leslie J. Perry, and Joseph W. Kirkley, *The Official Military Atlas of the Civil War* (Washington, D. C., 1891–1895), plate VII.

16. The 19th Indiana was transferred into Virginia, just across the Chain Bridge from Washington, D. C., on September 3. There the men began constructing Fort Marcy, an earthworks guarding the approaches to the bridge. The first attack mentioned by Jones refers to a skirmish that occurred near Lewinsville, Virginia, on September 10, 1861. Lewinsville was four miles from the bridge. As Jones indicates, the 19th was also engaged on September 11 near Fairfax Courthouse, Virginia, where several Civil War skirmishes occurred. Nolan, *Iron Brigade*, 12, 22–23. Jones's estimates of casualties at Lewinsville and in subsequent battles are, of course, often erroneous. For more exact figures see relevant reports in U. S. War Department, *War of the Rebellion: A Compilation of the Official*

Records of the Union and Confederate Armies (128 vols., Washington, D. C., 1880–1901). These volumes are hereafter referred to as *Official Records.*

17. Jones probably refers to Patrick Carmichael since there was a family of that name in the Muncie area.

18. Jones was among the 40 percent of the 19th Indiana that became ill at this time. For a while Federal authorities feared that Confederates had poisoned wells in the area, but this rumor proved unfounded. More likely, the lack of sanitary conditions caused the outbreak of typhoid. Jones's illness must have been severe, for only the worst cases were taken to the hospital. Nolan, *Iron Brigade,* 20–22.

19. Jones may well have written this letter in brief stints since it appears to be addressed first to Celia, then to John and Rebecca Abrell, and finally, after Jones's first signature, again to Celia.

20. Following are the words of a song entitled "Ever of Thee" by George Linley and Foley Hall. For words and music see *Heart Songs Dear to the American People* (New York, 1909), 222–23.

21. Fort Craig was located approximately one mile south of Arlington. Davis, Perry, and Kirkley, *Official Military Atlas of the Civil War,* plate VIL.

22. A military expedition under General Benjamin Butler captured Cape Hatteras in August, 1861. On October 4 Confederates attacked an Indiana regiment stationed near Chicamacomico, North Carolina. Apparently Jones's comment was made in response to rumors about increasing troop strength in the Hatteras area. The 19th Indiana, however, remained near Washington, D. C. See Long, *The Civil War Day by Day,* 24.

23. Volentine, or Valentine, Kiger from Delaware County served with Jones in Company E of the 19th Indiana. Later, in July, 1865, Kiger was transferred to the 24th Indiana Volunteer Regiment and was mustered out of service in October of that year. [William H. H. Terrell], *Report of the Adjutant General of the State of Indiana* (8 vols., Indianapolis, 1866–1869), IV, 398; Kingman Brothers, pubs., *History of Delaware County, Indiana* (Chicago, 1881), 95. An Isaiah S. Pruitt from Delaware County—possibly the Sam Pruitt to whom Jones refers—also served in Company E of the 19th Indiana. Later, in 1864, Pruitt was transferred to Company E of the 20th Indiana (Reorganized) and from there was apparently moved to the Veterans Reserve Corps before he was mustered out of service. *Report of the Adjutant General,* IV, 398, 438. David T. Haines was engaged in the wholesale and retail grocery business in Muncie between 1848 and 1853. His later entrepreneurial ventures include railroad development and the grain business. G. W. H. Kemper, ed., *A Twentieth Century History of Delaware County, Indiana* (2 vols. in 1, Chicago, 1908), II, 643.

24. William Howard Russell, special correspondent of the London *Times,* described the review as follows: "Today a grand review, the most remarkable

feature of which was the able disposition made by General McDowell to march seventy infantry regiments, seventeen batteries, and seven cavalry regiments into a very contracted space, from the adjoining camps.... Among the 55,000 men present there were at least 20,000 Germans, and 12,000 Irish." William Howard Russell, *My Diary North and South*, ed. Eugene H. Berwanger (Philadelphia, 1988), 327–28. Bailey's Crossroads was located about three miles south of Fort Craig.

25. The incident occurred on May 24, 1861. James T. Jackson, proprietor of the Marshal House in Alexandria, shot Colonel Ephraim E. Ellsworth as he attempted to take down a Confederate flag that Jackson insisted on flying from the roof of his hotel. See Russell, *My Diary North and South*, 163–64, for a full account.

26. Isaac Branson from Delaware County served as sergeant of Company E, 19th Indiana from 1861 until April, 1863, when he was commissioned as second lieutenant; still later, in January, 1864, he became first lieutenant of the company. *Report of the Adjutant General*, II, 172, IV, 398.

27. If Jones did indeed include another sheet with this letter, it is no longer extant.

28. Jones's unit was prepared to embark for the Peninsular Campaign, which took place between April and July, 1862. The 19th Indiana, however, was part of Irvin McDowell's division, a division that Lincoln insisted on keeping in northern Virginia to protect Washington, D. C., from Confederate attack. Instead of going to the peninsula the 19th was moved toward the Rappahannock River and Fredericksburg, Virginia. Nolan, *Iron Brigade*, 47–52.

29. Luther B. Wilson of Muncie was captain of Company E, 19th Regiment from its organization in 1861 until he was mustered out of service in April, 1863. *Report of the Adjutant General*, II, 172.

30. Some troops of the 19th Indiana were given the detail of keeping the Richmond, Fredericksburg & Potomac Railroad between Fredericksburg and Acquia Creek Landing in repair. Nothing in the letters implies that Jones was part of the repair crew, but if he were camped near the line, he certainly would have been aware of the damage done. Nolan, *Iron Brigade*, 58–60.

31. The best study on morale among northern troops is Bell I. Wiley, *The Life of Billy Yank: The Common Soldier of the Union* (Garden City, N. Y., 1971). Wiley notes that morale fell when soldiers suffered long periods of illness and when conditions in camp became difficult. He writes that no reliable figures on suicide exist but notes that "accidental" shootings of soldiers with their own guns were very common. See pages 275–96. Thomas H. Gilbert of Delaware County served as wagoner for Company E, 19th Indiana during its entire three years of service. He was mustered out of the army in July, 1864. *Report of the Adjutant General*, IV, 398.

32. Although Jones was never listed as a corporal in the Indiana adjutant general's report, in his service records the muster of December, 1861, indicates that he was a private, that of March, 1862, lists him as a corporal. *Report of the Adjutant General*, IV, 398; Jones file, "Service Records of Volunteer Soldiers who served in Organizations of the State of Indiana."

33. On June 26, 1862, McDowell's corp was incorporated into the Army of Northern Virginia, commanded by John Pope. The new army consisted of units stationed in northern Virginia and in the Shenandoah Valley. Although Jones does not say, the 19th was moved from Fredericksburg to Gordonsville to protect approaches to the Shenandoah along the Virginia Central Railroad. Nolan, *Iron Brigade*, 61.

34. This comment is made in response to numerous rumors that England and France planned to recognize the Confederacy, a move which would have almost forced the Union to declare war on the European powers. Following the battle of Antietam (Sharpsburg), such rumors became less frequent, and they were no longer heard after the Federal victory at Gettysburg. James Rawley, *Turning Points in the Civil War* (Lincoln, Nebr., 1966), 113–14.

35. This was one of a series of raids undertaken by the Iron Brigade between Richmond and the Shenandoah Valley in early August, 1861. The purpose was to break Confederate communications between Richmond and the Valley. Long, *Civil War Day by Day*, 247.

36. Nathaniel P. Banks, commander of Union troops in western Virginia, was encountering Thomas J. ("Stonewall") Jackson's troops in the Shenandoah Valley. Allan Nevins, *The War for the Union: War Becomes Revolution, 1862–1863* (New York, 1960), 123ff.

37. Jones refers to the Battle of Cedar Mountain, August 9, 1862. This was the first fighting that led to the second Bull Run campaign. The Battle of Cedar Mountain is also referred to as the Battle of Slaughter Mountain. See Jones's reference in his letter of September 6, 1862. James G. Randall and David Donald, *The Civil War and Reconstruction* (2nd ed., Boston, 1961), 218ff.

38. By midsummer, 1862, the early eagerness to volunteer for military service had waned in Indiana and in other states, and calls for additional troops in June and again in July made the prospect of conscription to fill quotas very real. On July 17 Congress authorized the states to draft members to fill their militia quotas if necessary. The draft was to be administered by state officials, and by the end of July steps had been taken in every township in Indiana to enroll men subject to conscription. Resentment led to violence in a number of instances. In October, 1862, after still another call for soldiers, three thousand men were drafted to fill Indiana's quota of forty-two thousand. A subsequent accounting indicated that the draft had in reality been unnecessary and that the number of volunteers had exceeded the quota. In March, 1863, a second conscription act that provided for

the enrollment of eligible men by Federal officials was passed. William H. H. Terrell, *Indiana in the War of the Rebellion:* Vol. I, *Report of the Adjutant General of the State of Indiana* (1869; reprint, *Indiana Historical Collections,* Vol. XLI; Indianapolis, 1960), 49–54. Apparently men were drafted from Delaware County in 1862, but the county experienced no subsequent drafts. Kingman, *History of Delaware County, Indiana,* 113. For a general discussion of conscription during the Civil War see James W. Geary, *We Need Men: The Union Draft in the Civil War* (DeKalb, Ill., 1991).

39. Barton S. Harter was from Delaware County and served with Jones in Company E of the 19th Indiana. Harter was killed at Antietam on September 17, 1862, just one month after Jones's letter to Celia. *Report of the Adjutant General,* IV, 398.

40. This letter was written following the Second Battle of Bull Run. The 19th Indiana and other units engaged in the battle were brought closer to Washington in order to rest and recuperate. Fort Warren is perhaps the name given to the bivouac area, for at this time the unit was stationed on Upton's Hill about two miles southeast of Arlington. Fort Warren was located in Boston, Massachusetts. Nolan, *Iron Brigade,* 111.

41. Gainesville lies thirty-five miles southwest of Washington, D. C.

42. Jacob Miller of Delaware County served with Jones in Company E of the 19th Indiana. He was wounded in this encounter at Gainesville but continued to serve with the regiment until he was mustered out in July, 1864. *Report of the Adjutant General,* IV, 398.

43. For Barton S. Harter see note 39 above. John F. Harter of Delaware County also served in Company E of the 19th Indiana. When the regiment's three-year term of enlistment was completed in July, 1864, John Harter reenlisted and served until he was mustered out of the army in July, 1865. *Report of the Adjutant General,* IV, 398, 438.

44. Isaac M. May from Delaware County had been mustered into service as captain of Company A of the 19th Indiana. In February, 1862, he was promoted to major of the regiment. May was killed at Gainesville on August 28, 1862. *Official Records,* ser. I, vol. XII, p. 378; *Report of the Adjutant General,* II, 168, 169.

45. Lieutenant Colonel Solomon Meredith had his horse shot from under him at Gainesville and was forced to withdraw from the field. Nolan, *Iron Brigade,* 131; see also [Catharine Merrill], *The Soldier of Indiana in the War for the Union* (2 vols., Indianapolis, 1866, 1869), I, 587.

46. The second sheet of this letter is no longer extant. This was the last letter that Celia received from Joshua, or, at least, it was the last that she kept. On September 6, 1862, the day that Jones wrote it, "Stonewall" Jackson occupied Frederick, Maryland, and Confederate troops began the push northward that culminated in the Battle at Antietam (Sharpsburg). The battle, known as the

"bloodiest day in the war" occurred on September 17 and resulted in the death of 5,100 men, with 18,000 wounded. James M. McPherson, *Ordeal by Fire: The Civil War and Reconstruction* (New York, 1982), 282–87.

47. Keedysville was a hamlet midway between Sharpsburg and Boonesboro, Maryland.

48. George W. Greene from Delaware County first served as lieutenant of Company E of the 19th Indiana. He was promoted to captain in April, 1863, and was honorably discharged from service in March, 1865, after having been a prisoner of war at Libby and other southern prisons for twenty months following the Battle of Gettysburg. *Report of the Adjutant General*, II, 172; Kingman, *History of Delaware County*, 114–16, 119.

49. Jacob Ebersole from Aurora, Indiana, was surgeon of the 19th Indiana from April, 1862, until he was mustered out of service in October, 1864, when the 19th was consolidated with the 20th Indiana (Reorganized). *Report of the Adjutant General*, II, 169.

50. Henry C. Marsh of Muncie joined the 19th Indiana in November, 1861. He is listed in the adjutant general's report as an unassigned recruit. When the 19th and 20th regiments were combined in January, 1864, Marsh was mustered into the 20th (Reorganized). He is listed there under regimental noncommissioned staff as a hospital steward. *Report of the Adjutant General*, IV, 409, 432.

51. J. N. Green of Indianapolis served as assistant surgeon of the 19th Indiana from September, 1861, until he resigned in December, 1862. *Report of the Adjutant General*, II, 169.

2

★ ★ ★

Democratic Attitudes in Johnson County during the Civil War Era

A Look at the Demaree Papers

EDITED BY WILLIAM G. EIDSON AND VINCENT AKER

THE DEMAREE FAMILY OF NORTH central Kentucky and Johnson County, Indiana, has left an absorbing legacy in a collection of more than seventy unpublished letters.[1] Full of politics, religion, farming, and family news, the letters offer a valuable commentary on life in Indiana and Kentucky during the turbulent middle decades of the nineteenth century. The patriarch of the family was Samuel Demaree, a prosperous farmer in Henry County, Kentucky. Of French Hugenot and Dutch ancestry, Samuel was born in 1792, the year Kentucky became a state. His father and grandfather had moved to Kentucky in the 1780s with a large migration of Dutch families from Pennsylvania and New Jersey. Within a few years after Samuel's birth his father had moved to the "Low Dutch Tract" in Shelby and Henry counties. Here many of the Dutch families had pooled their interests in 1786 to purchase a tract of over 8,000 acres. The land was held by the Low Dutch Company until deeded to individuals in the 1830s. Samuel's farm was carved out of the portion of the tract lying in Henry County.[2]

While Henry County magistrate in the 1820s and 1830s Samuel watched seven of his younger brothers and sisters migrate to Johnson County, Indiana, where the younger Demarees and many of their Dutch relatives hoped their financial prospects would be better.[3] Samuel, a slaveholder, did not follow their example. Samuel and his wife, Rachel, raised thirteen children in Kentucky, a border state becoming increasingly divided in the years just prior to the Civil War. In order of their birth the thirteen were: David (1814–1874), Henry (1816–1890), Elizabeth (1818–1907), Peter (1819–1888), Mary (1820–1908), Ann

(1822–1907), Susan (1823–1882), Albert (1825–1841), Samuel (1827–1871), John (1829–1915), George (1832–1915), Joseph (1833–1858), and Cornelius (1836–1898). The letters printed below are from their fourth child, Peter, and from William T. Shuck (1824–1900), the husband of Susan, their seventh child.[4]

Susan and her husband moved to Johnson County, Indiana, shortly after their marriage in 1847. There they settled in the Shiloh community in Union Township where Shuck farmed and became a leader in the local Presbyterian church. His behavior, however, puzzled many of those who knew him well. Always a faithful church attender and a staunch Democrat, he nevertheless gained a reputation for being one of the most cantankerous and stubborn men in the county. One of his six children wrote of Shuck: he was "the most unreasonable, wicked man I ever saw."[5]

Peter Demaree, nearly five years older than Shuck, did not move to Johnson County until 1856. Like other Demarees he was a devout Presbyterian and an active Democrat. Many of his letters reflect these two interests. Following in his father's footsteps, Peter dabbled in local politics and was elected Johnson County commissioner for three years.[6] Peter also felt the wrath of his younger brother-in-law. The two men lived in the same community, attended the same church, and visited in each other's homes; but they did not always do so harmoniously. Once, after Peter accused William of opening a letter which did not belong to him, Shuck angrily implied that Peter and his whole family were liars.[7]

All the letters printed below were written to George Whitefield Demaree, Samuel's eleventh child. While a young man George did some pioneering in Missouri; but by 1856 he had returned to Kentucky, where he lived the remainder of his life. He was a Kentucky Democrat with strong beliefs in states rights and slavery. Outwardly he remained neutral during the Civil War, but inwardly his sympathies were with the Confederacy. George was a deeply religious, Presbyterian elder who penned many articles expressing his premillenial beliefs. His chief fame and main source of income, however, came as a beekeeper. Through numerous articles and noteworthy experiments, George became a nationally known apiarist. He was also interested in history and preserved most of the letters now found in the Demaree Collection.[8]

In the first letter printed below Shuck provides some insight into the crippling effects a drought can have on a farming community and observes the cooperative method for dealing with crises. He sounds particularly modern, however, when he complains about the price charged by and the "speed" of the men who were building his home. The latter half of the letter touches on the 1856 elections in Indiana. The Willard referred to was the youthful and charming Ashbel P. Willard whom the Democrats succeeded in electing governor that year. Willard's rise in politics had been swift. As a New Albany lawyer he had become the Democratic leader of the Indiana House of Representatives and was elected lieutenant governor in 1852. The People's party, as opposition to the Democrats called themselves in 1856, supported for governor an even younger candidate, thirty-two year old Oliver P. Morton. Willard carried the state but not without the opposition's shouting fraud. The People's party maintained that the Democrats won by importing scores of voters from other states, especially Kentucky.[9] Shuck obviously believes these rumors.

Johnson Co. Ind Oct. 26, 1856[10]

Dear Bro

Through the mercy of a kind Reedeemer we are yet the Spared number of the liveing & Blessed with usuel helth health here is very good.

We have avery dry fall here & very Smoky Indian Summer wether & agreadeal of damage has Been done with fire & More Expected Ef the drouth continues our wheat Surely wil perrish for the want of rain & perhapse we wil hafto Sow over My workman are getting along Slow with my house it wil push u[s t]o get mooved this winter it is my calcu[la]tion to have the chimbleys put up this week & wil get my plastering done next week Ef the floars are layed[11]

I am feading 18 hogs 11 [t]o 12 for Sale hafto pack water to them which is an up hil Business i have apretty fare crop of Corn & Some old corn Sold Some old Corn at 50 pr Bu new corn 40 appels 50 & 60 wheat $1.00 cattel kno Sale horses hy I took my colts to the fare But Being Rather much rabbit Sine there i come out whare i Began ownly with less money & loss of time[12] old dad [started] to Switzerland Some time ago [ha]ve not heard from him Since Ef he is in y[o]ur State tel him we have heard from andrew & andrew wished him to write direct to west point Mo[13] Susan cooks for all our hands complains Agoodeal but Stil works on

we would be more than glad to See you All & you must all come to See us

Isaac Johnson took Suppr with us the other night but they Sent for him About bedtime to help about fire I must close as uncle P. Shuck & John[14] are here on a viset have preaching this Evning at Shiloh by mr allen[15] At 3.ocl Su[s]an Sends her respects to all you[r]s &c

fare wel

G. W. Demaree *Wm. T. Shuck*

Nov. 2[16]

Again the drouth Stil [c]o[n]tinues & fire Stil rageing in the woods & pastures A few Evnings ago i was invited to help Extinguish afire on Mrs Vannices[17] farm which was makeing towards her Barn But we removed Several thousand rails & rather Stoped the fire Since time i have been Very hoarse & have a very bad cold by over doing my Self my chimbley Builder come on last monday at 12 o clock put me up 2 Chimbleys & one flue finished friday at 4 Charged me $13.50 waited on him my self Nearabout put me through. The carpenters wil get reddy for the plasters this week.

I received aletter from [b]ro A. T. Shuck[18] Last thursday he says they have had Terabel times in Kanzes but have peace At presant but no Secu[ri]ty for life or property for what one pa[r]ty dose not destroy the other dose fine wether there grass green cattel fat plenty of melons up to the 16 Oct. & he voted the proslavery ticket & Expected to give buck alift & that he never Expected to be an Abolitionist & he had took kno part in the affairs yet but he Expected to Join the goveners army as he was for peace[19]

But willard is Elected i can Standit we beat the [bl]ack republicans abolitionis Negro Steal[e]rs ownly 7000 Stick this in your hat they are the worst Beat people you Ever Seen hogs have Been drive[n] from here to madison & not lost as much flesh In the Same length of time as they have Since the Election Ef you kyans [Kentuckians] had not of come over & voted they would have Beatenous they Say you must all stay at home on Election days[20]

old Squer Shuck[21] looks nearly as Black as nase Sence the Election

Ef they had of Beatten us we would have had to of left the State But we jist ask them have you heard from pennsylvania & Indiana [th]at kills a free monter[22]

We Expect to [illegible] franklin Before long & [illegible] river

I have many things to write to you But time & Space wil not prm[i]t J. More wars marryed to Jmima forsythe thursday night last[23]

you wil parden me for not writen Sooner as I have been uncommon Busy that i have quit chopping Stove wood for the old lady make the Buoys packit & you kno Jo & Sam[24] are workers i would like to heare from all Especially Saml & John give my respects to all &c

G. W. Demaree/Wm. T. Shuck

I wil perhapse send you one number of the Jeffersonian[25] 3rd you must all write Soon Stil cloudy but no rain yet us old liners gave our governer ownly 7000 majority Stick this in your hat hat hat & keep the woolies down[26]

5 oclock morning it Surely is raining Some but i fear By day light it wil be over But it is thundering very heavy which is a good prospect. Ef dad is with you let me kno

W. T. S

The second letter, from Peter Demaree to his brother in Kentucky, reflects the concerns of a typical Indiana farmer at this time in history. Health, money, and the war are uppermost in his thoughts. The Missouri lands mentioned were inherited when Peter's father died in 1858. Samuel had been given land in Missouri for service in the War of 1812. At the same time he bought cheaply large tracts of additional Missouri land from other veterans who preferred ready cash to uncultivated soil. By this method the elder Demaree acquired thousands of acres in Missouri, which were then divided among his heirs.[27] The depressed prices on sugar, coffee, and cotton remained low throughout the latter half of 1861, but the hog price of two dollars was only half what hogs had been bringing three months earlier.[28]

An 1860 satirical print depicting Republican presidential candidate Abraham Lincoln leading his party to the Lunatic Asylum. *Courtesy Library of Congress, Prints and Photographs Division.*

Johnson Co Ind
Nov 13th 1861

Dear Brother

I have bin thinking of Wrighting to you for Sum time but have neglected it I now make the attempt

We ar in usul helth at present. tha ar a good eal of cickness about feever of typhared forme Seemes to predominate then tha ar other grades of feever & a good eal of diptheara & Sor throat

We have not had the deeds of our masoura lands recorded yet the trobeld State of a fairs in that State We have bin afraid to risk Sending them, & it Seemes to get nobeter[29]

tha Will have to be Sum araingments maid to paying the tax on it I Will be glad if you Will give me Sum information concerning it I Supose it has bin all assessed together With out [a doubt] the rest of you have had your deeds recorded befor it Was assessed[30] I hav no ida how Wel manage to Pay our tax on the acount of the trobeld estate of goverment a fairs in mo it is very hard to tell hoo is the leagel oficers thar times is very hard her ever thing We have to Sell is very low & every thing We bui is very high Suger is 12½ ce lb coffe 20, [bown ?] coten 15 & ever thing elce in perporion tha ar only ofering $2.00 for hogs grosse I have a good too year old seear [steer] that I have bin ofering at 10 dolars & I hav not had one man to come to loock him eaven

I am very Sory that Ky has becom the Seit of War[31] War Such as the present one is the graitest calamatys that ever befell A nation my advise to you is to act as much as posibel With a christon Spearit not act rashly nether in Word or deed

you know how I Stand I have bin graty trobeld about goverment a fairs but I find it is no use to fret I try to be recncile as much as posibel beliving that god Will be wih the Wright.

if tha ever ar a thine that christions Should Pray more then another it dus Seemes to me that now is the thine but O What A coldness Seemes to exist in the church it Semes that We ar left to our Selves to go a Stray.

the cry Seemes to be blood blood. O What a glorious day it Will be When Peac & harmony Shall onst more rain. When the christion heart Shall flow With love to god & good Will to all men

may the Lord keep us & help us to liv faitful to the end

yours as ever

to G. M. Demaree ***P. Demaree***

Write Sone tell me What bro Samuel is Dooing

Shuck wrote the next letter only five weeks after Peter penned the one above. Again there is complaint about low farm prices. Actually from 1859 to the outbreak of the war in 1861 farm prices had risen steadily in Indiana. Then prices fell and remained low for several months. Recovery came in 1862, and prices continued to rise for the remainder of the war. Shuck mentions selling corn for twenty-five cents per bushel. This is as low as the price dropped. By 1864 corn was selling for ninety-five cents per bushel, the highest figure reached during the war.[32]

The Wild Cat Battle was not as impressive a Union victory as the letter indicates. Northern troops pursued a Confederate force from Perryville, Kentucky, toward the Cumberland Gap. The southerners, who were heading for Tennessee, tried to slow the Yankee pursuit by blocking roads with fallen trees. The battle occurred in October, 1861, near London, Kentucky, when some northern soldiers overran a small detachment of Confederates engaged in delaying tactics. A few hundred men on each side participated in the skirmish with total casualties amounting to less than seventy-five.[33]

Johnson Co Ind December 23, 1861.

Dear Brother & Sistr,

After long delay I Shal address a few lines to you in the way of news, &c.

I Shal Jest write to you on Such Subjects as tho we ware togather.

as the war is uppermost in evry mans thoughts you wil pleas pardon me ef I should write you a random Shot letter, that is miss the subject I ame at & lead off on the war.

we have had a beautiful fall of fine warm wether which gave the farmers a fine chance to Build repair dig & wall wels gather in there corn & get up there wintr wood tho there is allways Some one behind the times, or as the old Saying is put off the evel day as far as possible or think thre never wil be a change

we finished gathering corn the 17. inst   we have cribed near a 1000 bushels of corn   we husked Some 85 bbl on the Stalk   then we made a husking filled our crib & yet have a large pile on the floar   put up 7 loads in a pen for our out hogs & put the ballance in the old house.

yestureday was rather a rainy day or rather Sleet upon the Snow that fell Satureday night   this morning was quite cold & today has been a very good winter day, tho a very good day to chop & hall wood on the Sled, prepareing for christmas &c

tomorrow I expect to go to Franklin as that is the day of reconing between man & man that is in the way dets. there is no complaint needing in regard to the scarceity of money for it is as plenty as you ever Seen it but the rub is to get it. when our stock go off at half value to former years we think it quite a Sacrafice, beside paying dets quite slow but we must indulge with old father Abraham [Lincoln] for alittel Season & *Then.*

I have Sold two fine horses this fall for $160. I have Sold horses cattel & Sheep with one hundred & 25 bu old corn at 25 pr Bu to the amount of over $300. when it Should have Brought $500.

our children are going to School that is 3 of them Mary Jane Saml & Joseph   Jo is about as figity as ever   he has a great nack for beating the Drum   Sam whistels for the fifeer he has all the Barn doors & tabels nearly caved in   I wil either haveto get him a drum or go to *repairing.*

the war.   wel we have had Several months of war with Blood Shed deth & distress But whether we are any nearer great ness that at the Start I cannot tel.   it is vey Strange that as inteligent a people as the Americans are they cannot Settel a question without resorting to the Soard.

the papers Say the Wild Cat Battel in Ky was the greatest uneion victory that has been atcheived Sence the war Began, as we get but littel Southern news you wil give me ahistory of all the affairs of your Sate as we are deeply conserned about Ky as that is our Mother country.[34]

there is a greadeal of Sickness in the Regiment[35] our neighber boys are in Virginia. there has a good many returned home from that Regiment Sick perhapse wil die from the exposeure.

wel G. W. we have another fine Boy Born the 31. Aug we have not entirely named him yet we talk of calling his name George Thomas & ef we do you are to Send him a pair of Boots or a dog knife or Some other fine presant.[36]

the old lady[37] has quit Smoking except once a day we are all in usuel helth the kinfolks are jenerally wel.

Sister Mary wanted to kno what had become of cousin Voris He is roveing around Teaching Singing School & He entertains the same principal that Her husband *dose*.[38]

Peter told me He had received a letter from you & promise to Send it to me but has not.

We wil expect Samuel to attend to paying the tax on the Mo lands as usuel as there are none of them deeds yet Recorded Ef other wise we should be informed. I think it unnecessary to have them Recorded under the presan distracted affairs

I shal direct this to consolation[39] thinking this to be your nearest Post-office write soon donot delay as I have done. I must close.

Hoping that this wil find you & yours in the enjoyment of helth & prosperity & that I shal hear from you Soon

I remain yours as ever.

G.W. ***W.T.***

P.S. as I failed to mail this when I was at Franklin I have retained it up to the presant date 31s. Dec thre has been considerabel Stir the past week in collecting & paying dets there is but few that meets there contracts owen to the presure of times my payment was $400 I have paid $200. & have $100 Due me that I wil not get which leaves me $100. Minus. I expect to go to Franklin to day ef there is any thing new I shal add another PS.

the wether is quite fine at presant, two New moons this month.

> Buckner of this state has Jest returned from Newcastel Ky He says the people there are much dissatesfied & wil finally *secede*. He says they are crazy.
>
> you wil pleas write me the helth of John I. Vorises dauter

In the first paragraph of the next letter Peter mentions money received from his brother George. Since Shuck and Henry Demaree also received money about the same time, Peter is undoubtedly referring to an inheritance from his father's estate.

The substitutes mentioned in paragraph two were men who, for a substantial sum of money, agreed to take a draftee's place in military service. Four hundred dollars was not an excessive amount, however, for in some sections of the North substitutes were paid more than a thousand dollars.[40] Then, as now, no one wanted to be drafted, especially one who totally opposed the war as did many in Union Township and Johnson County as a whole.[41] Townships did all possible to raise their quotas without resorting to the draft. It is doubtful that

An 1864 print contrasting Lincoln and Democratic presidential candidate George McClellan, shown shaking the hand of Confederate president Jefferson Davis. *Courtesy Library of Congress, Prints and Photographs Division.*

the citizens of Union Township raised subscriptions so much out of patriotic enthusiasm as out of the desire to avoid sending their young men to a war they did not favor. Also, by raising their quota through subscription, the citizens avoided the stigma of cowardice that was sometimes attached to anyone who was drafted. That some of the townships had to draft is not difficult to explain. This was the third time in six months that the national government had called for additional troops. Johnson County's quota for these three calls was 920.[42] Most of the Johnson County residents were unhappy with the Lincoln administration. Peter wrote that he intended to vote for George B. McClellan; so did most of his neighbors. Johnson County was so thoroughly Democratic that it voted for the Democratic presidential candidate in every election from 1824 to 1920. In 1864 the county cast 1,713 votes for McClellan and 1,532 for Lincoln. The state, however, gave Lincoln fifty-four per cent of its vote.[43]

Brother Samuel, referred to in the last paragraph of this letter, joined the Confederate army in 1863 rather than be drafted by the Union in Kentucky. He rode with John Morgan's raiders in their romp through Indiana and Ohio but was eventually wounded and captured. He spent several months in the prison hospital at Camp Chase, Columbus, Ohio, before Henry obtained his release. He lived with Henry's family in Johnson County for a year before returning to Kentucky.[44]

Johnson Co Ind Oct 12 1864

Dear Brother

I Recievd A leter from you A few days agou & owing to the pressur of work I have not had A chance to write you. We Recievd the money you Sent us & have neglected to acnolage the Reciept or Send Reciepts for Same Bro Henry & W T had Bought A Seperater & had comenst thrashing When the money come & Was So Engaged With that tha thought of but litel Els I maned it to them & told them that We ought to atend to it but it was Still neglected I doo not know the Exact form of the reciet or I Would get them up & have them Sinde you had beter Send reciepts & I Will have them atended to & Return them. It Would allways be best for Reciets to accompany the money & then tha Would be no neglect

the peopel of this State has just Past thrugh a draft our touwn Ship Raisd money by Subcription & hierd Subistuts We had 30 men to furnish tha cos $400 each making 12000 dolars & this Saved our township of a draft. tha Was 3 other townships dun the Same the Rest of the County Was Drafted tha ar all trying hard to get Subistuts Cozen D D Banta[45] Was Drafted the State Election has went of I Supose the abeys has beeten us[46] it is as easy for them to beet us 50000 as 1000 as tha Resort to all maner of frauds

I See from your last leter that you ar not Pleasd With McClellan it makes but litel difernce hoo is the canidate for tha Will Elect old Abe at all hasards & Mc had as Well be Slauterd as eny other man if tha Was eny chance to Elect A Deocrat President I would rather have an oth man but I have no hopes I think the Sun of american liberty is a bout Seting never to Raise a gain

I in tend to voat for Mc if I am Spaird Bro Henry has bin to Washing city to get Bro Samuels Release he accomplished it Samuel as at Henry's he Saml Stood his trip beond Expecttation he is geting along Very Well he is quite Weak tho quite cherfull I think if he Would try to Excercise A litel he Would gain Strenth but he Seemes perfecly giv up I heave Seen Worse looking men then him going a bout. We are in usuel helth

yours as Ever

to G. W. Demaree *Peter Demaree*

I have Writen this A great hury look ore Blunders

The next letter from Shuck is interesting for the observations he makes about the end of the war, Lincoln's assassination, and John Wilkes Booth. The letter also demonstrates that to a farmer national events were important, but so were the spring rains and the price of land.

Shuck's letter exemplifies the phonetic spelling of that era. A clear distinction was not made between the "e" and "i" sounds in many words. Thus Shuck wrote "sence," "ef," distroyed," and "distruction." Other words, while not conforming to current spelling practices, are easily recognized and make for delightful reading. Some examples are: "broak," "deth," "helth," "littel," "reddy," "rool," and "wo."

Johnson co Ind May 2, 1865.

Dear Brother & sistr,

perhapse you wil think I am in a hurry in writing you so often, But the many great changes that have taken place sence we saw each other affords plenty of news &c.

it seems that the Rebellion is over that the spirit of the southern people has departed & they are ownly fit subjects for the yoke & chains that have been prepared for them   there doom is yet untold   there case is deploreabel in the extreme. ef they could be allowed to return home in peace & follow there daily ocupation with there slaves around them they would be doing wel, but there slaves are proclaimed free there country distroyed there lands to be confscated the public ded [debt] perhapse to be saddeled uppon them, wo to there misery & there *folly.*

I fear they wil be a people without a *country.*

There has been a great ado here about the deth of President *Lincon* who has been shamefully *assassinated.*   his corps was at Indianapolis Sunday   last they say there was 40000 people there all tho a very rainy day   rumer Says thre was thousands of dollars worth of Bonnets & dresses spoiled But they all braved the storm & mud to see the *chieftain.*[47]

it seems from the best proof that poor *Booth,* has payed the penelty that is layed down in Holy writ, wo to our nation & our beloved country.[48]

may the prayers of the Just wise meek lowly yet prevaile & save the nation from distruction.

we are haveing quite a wet spring   the most of farmers has but littel Broak for corn from 5, 10, to 15 Ac.   Some few are done but there is But littel planted yet. Some hardy ones are plowing up the mud But it may be dry after while. wheat has come out beyond all expectation   grass is plenty.

Wel G.W. we have waited Some 2 months on Mr Ellis & yet there has no money yet.[49] I informed you in my last that I had Bought land at the high price of $50 pr Acre my first payment being christmas   Sence I Bot I have a chance to Shave paper from 10 to 15 pr cent[50]   this I could have done the first of march, therefore Ef Mr Ellis is not reddy for settelment He must Expect to pay at least 10 pr cent.

we are Seling our produce at Reduced prices to meet our contracts therefore the golden Rool. I saw Peter yestureday   He is kneeding his money.

I Started a letter to Missouria yestureday in Regard to our Lands there. Ef you have any thing new on that subject pleas inform me. you wil also inform me whether thre is any ajents employed in each county.

we learn that David Johnston has been killed on his farm.

I was to see Brother Saml Sunday his helth is about as usuel he was quite talking & seemed cheerful.

Susan has been quite complaning with pain in her side & Back for several days but is Bettr.

Jes Demaree has lately marryed Molly Miller thompsons sister. Ellen has lately died with scrofula[51] She is next to Jane, there has been 4 deths in aunt Sallys family in a littel over a year, there is but 3 of the family left.[52]

we are all in usuel helth &c.

write soon
I remain yours affectontly

G.W. Demaree ***W T Shuck***

there is a great prospect here for fruit. Plery *Shuck is at home* give me all the news & the price & prospect of *tobacco.*

our George Boy is growing fast & fine

we have Broak 15 Acres for corn we sowed some oats we Broak 10 last fall we wish to plant 36 Acres.

The last letter from Peter Demaree is in many ways the most fascinating of the six printed here. The letter and the newspaper article following it picture in a few words the attitude of the average Hoosier toward blacks in 1867. One historian who has studied attitudes toward blacks during the Civil War wrote that of all the midwestern states Indiana was the most conservative by far. The racial situation did change somewhat after the war when the Indiana Supreme Court declared null and void the provisions of the Indiana Constitution which excluded blacks from entering the state and when the state legislature modified the law which excluded blacks from testifying in court. Nevertheless, many Indiana communities strongly discouraged blacks from settling in their midst, and it continued to be unlawful for black children to attend public school. The latter law was not changed until 1869.[53]

The last paragraph mentions an incident which resulted in the only lynching in Johnson County's history. David J. Lyons, an elderly Greenwood man, was murdered August 10, 1867, in an attempted robbery. The five men to whom

Peter refers were an old man, his two sons, and two sons-in-law. They were arrested for murder and robbery but later were cleared of the murder charge after implicating three men named Patterson, Simmons, and Hatchell. Patterson and Hatchell were eventually arrested, but Simmons escaped and reportedly was killed in Kentucky. During the night of October 31, 1867, an angry mob from the Greenwood area broke into the county jail at Franklin, removed the two suspects, and lynched them outside the town.[54]

Johnson Co Ind August 18 1867

Dear Brother

I recievd [your] leter I am very sorry to lern Bro Samuels condition I try in my Pore Way to Pray the Lord that he may Deliver him out of his affliction & give grase to suporte him in his trials & afflictions

We have very dry Wether corn crop is bound to be short

I have nuthing New to Write you Except A dificultia that I am in I Will giv you the pertícklers the trobel is between old John Shucks[55] my Self he has bin thrying to get me tryd in the church for more then A month the first of June tha Was a sabath school selabration in Franklin Shilowh Sc[hool] was in vited to atend bro Henry When the invitation Was Presented to the school for thar excptance oposd it on the grounds that We did not know What the program of the day Was & tha might be sum thing that We did not a prove of but the faithful put thare sholder to the Whel & excepted the invitation but tha Was A funarel at Shilowh on the day of [ce]libration[56] & tha Was but few of the school Went now for the program of the day the city schools of the difernt de[nomin]ations Was Put in front in persesion With A class of negrows next then come the contry schools this causd A goodeal of talk. Shortly after this Samuel & my Self Went to Franklin in A Wagon with Isack Vandivear.[57] Marggaret Shuck[58] got in Iks Wagon as We came home I asked her if she had bin at the selibration she said she had I asked What for time tha had only tolarble she said I told her I under stood tha had sum Negrows in thar Persesion she sed she believd tha Was A few I told her I did not A prove of such A coarse & had understud sum had taken thar children out & had I had [chil]dern in the Persesion I would have taken them out. What ses she dont you beleave the negrow aught to have the Gospel yes said I but in giving them the Gospel it dos not nesesarly leed to the sosial equality of the Negrow & I though that Was What it Was leeding to she said she Was not eny more in favor of negrow Equality then I Was but she Would not A felt the least bit degraded to march in persesion with A few litel negrows I told her that I thought it Would not be long till tha Would try to put them in the comin school With the Whites & Would you be Willing to teach A mixt school she said no but I Would as soone teach A negrow school as A White one provided I got the Dimes for it I ancerd her that I Would Rather be in a Rose Bush then in goards vines here the subject droped. I told this conversation to severL of [meny ?] Democrat friends sum one Roat an article for the County Paper [giving her line ?] tha acusd me of Writing or having hand in the article refurd to I told them I had no hand in it nor I did not know hoo ha[d roa]t it tha told me I ned not Deny it for I nod I had hand in it & Brow beat & villifyd me to the last & told me that tha Was going to have me before the church seshion. he has had it formely before the seshion for A month the seshion has bin dragen me Round trying to get sumthing out of me I tell them that I neather Roat dictated nor counsield the Writing of the article refurd to & I have told nothing but the trueth & Intended to defend it I dont know Whar the thing Will end bro H stands suar up to me in my dificultia

She [does] not deny What she said but tha say it Was cowardly in me in telling it

Shuck is clamering for the church seshion to Pas sum order to pertect thar Radicals members aganst talk A ganst the negrow eliment the ida is Il say What I pleas & you don tel it

When if eve[r] this Dificultia is seteld I Will Write you the result We expect to see the thing though We expect to take it to Presbytery if nesary.

murdering Robing & theaving has become the order of the day last monday morning tha Was a gang of men Went to A mans home a bov franklin baterd Down [his d]ore with a rail the man Resisted & tha shot him & Robd him & left the man has died I believ tha have Arested 5 men & have them in jail at Franklin tha ar sitizens of this county you must write

yours as ever

Peter Demaree

Following is the article to which Peter referred:

Black or White

MR. EDITOR:—It is very natural for persons to look and see who will take the lead in new things, and who is willing to condesend to teach the colored children in our midst.

There is a blooming maid of some 25 summers, living in Union township, by the name of Miss N. S. . . . [*sic*], who has publicly expressed her willingness to teach the young negroes of this or some other county,

> provided she can get the dimes for her services when rendered, and says some one has this NOBLE OFFICE to fill, and expresses her entire willingness to teach and associate with the loyal "Americans of African descent." "She has had some experience in teaching the white children of this vicinity, and no doubt she would do well teaching the MORE NOBLE RACE," and thus advance the reputation of the poor white children whom she has taught in days gone by and make the hearts of those poor parents rejoice to know that the minds of their children have been directed onward and upward. Would not some young and dashing youth do well to call at her father's house and see this fair and lovely maid, who has such a good heart, and try to pursuade her to cast her lot with his and travel life's weary journey together. It might not be amiss for some young gentleman of color to give her a call; he would no doubt receive a cordial welcome, and the "twain might be made one flesh," and bring into existance something more grand, more noble and more sublime than has ever yet graced our neighborhood.
>
> UNION[59]

The Franklin (Indiana) *Johnson County Press* was the county's Democratic paper. It was extremely anti-Republican, antiradical, and anti-Negro. It made all manner of charges against the Republicans—perjury and stuffing the ballot box being the most frequent. Three months later, on October 17, the paper added: "it has been settled by a church in our county that if a man tells an ordinary lie he is not a fit person to be a member, but if he will cast an illegal vote and commit perjury in the bargain, his conduct does not deserve even a censure."[60]

The Shiloh church session records have not been located and with them rests the final outcome of Peter's trouble with John Shuck. It is interesting to note, however, that Peter and his wife left the membership of the Shiloh church on December 8, 1867.[61] Since Peter denied writing the newspaper article, he probably was not expelled from the church but more likely quit in disgust.

The six letters printed here reveal an interesting change in the attitudes of two northern Democrats during the era of the Civil War. In the first letter Shuck is nearly ecstatic as he brags that the Democrats have outsmarted the Republicans in the 1856 elections. The war, however, changed that attitude abruptly. No expression of triumph, no sense of bragging are seen in the letters of the 1860s. Both Peter and Shuck cry out against the futility of the war in 1861. By 1864 Peter exhibits a feeling of political frustration and hopelessness. Instead of lauding the Democrats he laments that the Republicans have probably won again in Indiana and that no one the Democrats nominate can defeat Lincoln.

Shuck and Peter were never stalwart supporters of the war or of Lincoln's administration. It is not surprising then to find in Shuck's 1865 letter no attitude of vindictiveness. No "bloody-shirt" phrases come from his pen. Instead the former Kentuckian expresses fear and concern for the fate of defeated southerners. He had not agreed with their secessionist stand, and he had not supported them in the conflict that followed; but he fears that their punishment will be greater than their crime. And 1867 finds Peter, a Hoosier who had signed slave deeds less than ten years earlier,[62] in the midst of postwar difficulties relating to social equality of the blacks. Such difficulties were not unusual for residents of Indiana in the post-Civil War era, nor have they been completely resolved today.

WILLIAM G. EIDSON was Associate Professor of History at Ball State University, Muncie. Vincent Akers was a CPA with Price Waterhouse & Co. and a Demaree descendant with a special interest in Johnson County history. This article originally appeared in volume 70, March 1974.

NOTES

1. The original letters are in the possession of David B. Demaree, Pleasureville, Kentucky. Transcribed copies of the letters may be seen at the Indiana Historical Society Library, Indianapolis. All pictures are from the collection of Mr. Akers.

2. Information on the early family background and "Low Dutch" connections comes primarily from family papers, grants, deeds, depositions, and memoranda in Mr. Akers' possession. Samuel Demaree's deed from the Low Dutch Company, dated September 12, 1836, is recorded in Deed Book, XVIII, 6–7 (Henry County Courthouse, New Castle, Kentucky).

3. The Dutch were instrumental in the founding of four Johnson County, Indiana, communities: Franklin, Greenwood, Hopewell, and Shiloh. The Demarees were most closely associated with the farming communities of Shiloh and Hopewell. The basic sources for the history of these communities are David Demaree Banta, *Making A Neighborhood, Delivered at the Shiloh Reunion, May 26, 1887* (Franklin, Ind., 1887); and Robert Allen Brown, "The Making of Hopewell, 1831–1915," typescript (Indiana State Library, Indianapolis).

4. For a genealogical record of the Demaree family see Voorhis D. Demarest, *The Demarest Family* (2 vols., Hackensack, N. J., 1964).

5. Emma Shuck to Elizabeth Demaree, August 20, 1890, Demaree Collection. Various letters and memoranda in the Demaree Collection are the sources for the background information on Shuck.

6. Peter Demaree's obituary, Franklin (Indiana) *Democrat*, May 25, 1888.

7. Peter Demaree to George W. Demaree, April 6, 1860, Demaree Collection.

8. George W. Demaree wrote hundreds of articles for beekeeping magazines during the period of 1880 to 1900. His name became known internationally through his method of swarm control, first publicized in 1892. George W. Demaree, "How to Prevent Swarming," *The American Bee Journal*, XXIX (April 21, 1892), 545–46. The term "Demareeing" was generally adopted to describe the necessary manipulations. Two biographies are: [L. L. Langstroth], "Biographical—G. W. Demaree, Esq.," *The American Bee Journal*, XXXI (March 6, 1893), 328; and William G. Eaton, "Beemaster—Not Just A Beekeeper (A story about Kentucky's George W. Demaree, of Swarm-Control fame, in Retrospect)," *The American Bee Journal*, XCVI (December, 1956), 474–77. Sources for the background information on G. W. Demaree are various letters and memoranda in the

Demaree Collection. Demaree's Civil War attitudes are clearly spelled out in a series of newspaper articles which he wrote in 1903 entitled "Some Local History of the Dark Days of the Civil War," Shelbyville (Kentucky) *Shelby News*, June 18, 25, July 2, 9, 16, 23, 1903.

9. Emma Lou Thornbrough, *Indiana in the Civil War Era, 1850–1880* (*The History of Indiana*, Vol. III; Indianapolis, 1965), 71–72, 76–77.

10. The six letters in this article were transcribed from the original handwritten documents; photocopies of the originals were used for editorial purposes. Although decisions were at times necessarily arbitrary, every effort was made to determine and retain the capitalization, spelling, paragraphing, and punctuation intended by the correspondents. Unintentional word repetitions and what appeared to be superfluous or indiscriminate commas and periods were deleted. Spacing of headings, salutations, and closings was standardized; and in order to increase readability, space was left between sentences when there was no punctuation in the original letters. Brackets enclose letters or words which were missing because of torn manuscripts or possible explanations of illegible or confusing terms. Notes written in the margins of the letters were added following the signatures. Local individuals and family members mentioned in the letters have been identified through footnotes wherever possible.

11. "Mr. W. T. has not got his house finished yet nor wont have before christmas if then his workmen get along slow." John B. Demaree to George W. Demaree, November 25, 1856, Demaree Collection.

12. "Being rather much rabbit sine there" probably means that the buyers and sellers were too timid while there.

13. Henry Shuck, William T. Shuck's father, was then sixty years old and addicted to heavy drinking. He had evidently set out for a related settlement of Dutch families in Pleasant Township, Switzerland County, Indiana. Andrew was W. T. Shuck's younger brother. Information is from notes on the Shuck family by John Owen Demaree, Demaree Collection.

14. Uncle P. Shuck and John are either Shuck's uncles, Peter and John, twin brothers who had settled in the Shiloh neighborhood in the 1830s, or they are Peter and his son John. John O. Demaree's notes, Demaree Collection.

15. The Reverend Archibald Cameron Allen was pastor of the Hopewell Presbyterian Church from 1854 to 1859 and of the Shiloh church from 1868 to 1870. The two churches were closely associated since the Shiloh church was organized by Hopewell members in 1832. In 1888 the Shiloh congregation was combined with the Hopewell church. Brown, "The Making of Hopewell," 9, 33–35; D. D. Banta, *Making A Neighborhood*, 48.

16. Shuck resumed his letter to his brother-in-law on November 2.

17. Shuck is probably referring to Elizabeth VanNuys, widow of Isaac VanNuys. The VanNuyses had moved to the neighborhood in 1836. Isaac died in

1844, and Mrs. VanNuys moved to Franklin in 1858. D. D. Banta, Making A Neighborhood, 39.

18. A. T. Shuck, W. T. Shuck's younger brother, is undoubtedly the same Andrew who was requesting that his father write to him at West Point, Missouri. Shuck would have received this new letter from his brother on the intervening Thursday, October 30.

19. After passage of the Kansas-Nebraska Act in 1854, settlers had moved into Kansas determined to make that territory free or slave. Agitation between proslavery forces and free state forces led to disputed elections and bloodshed. In May, 1856, proslavery advocates sacked Lawrence, Kansas. Antislavery settlers under the leadership of John Brown retaliated by murdering five proslavery men at Pottawatomie Creek. The guerrilla warfare that followed led to many deaths and much destruction of property. The "buck" referred to is James Buchanan, successful candidate for the presidency in 1856. The "governers army" was the Kansas militia organized by Governor John White Geary to help maintain peace and to divert the turbulent energies of both the free state and proslave forces. Jay Monaghan, *Civil War on the Western Border, 1854–1865* (Boston, 1955), 92; Richmond (Indiana) *Palladium*, October 2, 1856.

20. Willard actually defeated Morton by slightly less than 6,000 votes. Charles Roll, *Indiana: One Hundred and Fifty Years of American Development* (5 vols., Chicago, 1931), II, 149; Richmond (Indiana) *Palladium*, October 23, 1856.

21. Squire John Shuck, William's uncle, was a justice of the peace in Johnson County. Theodore M. Banta, *A Frisian Family: The Banta Genealogy* (New York, 1893), 158.

22. A "free monter" was a supporter of John C. Fremont, Republican presidential candidate in the 1856 election. Indiana and Pennsylvania supported Fremont's Democratic opponent, James Buchanan. The Indiana vote was 118,000 to 94,000 in favor of Buchanan. In Pennsylvania, Buchanan's home state, the margin was much greater–230,000 to 147,000. W. Dean Burnham, *Presidential Ballots, 1886–1892* (Baltimore, 1955), 248.

23. Joseph J. Moore and Ermina Forsythe were married Thursday, October 23, 1856. Moore had been born in Union Township in 1831 and was destined to become one of the most prominent businessmen of the county. He at one time operated dry goods, grocery and clothing stores, a warehouse, tin shop, butcher shop, scale house, and lumber mill in Trafalgar, a town in Hensley Township, Johnson County, which he is credited with having named. David Demaree Banta, *History of Johnson County, Indiana* (Chicago, 1888), 562–64, 709–10.

24. Jo & Sam were William Shuck's two oldest children. Joseph William was eight and Samuel Nelson was seven at the time this letter was written. William T. and Susan Shuck family Bible in the possession of Mr. Akers.

25. The Franklin (Indiana) *Jeffersonian*, published from 1852 to 1886, was Johnson County's Democratic newspaper in 1856. The paper was never proslavery and was later to be the organ of the Stephen A. Douglas Democrats. When the Civil War broke out, it became a Republican newspaper. Elba L. Branigin, *History of Johnson County, Indiana* (Indianapolis, 1913), 412. The county papers published during the 1856 election are no longer extant.

26. The exact meaning of the term "woolies," as it is used here, has not been ascertained.

27. Information here and in footnote thirty regarding Samuel Demaree's estate is taken from the grants, deeds, letters, memoranda, and the administrators' receipts and records in the Demaree Collection.

28. Franklin (Indiana) *Democratic Herald*, August 15, 1861; January 2, 1862. These are the nearest existing issues to November, 1861.

29. In Missouri the conflicts between unionists and secessionists were particularly severe. By the summer of 1861 attempts to avoid bloodshed by conciliation had failed. The second largest battle of 1861 was fought at Wilson's Creek in August. Guerrilla fighting, neighborhood war, and the intervention of forces from Kansas continued to trouble the state for the next few years. James G. Randall and David Donald, *The Civil War and Reconstruction* (2nd ed., Lexington, Mass., 1969), 234–36.

30. The Missouri lands had been surveyed and divided into eleven equal parts in May of 1860. A drawing was held June 28, 1860, and each heir was assigned a ticket representing one of the eleven parts. Eleven deeds were drawn up, each of which had to be signed by all of the heirs and their husbands and wives. The brothers and sisters were at that time living in Kentucky, Indiana, and Missouri, and all the deeds were sent to each state to be signed and notarized. Even after the last of the heirs in Missouri had finally signed in October of 1860, the trouble was not nearly over. William T. Shuck in a letter dated January 20, 1861 (Demaree Collection), and addressed to Samuel Demaree, Jr., who was handling the division, brought up a matter of pride which further delayed the recording of the deeds:

"I feel that you have treated us with Scorn & contempt I kno that we wil get the Same Shear the way the deeds are, but what man wants to send a deed to the recorders office to be recorded in his wife's name I do not care Ef She is the Heir of inheritence, the Supposition arises that She is a widow otherwise her husband is a worthless bankrupt & not worthy to manage his wife's affairs."

"You Say those deeds must be Recorded next Spring, Ef you wil make them as they Should be made we will have them Recorded Ef not I care but littel what becomes of them that is my feeling about it. . . ." By the time this point was cleared up the war had made it unsafe to have the deeds recorded; thus, the recording was delayed until September 25, 1866.

31. In September, 1861, Confederate forces under General Leonidas Polk seized Columbus, and Union troops under Grant retaliated by occupying Paducah. During the reminder of the year Union troops moved into Louisville and Covington while Confederates advanced to Bowling Green and the Cumberland. Though no major battles occurred in Kentucky during 1861, the situation was tense as counties, cities, and even families divided their loyalties. Mark Mayo Boatner, III, *The Civil War Dictionary* (New York, 1959), 455.

32. Thornbrough, *Indiana in the Civil War Era*, 389–90.

33. *The War of the Rebellion: A Compilation of the Official Records of the Union and Confederate Armies* (70 vols., Washington, 1880–1901), Ser. I, Vol. IV, 205–14. Hereafter this work will be cited as *Official Records*.

34. Apparently many Hoosiers were concerned about events in Kentucky. Almost every issue of the Indianapolis *Daily Journal* in December carried letters from Indiana soldiers stationed in Kentucky, news articles about the border state, or items from Kentucky newspapers. For further discussion of Indiana's preoccupation with affairs in Kentucky see Thornbrough, *Indiana in the Civil War Era*, 108–109; Kenneth M. Stampp, "Kentucky's Influence on Indiana in the Crisis of 1861," *Indiana Magazine of History*, XXXIX (September, 1943), 263–76.

35. Shuck was undoubtedly referring to the Seventh Indiana Regiment, reorganized in the fall of 1861 for three years' service, with Company F being made up of Johnson County men. Seven Johnson County men in this company are known to have died in the period from November, 1861, to January, 1862. Five Demarees from the Shiloh and Hopewell neighborhoods belonged to this company, including two nephews of the correspondents. D. D. Banta, *History of Johnson County*, 731, 739; Demarest, *The Demarest Family*, II, 8, 9. Volume II of this work contains war records of the Demarest family.

36. George Thomas Shuck, the sixth and last child of William T. and Susan Shuck, was born August 31, 1861, and died January 21, 1935. Shuck family Bible.

37. The "old lady" undoubtedly refers to Shuck's wife, Susan Demaree Shuck, as both his mother and mother-in-law had died prior to 1861.

38. The exact identities of "Sister Mary" and "cousin Voris" are difficult to establish. Both Shuck and Demaree had sisters named Mary. Demaree's mother was one of fourteen children of Albert and Anna Banta Voris and was distantly related to Congressman Daniel W. Voorhees of Terre Haute, Indiana. Shuck also had Voris cousins and was in fact a grandnephew of Anna Banta Voris. T. M. Banta, *Frisian Family*, 157–58; Elias W. Van Voorhis, *A Genealogy of the Van Voorhees Family* (New York, 1888), 315–42, 543–54.

39. Consolation was a railroad depot and post office in northeastern Shelby County, Kentucky, near where George W. Demaree was living.

40. The original purpose of substitution was to allow those in critical jobs to aid the war effort by remaining at home while another took their place in the

service, but in reality anyone who had the resources and the desire could furnish a substitute without reference to the importance of his position. At the time Peter wrote this letter draft boards could exempt a man the whole term for which he was drafted if the draftee would provide a substitute who was not eligible for the draft. If the substitute was eligible for the draft, then the draftee's name was again placed on the rolls for future calls. Eugene Converse Murdock, *Patriotism Limited, 1862–1865* (Kent, Ohio, 1967), 9–10, 31–32; Jack Franklin Leach, *Conscription in the United States: Historical Background* (Rutland, Vt., 1952), 256, 396–97; U.S., *Congressional Globe*, 38 Cong., 1 Sess., Appendix, 140–42, 257.

41. D. D. Banta, *History of Johnson County*, 1735; Livy A. Young, *A Backward Glance at Old Union* (Franklin, Ind., [1940]), 37–39.

42. D. D. Banta, *History of Johnson County*, 738.

43. Burnham, *Presidential Ballots, 1836–1892*, pp. 238, 400–401; D. D. Banta, *History of Johnson Country*, 690–92; Branigin, *History of Johnson County*, 29; Edgar Eugene Robinson, *The Presidential Vote, 1896–1982* (Stanford, 1934), 188.

44. Samuel Demaree, Troop C, Fourth Kentucky Cavalry, died in October, 1871, in Henry County, Kentucky, of the wounds he had received in the war. Various letters and memoranda in the Demaree Collection, especially correspondence between Samuel and George W. Demaree, 1863–1865.

45. This is David Demaree Banta (1833–1896), who later became a circuit court judge, president of the Indiana University Board of Trustees, and dean of the Law School at Indiana University. He was fascinated by local history and wrote several Johnson County histories. The Banta Collection at Franklin College, Franklin, Indiana, is named after Judge Banta and consists primarily of material on Indiana and the Middle West. Banta's mother, Sarah, was the youngest sister of Samuel Demaree, Sr. Burton Dorr Myers, *Trustees and Officers of Indiana University, 1820 to 1950* (Greenfield, Ind., 1951), 296–99; Demarest, *The Demarest Family*, Vol. I, p. VII-20-1.

46. "Abeys" is the editors' conjectural transcription of the almost illegible word scrawled by Demaree. If this is indeed the correct term, it presumably referred to Republican followers of President Abraham Lincoln.

47. Lincoln was assassinated on April 15, 1865. His funeral train arrived in Indianapolis at 7:00 a.m., April 30. The body was taken to the State House, where visitors were able to view the fallen President from 9:00 a.m. to 11:00 p.m. One newspaper estimated that despite the rain which fell throughout the day 100,000 persons passed by the President's coffin. Indianapolis *Daily Journal*, April 30, 1865.

48. John Wilkes Booth, Lincoln's assassin, was captured and shot in a barn near Bowling Green, Virginia, on April 26, 1865. *Official Records*, Ser. I, Vol. XLVI, Part I, 1317–22.

49. William R. Ellis bought from the heirs, at $25.00 per acre, 173 acres of the Samuel Demaree farm in Henry County, Kentucky. Deed Book, XXIX, 50–51 (Henry County Courthouse, New Castle, Kentucky).

50. Bank notes which circulated as paper money during this period were frequently discounted at less than face value. This practice, known as "note shaving," was applied not only to bank notes but also to other types of commercial paper. For a discussion of the complex financial practices and conditions in early Indiana see R. Carlyle Buley, *The Old Northwest: Pioneer Period, 1815–1840* (2 vols., Bloomington, 1951), I, 565–632; II, 260–325; Logan Esarey, *State Banking in Early Indiana, 1814–1873 (Indiana University Studies,* No. 15; Bloomington, 1912), 219–305.

51. Scrofula is an antiquated term for a morbid constitutional condition which is usually hereditary and most common in childhood. It manifests itself in development of glandular tumors, particularly in the lymphatic glands of the neck, which usually degenerate into ulcers.

52. Jesse Young Demaree (1838–1902) married Mary Melvina Miller (1843–1871) on April 3, 1865. Two weeks later his sister, Rachel Ellen (1847–1865), died, the fourth death in the family in a little over a year. Only Jesse and two sisters remained of the family of George Washington Demaree (1812–1851), Samuel's younger brother, who had moved to Johnson County in 1835. Demarest, *The Demarest Family,* Vol. I, pp. VII-21, VIII-28-9.

53. V. Jacque Voegeli, *Free but Not Equal: The Midwest and the Negro during the Civil War* (Chicago, 1967), 170, 172; Thornbrough, *Indiana in the Civil War Era,* 231, 482, 543; Richard G. Boone, *A History of Education in Indiana* (New York, 1892), 239.

54. Branigin, *History of Johnson County,* 107–108; Franklin (Indiana) *Johnson County Press,* August 22, September 26, October 31, November 7, 14, 1867; Indianapolis *Daily Journal,* August 13, November 2, 1867. It was rumored that Hatchell may have been innocent of the murder charge, and in the following spring several leaders of the lynch mob were indicted for his murder. Although found not guilty and supported by the majority of the county, their indictment was an unusual aftermath for a lynching in that era. Franklin (Indiana) *Johnson County Press,* March 12, 1868; Indianapolis *Daily Journal,* March 6, 10, 13, 18, 19, 1868.

55. Squire John Shuck (1800–1878), William T. Shuck's uncle, was a first cousin of Peter Demaree's mother. He was described as "the neighborhood chimney corner lawyer" noted "for his wit and humor and power of declamation." His humor was evidently stretched by Peter's alleged insult to his daughter. T. M. Banta, *Frisian Family,* 157–58; D. D. Banta, *Making A Neighborhood,* 32, 34.

56. The sabbath school celebration was held June 4. The funeral Peter attended would have been that of Mrs. Serril Winchester who died June 3, 1867. The Winchesters were among the earliest settlers in the Shiloh community. Franklin

(Indiana) *Johnson County Press*, May 23, 1867; D. D. Banta, *History of Johnson County*, 674; D. D. Banta, *Making A Neighborhood*, 14–15.

57. Samuel (1847–1938) was Peter Demaree's son. Isaac Vandivier was an area farmer, then forty-one years old. Demarest, *The Demarest Family*, Vol. I, p. IX–26; Branigin, *History of Johnson County*, 822.

58. Margaret F. Shuck, daughter of Squire John Shuck, was at this time an "old maid" school teacher of thirty-three. T. M. Banta, *Frisian Family*, 158; Young, *A Backward Glance*, 78.

59. Franklin (Indiana) *Johnson County Press*, July 11, 1867.

60. *Ibid.*, October 17, 1867. There is no way to determine whether or not this notice was connected with the order which Shuck was clamoring for the church session to pass "to pertect thar radicals." Other churches in the county were also having political troubles at this time.

61. Membership roll of the Shiloh Presbyterian Church, published in D. D. Banta, *Making A Neighborhood*, 42.

62. The heirs of Samuel Demaree had sold slaves in 1859. Deed for the sale of Thomas Perce to Samuel Demaree, Jr., January 14, 1859, Demaree Collection.

Recollections of Morgan's Raid

MIDDLETON C. ROBERTSON

ON THE ELEVENTH DAY OF July, 1863, Gen. John H. Morgan and his army passed through Graham Township, Jefferson County, in the flight through southern Indiana from Kentucky to Ohio. Not being a trained soldier, Morgan did not rank in ability with a number of the generals in the Confederate Army but was recognized throughout the South as an able and valorous officer. In his military operations in Kentucky and Tennessee, he and his command constituted a destructive force with which the Union armies found it difficult to cope.

At the time of the Raid, I was not at our family home which was less than a mile from the line of march of the enemy army. I was away temporarily visiting an uncle, Dr. H. D. Gaddy, at Weston, in Jennings County, and so did not see any of the Confederates. There were no telephones or radios in those days, but we kept fairly well advised as to what was going on outside of our community. Hearing of a movement among the citizens to assemble at Vernon and engage the enemy in battle, my uncle joined them. I see him now through the eyes of memory as he rode away that Sunday morning in company with some of his neighbors, his rifle on his shoulder and enough bullets in his ammunition pouch, that I had helped him mould, to send the souls of scores of Morgan's men to purgatory. The day passed, but no sound of cannon came our way which led us to believe that there was no battle in progress. After hours of waiting for him, my uncle returned. He bore on his person no marks of carnage or strife, but did bring the glad tidings that Morgan had gone without unleashing his guns in the destruction of life or property.

Morgan's Raid as depicted in *Frank Leslie's Illustrated Newspaper*, August 8, 1863.

Not many years prior to his death, G. W. Whitsett, who, for a long period was well known in this part of the country by reason of his musical talent, informed me that he was in Vernon at that critical period of its history and that a regiment of Union soldiers from Michigan was there and also a considerable number of citizen soldiers. Mr. Whitsett stated that he was present and overheard a conversation between General Lew Wallace, who was in command, and the colonel of the Michigan regiment. The latter begged permission to lead an attack against the enemy, but the general was firm in his opposition, alleging that in view of the superior strength of the foe, such a move would result in a useless waste of life.

The most vivid remembrance that I have of any experience in those troubled times relates to something that happened a few days after Morgan had gone out of the state. Some men came along, riding fast and furious past my Uncle's place, pausing just long enough to tell us that the Confederate leader, General Forrest, had destroyed Paris by fire and was coming our way, burning buildings and killing men. My uncle assigned me two tasks—one to assist in burying a box of silver coins, amounting in value, I suspect, to several hundred dollars, and the other to walk to the home of his fatherin-law and give warning to the family of impending danger. The distance was about a mile, part of it through a dark woodland. I was younger then than I am now, being in my twelfth year, and not over-stocked with that admirable quality of the spirit called courage. I discharged my trust, but not without realizing that the sense of fear was a part of my make-up.

The supreme moment was yet to come. It was not long after Morgan passed until a body of armed men on horseback came into view. Surely, we thought, this must be Forrest and his army and the end of the world. We were unduly alarmed, for, when the men came close, they told us they were not Confederates but Union men. It was they who had been at Paris, they declared, explaining that it was through the distorted imaginations of some parties who had seen them that the rumors of disaster and death had been spread. An imaginary danger, for the time being, is as nerve-racking as an actual one, for, while one thinks he is in danger, to him it is real and palpable. Learning that we had been deceived, whether intentionally or otherwise, the black cloud of fear lifted and passed away. From that day to this I have never felt any danger imminent to myself or country from armed rebellion or foreign foe.

About a fortnight after Morgan had come and gone, I returned to my home in Graham Township. The perspective was about the same. No marks of vandalism were observable except the loss of three good horses. There had been a forcible transfer of the title to ownership from the family to the Confederacy. On the morning of July 11 (1863), my brother Philander, had gone to a mill about three miles east of our house. The mill was built on land now owned by Hiram Foster. The trip was made in a two-horse wagon and wheat had been exchanged for flour. The day was fair and no portents were in the sky of impending danger until on the return trip my brother reached a point in the road opposite Pisgah Church. Suddenly about fifty men appeared in view and soon demanded that he get out of the wagon and unharness the horses. Being slow to obey, they persuaded him to hurry by pointing their guns in his direction. The horses then taken were good ones. Philander was forced to walk in front of them to the creek about half a mile north of the Church, where the marauding band bade him go home. Before he reached the house, the band of riders had visited the premises and taken from the stable a fine young black mare, the idol of the family. My eldest sister, Nancy, though habitually of a mild and equable temper, became so angry when she saw her pet mare being taken away, that she told those sons of Dixie what she thought of them in the most abusive and bitter language at her command. She did not accomplish more than if she had given them her blessing instead, for they took the beautiful animal away and my sister newer saw her more. This was one of the great sorrows of her life.

Our home was not the only one visited by the raiders. Almost all the good horses near the line of march were taken.[1] There was one marked exception. James Dowen Robertson, better known in this vicinity as "Uncle Doc", lost only one horse and saved four. His eldest son, Melville, was at home from college on his summer vacation. Looking towards the South, he saw a large body of horsemen at a high point in the road where John Stuart now lives headed in the direction of his home. Acting with quick presence of mind, he went to the barn and rushed off four good horses to a thicket at the back part of the farm where he tied them near together so they would not get lonesome and break the quiet. These four horses escaped capture. Returning to the house, he found some Confederates ransacking it. Uncle Doc had recently become the owner of a new pair of fine boots, and one Confederate, evidently having some sense of humor, picked up the boots and said: "This fellow has some good boots, and I believe I will trade with him." By reason of some offensive remark, Melville was compelled to go with the rebels as far as Dupont where he was released. Later he joined the Union army, was captured in his first battle, and held for some months in a confederate prison. After his release, he contracted typhoid fever in the Union Camp at Vicksburg, from which he died.[2] Uncle Aquilla Robertson, better known as "Uncle Quill," a brother to Uncle Doc, was less fortunate than his brother in saving his horses, as all of his were taken.

The youngest daughter of Uncle Quill, Mrs. Rebecca McClelland of Deputy, remembers well the leading events of Morgan's raid. She lived with her father, less than half a mile from the road over which Morgan and his army passed. They could see the cavalry and artillery as they passed along the highway. They first saw them at about 8:30 in the forenoon. They were nearly all day passing. The most exciting scene in the drama came when several Confederates came into the yard clamoring for something to eat. One insistent fellow attempted to go into the kitchen in spite of a refusal by Rebecca's stepmother to admit him. To stop him the stepmother flourished a butcher knife in his face saying: "I'll let you know I am one of the blue hen's chickens from the State of Virginia, and if you make any further attempt to enter here I'll cut your heart out." Eyeing her intently for an instant, the Confederate said: "I know them Virginians will fight like the devil and I have no doubt you mean what you say." He went away and left her, for the time being, mistress of the situation.

Next morning (July 12) at about 6:30, while the family were at devotions, the father leading in prayer, several armed men in federal uniform entered. They disregarded the usual civilities on entering a home, and in a rough and overbearing manner demanded something to eat. Being Union soldiers, the family were glad to feed them. The father ended his prayer rather abruptly, as any other good man would have done under the circumstances. Regarding the number of men in each army, Rebecca's impression is that according to the estimates of the people at that time there were somewhere between four and five thousand men on each side.

My story would not be complete without some reference to another prayer, made a day earlier, that is, on the day of the raid. There then lived in Graham Township a local preacher, Reuben Rice by name. He was an ardent Methodist and a militant abolitionist. These facts, together with his heavy artillery voice when in prayer, made him a distinctive citizen in the community. It was currently reported and generally believed that some Confederates called upon him and under threat of death commanded him to get down on his knees and pray for Jeff Davis and the success of the southern government, which, being under duress, he did. "Prayer being the soul's sincere desire, uttered or unexpressed," it was really not prayer, but mere lip service. It accomplished no good. Rice lived for years and years after John Morgan and the southern Confederacy had passed away, and all through these years prayer was a part of his daily program. One week before this time, Lee and his splendid army were defeated at Gettysburg and retreated back across the Maryland border, and Grant, after long, patient and laborious effort, captured Vicksburg. Surely the clock had struck the hour marking the beginning of the end of the southern Confederacy.

Dr. C. H. McCaslin, now of Kansas City, Missouri, was at the time of the Morgan raid a boy about my age, but much larger and I think much braver. He lived on what is now the E. J. Wolf farm, the dwelling house being within 100 feet of the road over which the armies of Morgan and Hobson passed. From a letter that I received from him, not long since, I quote:

> When John Morgan's raid through Jefferson County occurred, I was plowing corn. I looked up the road and saw a company of soldiers on horseback. I supposed it was the home guard going to Washington, Indiana, where the company at Paris, Indiana, had been ordered. Morgan had telegraphed Governor Morton that he was going that way. My brother was at home on a furlough and he went with the Paris home guard. The Confederates were all day passing our house, and I wish to state that my mother was sick in bed and I was sent to the spring for water. It was surrounded with soldiers. An officer approached and asked if I wanted water. I told him my mother was sick and wanted a drink, and he ordered the soldiers to stand back and let me fill my bucket. They had several carriages which in those days were known as rockaways. Whether General Morgan was riding in one of them or not, I cannot say. They took all of the horses within the radius of two or three miles on each side of the road. They told us there would be a larger army the next

day and that they would burn houses and barns, but Generals Hobson and Shackelford of the Union army followed them.

There was an incident on the day of the Raid that gave a touch of comedy to the tragic side of the picture. A prominent woman of our community evinced considerable excitement when she learned that Morgan was near. She lived in a large house, well stored with valuable goods and furnishings. Wishing to salvage something of real worth from the coming destruction, in her confusion she selected a mirror and hastily took it to the garden and buried it. This seems ludicrous in view of the fact that she made no effort to save things more valuable, but perhaps there was method in her madness, for, after all, what is there about a home which a woman prizes more than a looking-glass?

If the searchlight of truth were applied to all the facts connected with the Morgan raid, it would awaken a memory not complimentary to the Federal Government. Morgan's men, about as fast as they captured and appropriated good horses, discarded those that they did not care to use longer, and quite a number of these were taken over by the farmers. They were fed, groomed, and taken care of until they were fit for farm work. My brother appropriated two of these horses but just when he, in common with his neighbors, felt that they had some amends for their losses, the Federal Government sent agents around and through might not right, took possession of these horses without any compensation to the farmers whatever. This was not only flagrantly unjust, but it was obviously unwise. Here was a government in a great war needing provisions to feed the armies and navies and depending in part on these very farmers to supply foodstuffs, but at the same time taking from them the means of production needful to help the cause along. Later a concerted effort was made to induce Congress to appropriate money to reimburse the farmers for their losses sustained by reason of the losses explained, but these claims were never allowed.

For more than three score and ten years, the body of John Morgan has slept in the dust of the earth, but the government that he sought to destroy still lives at Washington, and the flag under which the Union armies fought still waves in undiminished splendor.

MIDDLETON C. ROBERTSON was born in April 1852 in Jefferson County, Indiana, and died in April 1940. When the article appeared in 1938, the author noted that he was "now more than eighty-six years of age, and was more than eleven at the time of the Raid led by General Morgan." This article originally appeared in volume 34, June 1938.

NOTES

1. General Morgan and the main part of his troops passed northward on a road about one mile east of where Deputy is now located. This road was then, and is now, intersected by an east and west road that runs from Deputy to Madison, Indiana. The intersection of the two roads is about one hundred feet from the bridge on the Deputy and Madison road. The part of the road traveled by General Morgan which runs southward from the intersection long ago went into disuse, but the part running northward from that point remains for about a mile very much the same as it was in 1863. The Paris mentioned was about three miles north of Deputy. The latter is on State Road 3 about ten miles north of Scottsburg and nearly west of Madison.

2. The "Diary of Melville Cox Robertson" was published in the *Indiana Magazine of History* 28 (June 1932), 116–137.

4

The Battle of Corydon

EDITED BY ARVILLE L. FUNK

ALTHOUGH CONFEDERATES AND THEIR SYMPATHIZERS made various raids across the Ohio River into southern Indiana during the Civil War, the one led by General John Hunt Morgan exceeded them all in size. Morever, it caused more excitement, resulted in more property damage, and created more legends than did any of the other raids. The objectives and results of Morgan's raid continue to be interpreted with much diversity of opinion.

General Morgan's cavalry division included approximately 2,400 troops when it arrived at the little Ohio River town of Brandenburg, Kentucky, on the morning of July 7, 1863. During the previous day advance scouts had captured two steamers, the "J. T. McCombs" and the "Alice Dean," for use in crossing the river. Meanwhile, the Indiana Legion (Home Guards) and local volunteers called for reinforcements and girded for conflict.

On July 8 Morgan easily crossed the Ohio despite the opposition of the Indiana Legion and local volunteers. Proceeding northward against sporadic opposition from the Hoosiers, Morgan's cavalry spent the night several miles south of Corydon and about ten miles from the Ohio.

Next morning, July 9, the Indiana Legion and the local volunteers fought the invaders at the Battle of Corydon, a mile or so south of the former state capital. Morgan's cavalry were soon victorious and immediately marched into Corydon and looted the town, then headed toward Palmyra and Salem yet that afternoon.

The account of the Battle of Corydon which follows was written by Simeon K. Wolfe, editor of the Corydon *Weekly Democrat*, and a participant in the battle. Though his estimate of 4,500 men with Morgan is about twice the actual number, Editor Wolfe frankly admitted quick defeat for the defenders. The original punctuation and spelling have been preserved in reproducing the editor's account from the *Weekly Democrat* of July 14, 1863. Since the newspaper was a weekly, additional items were interspersed in succeeding columns after the main account of the battle as further news was received.[1]

The Morgan Raid Into Indiana.

The Battle at Corydon.

450 Home Guards and Citizens.
vs:
4,500 Rebel Cavalry and 7 Pieces of Artillery.

The Home Guards & Citizens hold the Rebels in Check 25 Minutes.

Home Guards and Citizens Overpowered by Numbers and Compelled to Surrender.

CORYDON CAPTURED

Union Losses four Killed and two Wounded.

REBEL LOSS 10 KILLED AND 40 WOUNDED.

GREAT ROBBERY OF THE PEOPLE IN TOWN AND COUNTRY.

Our town and community have been the scene of intense excitement during the whole of the past week in consequence of the invasion of the State at this point by the notorious guerrillas under the equally notorious John Morgan. A vast amount of damage by horse-stealing and other plundering has been done which it is impossible for us to detail at the present time with any great degree of accuracy, but we think it a safe estimate to put the loss to our citizens at the least at $100,000.

We will endeavor to give a reliable account of the raid from the time the rebels crossed at Brandenburg up to the time when they left Harrison county. But for the lack of due military organization and the consequent official information on many points, our details may not be in every particular correct, but the main features we *know* are correct, for we were present in the midst of some of the exciting scenes and have a

THE CORYDON DEMOCRAT.

SIMEON K. WOLFE, Editor

CORYDON, IND., JULY 14, 1863

The Morgan Raid Into Indiana.

The Battle at Corydon.

450 Home Guards and Citizens.

vs:

4.500 Rebel Cavalry and 7 Pieces of Artillery.

The Home Guards & Citizens hold the Rebels in Check 25 Minutes.

Home Guards and Citizens Overpowered by Numbers and Compelled to Surrender.

CORYDON CAPTURED

Union Losses four Killed and two Wounded.

REBEL LOSS 10 KILLED AND 40 WOUNDED.

GREAT ROBBERY OF THE PEOPLE IN TOWN AND COUNTRY.

Corydon Democrat, July 14, 1863.

very lively recollection of them; of the other matters we think we have reliable accounts.

THE FIGHT AT BRANDENBURG CROSSING

On Tuesday evening (July the 7th) the steamboat T. J. McCombs landed at Brandenburg, and was immediately captured by Morgan's advance guard then in possession of the town. The McCombs was taken by the rebels to the middle of the river and there she hoisted the sign of distress. Soon after the Alice Dean coming up was hailed to give relief. For that purpose she approached the McCombs and was thus also captured by the rebels. The news of the capture of these boats was communicated by some Union men of Brandenburg to Lieut Col: Wm. J. Irvin, of the Indiana Legion, then at Mauckport. A short time after receiving this intelligence the Lady Pike coming up was hailed by Col. Irvin at Mauckport, and turned back to Leavenworth for a six-pound gun and [*sic*] assistance; a dispatch was also sent to Col. Jordan at Corydon for reinforcements to intercept the rebels crossing. At midnight the Lady Pike returned with the Leavenworth gun and a small company to man it under command of Capt Lyons and Col. Woodbury. Before daylight, on Wednesday morning the gun was in position on the bank opposite Brandenburg, and as soon as daylight and the disappearance of the fog would render it practicable the gun was directed by Col. Irvin to be fired upon the boilers of the vessels with a view of sinking or disabling them and thus prevent the crossing of the raiders. This command, we are informed by Colonel Irvin, was countermanded by Provost Marshall [*sic*] John Timberlake who claimed precedence in command on the occasion, and an order was given by the latter officer, to shell the rebel cavalry on the bank. Another and different version, however, of this matter, we understand is given by Provost Timberlake; but we have not been able to see him and obtain it. This shelling was done for a short time with some success, causing the rascals to skedaddle to the rear of the town in fine style but before getting out of the way some thirty of them were killed and wounded. Soon, however, after our gun opened fire, two rebel batteries, one at the Court House at Brandenburg and the other towards the lower part of town, began to play with terrific force upon our gun with shells, making it too hot for our boys to hold their position. They abandoned the gun, but afterwards retook it and carried it farther to the rear. The rebel infantry from the Kentucky shore also kept up a brisk fire across at our forces; and our infantry, consisting of Capts. Farquar's Huffman's and Hays' companies of the Legion, in all not exceeding 100 men, returned the fire briskly.

But the superior artillery force of the enemy soon compelled our small force to abandon the gun again, and then under the cover of his batteries, the enemy began to cross their thieving forces to the Indiana side. Our boys held the ground as long as it was prudent or safe in the face of the forces coming against them, and then retired.

In this gallant little fight we lost two men killed and three or four wounded.—The killed were, Georia Nance of Laconia and James Currant of Heth township. Capt Farquar was pretty badly injured by his horse running him against a tree. The names of our wounded in this fight we have been unable to obtain.

SKIRMISHING ON THE ROAD

Failing in the effort to prevent the rebels crossing Col. Irvin and provost Timberlake ordered the men to fall back on the road to Corydon and by skirmishing and falling trees to obstruct the passage of the enemy as much as possible until reinforcements with artillery could be had from New Albany, to which place dispatches were repeatedly sent for help; but for some reason, which we hope the authorities of that post will be able to explain, *we never got a man or a gun!* Not deterred however by this neglect, or the overpowering forces in our front, the people went to work and by great exertions a force of Home Guards and citizens, number about 300 effective men, were got together on Wednesday evening and marched out on the Mauckport road to skirmish with the enemy and impede his progress as much as possible. The main body of these under command of Col. Jordan, went as far as Glenn's house four miles south of Corydon. Here the infantry remained until about 10 o'clock at night and returned to the neighborhood of Corydon, while the cavalry and mounted citizens to the number of over one hundred men were sent on the roads running south of Corydon as scouts to watch the operations of the enemy. Several small engagements between the skirmishers occurred on Wednesday evening and Thursday morning; in one of these one rebel was killed near Glenn's house, and two prisoners were captured. The rebels, shortly afterwards at the same place shot John Glenn, a son of Peter, through both thighs, and about the same time—shot and killed Peter Glenn, an old and well known citizen, and burnt his dwelling and barn. In their progress to Corydon they also burn Peter Lapp's Mills on Buck creek, which is all the burning of property we have heard of them doing in the county. Their principal depredations being in horse stealing and robbing houses and citizens of everything valuable.

Many "hair-breadth escapes" and gallant charges are reported by these skirmishers, but we have not the space for detailing them at this time.

THE BATTLE AT CORYDON.

About 11 ½ o'clock on Thursday morning our scouts brought the report that the enemy was approaching in strong force up the Mauckport road toward Corydon. Our forces, consisting of about 450 Home Guards and citizens under command of Col. Lewis Jordan of the Legion, assisted by Provost Timberlake (late Col. of the 81st Indiana regiment) and Maj. Jacob Pfrimmer (who up to this time had been engaged with the cavalry in scouting) formed a line of battle on the hill one mile south of town, the extreme right wing resting at the Amsterdam road and the left near the Laconia road, making the Mauckport road, along which the main body of the enemy would approach, about one third of the distance of the entire length of the line from the right wing. The ground on the left of the Mauckport road is a heavy woods and though not hilly is somewhat uneven, which with the logs and underbrush made it difficult for a cavalry charge. This portion of the line was well selected for the purpose of saving our men from the rebel fire, but bad for the purpose of enabling our men to operate effectively against them, the line being at least fifty yards too far north, being that distance from an elevation in the ground which prevented either party from seeing the other before the enemy arrived to that distance from our line. Temporary breastworks composed of logs and fence rails were hastily thrown up by our forces which did good service in impeding the charge of the enemy.

About an hour later, the enemy made his appearance in small force, probably one company, about three quarters of a mile a little to the left and in front of our line where they were handsomely whipped by the infantry under the command of Captain G. W. Lahue which had been placed there for picket duty. In that fight we lost one man killed, named Steepleton, and had none wounded. The rebels had several killed and six or seven wounded. Before this skirmish was fairly over, the enemy made their appearance in front of our main line along the Mauckport road in strong force. We (the editor) were with a squad of the Henry Rifles under command of Maj. McGrain, at the extreme right of the line on the Amsterdam road and had a full view of the approaching enemy. They completely filled the road for nearly one mile. As soon as they approached in range the Henry Rifles opened fire and did good work, the enemy being in full view. Soon the fire became general along the entire right wing, which checked the advancing column of the enemy, and compelled them to undertake to flank both our wings at the same time, a performance which the great disparity of forces enabled them easily to do.

Shortly after the flank movement was began [*sic*] and before it was executed, the enemy opened upon our forces with three pieces of artillery, making the shells sing the ugly kind of music over our heads. This shelling operation, together with the known fact that our line would be strongly flanked on both wings at the same time made it necessary for the safety of our men, for them to fall back. This was done, not with the best of order it is true, for our forces were mostly undrilled, but with excellent speed. From this time the fight was converted into a series of skirmishes in which each man seemed to fight upon his own hook mostly after the manner of bushwhackers.

In the meantime the enemy had completely flanked the town, having, before a gun was fired, taken possession of the plank road one mile east of town, where our men in their retreat were intercepted. Upon the right wing a large flanking force was sent against our lines and the fighting was very sharp for the space of 20 minutes in that quarter; twelve Henry Rifles and a squad of 30 or 40, some 100 yards to their left, armed with the ordinary rifle musket holding a heavy body of flankers in check for ten or fifteen minutes and compelling them to dismount.

Being completely overpowered by numbers our forces gradually fell back to Corydon and the cavalry and mounted infantry generally made their escape. After the field was taken by the enemy they moved forward, and planted a battery on the hill south of the town, and threw two shells into the town, both of them striking near the center of main street, one exploded but did no damage. Seeing the contest was hopeless and that a continuance of the fight would only result in unnecessary loss of life and the destruction of the town, Col. Jordan wisely hoisted the white flag and surrendered.

The enemy immediately marched in and took military possession of the town; and then the work of pillage soon began. Everything the rebels wanted in the eating and wearing line and horses and buggies they took. The two stores of Douglass, Denbo & Co., and S. J. Wright and the two Steam Mills were the heaviest losers. The two stores were robbed of about $300 each and a contribution of $700 each in cash was levied upon the two mills in town and a like sum upon Mauck's mill near town. This large sum Messrs. Leffler & Applegate, Wright & Brown and John J. Mauck were compelled to pay to save their Mills from the flames. Many other citizens lost in horses and other property from 100 to $600, Mr. Hisey was robbed of $690 in cash. But we have not space enough to enumerate the pecuniary losses—few or none escaped entirely.

LOSSES.

The Union losses, beside property, are as follows:

KILLED:

Wm. Heth; Nathan McKinzie and Harry Steepleton—3.

WOUNDED:

Jacob Ferree and Caleb Thomas—2.

Our loss in prisoners was about 300 all of whom were paroled.

The rebels admitted their loss to be 8 killed and 33 wounded.

FORCES ENGAGED.

The number of forces engaged was 4500 commanded by Gen. Morgan with 7 pieces of artillery. The Union forces, consisting of raw malitia [*sic*] and citizens, did not exceed 450. With these raw troops—*one* yank to *ten* rebs—Morgan's progress was impeded about five hours, which we hope will result in his capture.

Under all the circumstances we think our boys did exceedingly well. It was not expected at the start that so small a force could whip Morgan, but it was expected we could punish him some and impede his progress so that somebody else more nearly equal his strength could catch him and do him justice. That this will soon be done we have every reason to hope.

HIS LEAVING THE COUNTY.

About 5 o'clock, P. M., after robbing the town to his heart's contents, the King of American Freebooters left, moving north on the Salem road, stealing, as a matter of course, as he went. In Blue River township the rebels shot two young men named McKinstry and at Bradford they shot a German whose name we did not learn.

Morgan's Whereabouts.

It isn't safe to say one hour where Morgan will be the next. Our latest intelligence placed him in the neighborhood of Vernon in Jennings Co., on Saturday where he had a fight with Lew. Wallace. A small squad of the raiders were whipped and scattered at Perkin in Clark county, a portion of their scattered men were seen in the north part of this county on Sunday.

Facing, The July 14, 1863, issue of the *Corydon Democrat* carried news of the Union victories at Vicksburg and Gettysburg, as well as Morgan's Raid.

GLORIOUS NEWS!

Vicksburg Surrendered with Over 20,000 Prisoners!

We have the glorious news, officially announced, that Vicksburg surrendered to Gen. Grant on the 4th inst, at 10 o'clock, A. M. with the entire garrison. The number of prisoners taken is about 20,000 effective men besides several thousand disabled. By the terms of the capitulation they were all paroled, including Lt. Gen. Pemberton, the commander of the post. We have no room for details this week.

The Great Battle at Gettysburg Penn. Between Gens. Meade and Lee—Lee Badly whipped.

We have full and authentic details of the great Battle at Gettysburg Penn. fought on the 2nd and 3rd inst., but have neither time nor space to insert them this week. The substance of the thing is, that General Meade gained a great victory—Lee is badly whipped and was trying to escape to the south side of the Potomac. Meade captured about 15,000 prisoners. Lee's loss is fully 35,000 in killed and wounded; our loss about 20,000. Unless Lee manages to effect a crossing of the Potomac another heavy battle will soon take place.

After leaving this county Morgan went to Salem and captured the town without any resistance. After burning the depot and committing all the depredation he wanted, he left, going east.

Shot and Mortally Wounded.

At Salem, Wm. Vance, a son of the late Arthur Vance of this place, was shot by the rebles and mortally wounded, but under what circumstances we have not been able to learn.

★ ★ ★

6 Rebs and 19 Horses Captured.

Six of Morgan's men and nineteen horses were captured by the citizens near Fairdale, on Monday morning, and brought to this place. They are a portion of those that crossed at Twelve Mile Island. They were cut off from their main force in a skirmish at Pekin on Saturday evening last. The 13 who had the other horses have not at this time (Monday evening) been captured, but will be, unless they dodge equal to Morgan himself. The horses are mostly very fine ones.—The Rebs came to a house unarmed, gave themselves up and told where the horses were hitched in the woods.

Hurrah for Old Harrison!

Morgan, at last accounts, was at Aurora, Dearborn county, having left Vernon. The Home Guards and citizens, in no other county but Old Harrison, stood and gave him a fight. We fought him twice.

In the hurry and confusion with which we have been surrounded for the past few days we have not, in our account of the rebel invasion and the battle, been able to give a statement of the different companies of the Legion engaged. Nor are we able to state fully the assistance we received from other counties. We saw some gallant boys from Georgetown and Edwardsville. The "two hundred from New Albany," mentioned by the Louisville Democrat, we have not heard of.

We have every reason to believe and hope that Morgan cannot escape from the State. Ample preparations are on foot to capture him.

Another contemporary document which describes the Battle of Corydon is the following letter written by Attia Porter, a young Corydon girl, to her cousin Private John C. Andrews, Forty-third Indiana Infantry Regiment, Company C, who at the time was with the Union army in Helena, Arkansas. This letter is the property of the family of James P. Andrews of Terre Haute, and is here reproduced with the permission of the Andrews family.

Corydon Ind. July 30/63

Dear Cousin

I was just studying the other day whose time it was to write mine or yours and could not come to any satisfactory conclusion, when your letter arrived and as a matter of course I was the debtor and I have since found out I owe you two letters instead of one. I received yours with the miniature three weeks ago, but never could manage to sit down and write. We have had rather exciting times in Indiana for the last few weeks, and have had a few of the miseries of the south pictured to us though in a small degree. On the doubly memorable ninth of July a visit was paid to the citizens of Corydon and vicinity by Morgan and his herd of horse thieves. We heard Tuesday night that they had crossed the river and had disgraced the soil of Indiana with their most unhallowed feet. Our home guards skirmished with the rebs from the river to [Corydon] and on one of the hills overlooking the town had a grand *battle*. The battle raged violently for *thirty* minutes, just think of it! and on account of the large number of the rebs we were forced to retire which our men did in good earnest every one seemed determined to get out of town first but which succeeded remains undecided to this day. After the general skedaddle, Col Jordan wisely put up the white flag—and we were prisoners to a horde of thieves and murderers. I don't want you to think I am making fun of our brave home guards for I am not in the least. But now, that all the danger is over, it is real funny to think how our men did run. Gen. Carrington awarded great praise to us and we all think that is something. What could 350 undrilled home guards and citizens do against 4,000 well drilled and disciplined soldiers (?) We did not even know Hobson was following him. We sent to New Albany time and again for help and not one man or gun did they send us. Though we have found out since that it was the fault of Gen. Boyle and not the people of New Albany. It made Morgan so mad to think a few home guards dared to fight his men. I am glad they done it just to spite him. However they captured most of the guards and parolled them and killed three of our men. Father was out fighting with his Henry rifle but they did not get him or his gun. One of Morgans spies was in town three or four weeks visiting his relatives and some of his men helped our men to build the entrenchments. I guess none of the rebels down south are that accommodating are they? One of our brave boys run three miles from the rebels, and really run himself to death. He stopped at a house and fainted and never came to. Dident he deserve a promotion?

I think that was the awfullest day I ever passed in my life. The rebels reported around that they shot father because he would not surrender, but it was all a story. The rebs were pretty hard on the copperheads but they did not take a thing from us. The[y] kidnapped our little negro and kept him three weeks but he got away from them and is now at home safe. We killed six or eight of theirs and wounded twenty five or thirty. I expect you are tired of hearing about Morgan so I will stop. I forgot my letter till so late this morning, and I have not got time to write much more or I will be too late for the stage so Goodby.

Attia

ARVILLE L. FUNK was a teacher at Perry Township Junior High School, Marion County. This article originally appeared in volume 54, June 1958.

NOTES

1. For a general account of Morgan's Raid see Cecil Fletcher Holland, *Morgan and His Raiders* (New York, 1943); Louis B. Ewbank, "Morgan's Raid in Indiana," Indiana Historical Society Publication, Vol, VII, No. 2 (Indianapolis, 1923); and Logan Esarey, *History of Indiana* (2nd ed., 2 vols., Indianapolis, 1918), II, 771–775.

5

"This Just Hope of Ultimate Payment"

The Indiana Morgan's Raid Claims Commission and Harrison County, Indiana, 1863–1887

STEPHEN ROCKENBACH

FOR MORE THAN A CENTURY, hundreds of depositions, still sealed in the envelopes in which clerks had placed them in the 1880s, lay in boxes in the National Archives. Forgotten and crumbling with age, the evidence of southern Indiana's losses from the July 1863 depredations of John Hunt Morgan and his raiders (and the Union troops who pursued them) sat unread, even as romanticized versions of the raid—and its effects on hundreds of Hoosiers—continued to circulate as history. Few of the residents of Harrison County, Indiana, who waited in vain for more than two decades for some reimbursement for their wartime losses would have been surprised by the fate of their depositions.

On July 10, 1863, Henry Richard stood watching General Edward H. Hobson's Union cavalry pass in front of his farm in pursuit of Confederate raider John Hunt Morgan. One of the young troopers approached Richard carrying a saddle and bridle—his horse had dropped dead several hundred yards behind. The patriotic Richard offered the only mount he had at hand—a mule—to the beleaguered cavalryman, who remounted and joined the chase. Like many other civilians in the area, Richard hoped that his loss would be compensated, especially since he had given his mule to Union troops; instead, he found himself among the hundreds of southern Indiana residents who lost property to either Confederate or Union troops, only to be frustrated by a long and fruitless effort to receive payment. It was not until 1882 that clerks at the federal Office of the Quartermaster General reviewed Richard's claim for $150 for the loss of his mule. Although his story seemed likely, the quartermaster refused the claim.

In his efforts to aid Union forces and avenge the rebel incursion into Indiana, Richard had forgotten to ask the officer in charge for a receipt.[1]

On July 7, 1863, Morgan's raiding party of almost 2,500 cavalry, backed by four artillery pieces, occupied the hills above Brandenburg, Kentucky, and then crossed into Harrison County, Indiana. Morgan's raid on the county seat of Corydon on July 9 culminated in roughly thirty minutes of fighting—a skirmish commonly referred to as the battle of Corydon—between Confederate forces and elements of the state guard aided by local volunteers. The significance of Morgan's raid into southern Indiana lies not only in the brief fighting that took place that day, but also in the subsequent inability of state officials to deal properly with local residents' claims for the extensive losses that they incurred in its wake. Historians and popular writers have neglected the raid's lasting financial impact in favor of more romantic accounts of Morgan's Confederate raiders and residents' sometimes inaccurate, but intriguing, tales passed down through generations.[2] Three main misconceptions continue to distort Hoosiers' thinking about the event. First, popular conceptions of Morgan and his troops as a latter-day Confederate version of Robin Hood and the Merry Men have led some to assume that citizens were not adversely affected by the raid, and may have even benefited in some cases. For example, folklore surrounding the raid claims that many Hoosier farmers were happy to learn that the raiders left them quality Kentucky thoroughbreds, which eventually made fine race horses.[3] Second, several writers have misinterpreted an 1867 ledger recording claims as proof that the state paid victims for their losses—it did not. Finally, many historians view Morgan's raid as a pointless sideshow of little historical importance. It was, instead, a well-timed strike at the midwestern homefront, and it brought the pain and destruction of war to families north of the Ohio River.

A careful study of the raid's effect on Harrison County and the fate of residents' claims for compensation proves the error of these assumptions. In the aftermath of the raid, U.S. military authorities in Indiana rounded up horses confiscated by Confederate and Union troops, but then only temporarily loaned them out to farmers to harvest the wheat and corn ripening in their fields at the time of the raid. During three successive sessions of the Indiana General Assembly, residents of Harrison County and other affected counties filed petitions for relief from their losses at the same time as their representatives and senators introduced legislation intended to collect, adjudicate, and pay legitimate claims. In 1867, legislators finally authorized a commission to investigate the losses related to Morgan's raid; 468 Harrison County residents filed a total of $86,552 in claims for property and monies lost to Confederates,

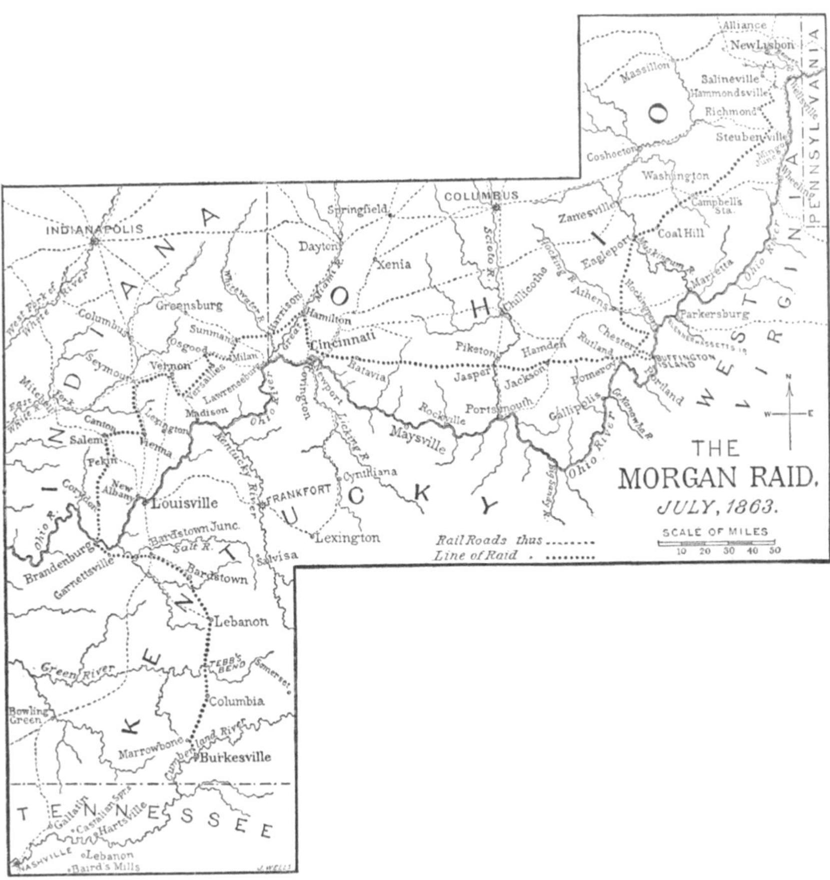

A map of Morgan's Raid, from Robert Underwood Johnson and Clarence Clough Buehl, *Battles and Leaders of the Civil War* (1887).

Legion members, and Union troops. The amount totaled about five percent of all personal property listed for the county in the 1860 census.[4] However, Indiana lawmakers failed to pass the necessary legislation to settle the claims. In the 1870s and 1880s, residents and their descendants submitted requests for payment of $81,558.07 to the U.S. Quartermaster General (USQG), but by law that office could consider only legitimate and properly documented claims against Union troops, and thus the quartermaster paid out $8,659.[5]

From the start, county residents considered state and national authorities to be partially responsible for Morgan's troops having crossed the Ohio River and for the absence of a sufficient number of Union troops to prevent Morgan's capture of Corydon. The defense of Corydon was not, contrary to popular belief, led by a ragtag collection of home guard. Instead, the companies that assembled outside of town were but a small part of the 6th Regiment of the Indiana Legion, a state-funded military organization created to defend the southern counties and made up of men from those counties.[6] However, the Legion mustered only about 400 members and volunteers to stand against several thousand Confederates. Gen. Jeremiah T. Boyle, who commanded the state and federal troops in the Louisville area, believed that Morgan intended to attack New Albany, and as a result refused to let the Legion companies go to the aid of their comrades in nearby Corydon. Two weeks after the raid, Harrison County treasurer William Hisey wrote to Gov. Oliver P. Morton asking for Boyle's resignation on the grounds that the Union commander had let "rebel cavalry, with artillery, destroy a country town."[7] Although Hisey was justifiably bitter after losing $786.87 in cash and property to the raiders, he was right to criticize Boyle for subverting the Legion's organization and holding back part of the regiment.[8] Three weeks before Morgan's incursion, more than one thousand state troops had garrisoned the town during an invasion scare.[9] Corydon's citizens believed that federal and state governments could have taken greater measures to protect against the raid, and that they therefore shared at least partial responsibility for the loss and destruction that followed.

The raid's greatest immediate impact fell upon merchants and business owners, who suffered the highest monetary losses. The raiders charged local businessmen a five-hundred-dollar protection fee for three of the community's mills, and although they largely avoided needless destruction, some of the men burned a flour mill outside of Mauckport because snipers allegedly fired from the building.[10] Theft was much more common—Samuel J. Wright lost $5,524 in merchandise from his Corydon store and became so financially burdened that he placed an ad in a local newspaper asking all of his customers to pay their debts to him, because "Morgan's band of thieves robbed me of at least half my goods."[11] At the beginning of the war, Wright had accepted the potentially lucrative position of quartermaster for the Legion's 6th Regiment. In January 1864, he resigned, citing the financial burden of the post, supply difficulties, and the raid's effect on his business. Wright eventually sold his store and fell back on his legal training.[12]

Farmers, laborers, mechanics, and tradesmen also risked privation—especially farmers trying to finish the wheat harvest. Those who had already cut their wheat lost some of their crop to both raiders and their pursuers, who stole fodder and even resorted to taking wheat out of the shock to feed hungry mounts.[13] Both Confederate and Union cavalry also took local farmers' horses, which were essential for harvesting and marketing agricultural goods. Farmers who could not afford cutting and threshing machinery usually cut by hand, but they still used horses for treading, to stomp the wheat away from the stalk. Wheat growers who owned, or had access to, a threshing machine needed horses to power the equipment. Large machines needed as many as ten horses, requiring neighbors to combine their resources during the harvest.[14] The raiders took between 300 and 400 horses in Harrison County, while the Union cavalry in pursuit of Morgan took an additional 150 mounts.[15]

A number of local men remained at their homes and attempted to hide their property, while others joined Legion companies and left the job to their wives and children—most to little avail. To maximize their speed, the raiders and their Union pursuers commandeered new mounts in a frenzied and relentless manner. Rebel horsemen often left behind one worn-out mount when they took a fresh horse, and on several occasions, successive groups of raiders took and replaced the horses left by their comrades. The baffled citizens could do nothing but watch as the Confederates recycled their own spent mounts.[16] Union pursuers then picked among the animals that had been overlooked, hidden, or left behind in order to replace their own tired mounts. Isaac Pittman formed up with the Legion while his wife Mary hid one of their horses. The couple left two plow horses in the stable, and Isaac was able to return to his fields the day after the raid to cut wheat with his three horses and one borrowed animal. A group of raiders had overlooked the animals when Mary made them breakfast on July 9, but the following day Union cavalrymen took two horses and left Isaac to finish his work with half a team.[17] In disrupting the harvest, the raid jeopardized the economic stability of this rural community.

Morgan and his men had been relatively lenient on civilians in the bluegrass, often taking only food or fresh mounts. Once in Indiana, however, the Confederate raiders were determined to exact retribution from inhabitants and reap the benefits of raiding a state not yet touched directly by war.[18] Thirteen claims mention cash among the stolen items. Including the protection money paid by business owners and the cash taken from citizens, the Confederate raiders probably robbed residents of more than two thousand dollars. Some claimants listed both guns and cash lost to rebel forces, which suggests that the Confederates relieved captured townsmen of their weapons and whatever cash they had in their pockets.[19] The raiders made off, as well, with a variety of personal items, including various articles of clothing and at least nine pocket watches. The community also lost at least ten boats of various sizes. It is unclear whether Confederate soldiers damaged and destroyed boats to slow their Union pursuers, or residents themselves caused the losses. James Trotter indicated in his claim for $40 that his wooden boat had been damaged while he tried to "prevent rebels from crossing the Ohio River."[20] None of these claims was covered by the laws governing the quartermaster's reimbursement procedure. Clerks denied payment and marked the files "Taking and Use Not Proven."

The skirmishes also caused loss of property and, more importantly, of life. On July 9, the Legion cavalry and a number of mounted minutemen spread out along the roads south of Corydon and prepared to ambush the Confederate attackers. The defenders knew that they could not stop the larger opposing force, but they hoped to cover the approaches to town, slowing down the enemy and giving the expected troops from New Albany time to arrive. Capt. William Farquar ordered detachments of cavalry, including a small group of twenty-two Legion men, to form a skirmish line along the Corydon–Mauckport Road, approximately four miles south of town. The squad prepared to make a stand near Rev. Peter Glenn's house. Glenn's son, John, was a member of this unit and probably suggested his father's farm as a defensible position. The Hoosiers charged forty advancing Confederate cavalry and killed Private John Dunn of the 5th Kentucky. When the remainder of the Confederate regiment arrived, the Hoosier horsemen withdrew towards Corydon. Elsewhere, citizens, determined to protect their property and livelihood, distracted the approaching raiders by firing from concealed positions and then withdrawing.[21]

Events at the Glenn farm exemplify the sorrow and loss caused by the raid. Shortly after the cavalry retreated, Confederate troopers shot Peter Glenn and set fire to the house. A number of variations on the incident appeared over time, including one version that suggested that raiders murdered Glenn because they recognized him as an abolitionist.[22] Later newspaper reports indicated that Glenn's wife, Catherine, and his daughter-in-law were in the house when Confederate reinforcements arrived and discovered Dunn's body nearby. Concluding that gunmen inside the house had killed him, rebel officers ordered the house to be destroyed. Confederate accounts depict Glenn and his son as "bushwhackers" who resisted cavalrymen's attempts to burn the house—common retribution when civilians fired on troops from buildings. Legion reports claimed that the rebels told the minister to surrender and then murdered him in cold blood. In 1881, William Weaver testified in a sworn affidavit to the U.S. quartermaster that Peter Glenn had helped the Legion troops during the skirmish; the account matches the Legion's version of events. Weaver attested that rebel troopers killed Glenn: "When he came forward he was shot and murdered and his dwelling house and barn burnt."[23] Regardless of the details of varying accounts, Confederate troops killed Peter Glenn, wounded John Glenn, and destroyed the Glenn farm because the minister and his family opposed the Confederate advance. Ironically, the family hid their horses during the raid, only to have Union troops take one of the mounts from a nearby field as they stopped at the smoldering ruins of the farm the next day. The Glenns were among the most prominent victims of the raid, and their losses should have been reimbursed—but they were not. State and military authorities took steps to restore order after the raid, although not all of the regulations worked in favor of farmers. Gov. Morton ordered Gen. Henry B. Carrington, commander of the Indiana military district, to issue a detailed description of the procedure for reporting and recovering stolen or appropriated horses. The message detailed the policies and procedures needed to remedy "the exigencies of the harvest and the interruption of the farming interests by the John Morgan raid." Carrington ordered all citizens who had replacement horses to give these animals to the provost marshal, who gathered all of the recovered horses in each locality and redistributed them to farms based on individual need. Farmers who had lost horses were able to bring in the wheat harvest and transport it to market. Citizens who did not turn in animals after that time were open to prosecution, and those who tried to gather stray horses and sell them to the quartermaster faced severe punishment under the martial law which was still in effect.[24]

Civilians encountered a number of problems with the procedure for claiming animals and applying for reimbursement. Owners were responsible for finding and identifying their horses. They filed descriptions and affidavits, often traveling as far as Cincinnati to find their animals. By the time Morgan's command was finally captured near West Point, Ohio, Union regulars and state militia had caught every missing horse. The U.S. Quartermaster Department, however, made no attempt to return animals that Union forces had captured, instead offering them for sale with the government keeping the proceeds. The department also required each claimant to produce a receipt or at least two sworn witnesses' statements indicating that Union forces had taken the property. In the confusion and urgency of the pursuit of Morgan, many claimants had not obtained valid receipts and those who did could not always produce them.[25]

The romanticized, anecdotal accounts compiled by local and amateur historians do not depict the lasting economic impact of the raid on Corydon and the surrounding area.[26] Individuals needed to replace what they had lost and resume their daily routines; the loss of important community assets threatened to have long-lasting effects on the local economy. In 1865, when the Indiana General Assembly finally reconvened, victims in Harrison County and elsewhere in southern Indiana turned to what they believed to be their only source of relief—the state government.

Unfortunately, Indiana's bitter political partisanship prevented victims of Morgan's raid from receiving the swift action they needed to replace property and pay debts. Ohio's legislature had taken immediate action, evaluating and paying the majority of claims related to the raid by 1865; the U.S. Quartermaster General's office then reimbursed the state for claims against Union troops.[27] In contrast, Indiana Republicans rendered state compensation impossible, as they attempted to maintain control of the state's government. After Democratic gains in the 1862 election and that party's subsequent attempt to take away the governor's control over the state Legion, Republicans left the capital in mid-session in 1863, and left the legislature without a quorum to conduct its business. For the remainder of that year and all of 1864, Gov. Morton operated the state with a combination of government and private funds.[28] The legislature did not meet, and for seventeen months claimants had no chance of appealing to the state.

When the Indiana General Assembly finally met in January 1865, Republicans and Democrats jockeying for advantage concerned themselves more with political matters and issues of loyalty than with the plight of southern Indianans who had lost property in 1863.[29] In his address to the assembly on January 6, Gov. Morton indicated that compensating the victims of Morgan's raid was the duty of the state, and he called for the payments to be made from the state treasury. However, the governor also outlined the creation of a commission to assess and adjust the losses, so that the people of Indiana were not burdened with paying false or exaggerated claims. Although Morton's charge was reasonable and straightforward, efforts to pass legislation were met with political maneuvering and squabbling. Some representatives, including many from southern Indiana, supported House Bill 13, introduced by Rep. Hiram Prather from Jennings County. But political and geographic divisions led Rep. M. F. Shuey (representing the northern towns of Elkhart and LeGrange) and others to derail discussion of the bill. Shuey demanded that a provision be added to disallow payment of claims to citizens associated with any disloyal organization (a reference to the Knights of the Golden Circle, the Sons of Liberty, and other groups of "Peace" Democrats opposed to the war). Senate Bill 15, intended to create the claims commission which Morton had requested, met with similar opposition. Senators argued about the commissioners' pay and whether John Hunt Morgan should be referred to as a legitimate "General" or simply as "the guerrilla chief." In spite of Gov. Morton's statement that Indiana should bear the cost of paying the claims, Senate proceedings soon devolved into political debates over the responsibility of state versus federal government for wartime damage claims. When the assembly finished their winter session, neither chamber had passed any legislation.[30]

When the legislature met again in 1867, southern Indiana politicians reintroduced legislation to pay for the losses. In March, the Senate committee considering House Bill 14 returned it with a recommendation for indefinite postponement. The last chance for payment during the session then lay with House Resolution 13, which simply called for the Senate and House to pass a bill allowing for payment of the claims. Opponents of the Morgan's Raid bill believed that the question of appropriating money to pay the claims had been settled by previous votes rejecting such a proposition. One of the Senate's final actions during the 1867 session was the passage, 27 votes in favor and 7 against, of a resolution to create a committee to assess the claims.[31] The result was a "non-binding concurrent resolution" that allowed new governor Conrad Baker to "appoint three commissioners to . . . hear, determine and adjust all claims, for losses" to Confederate, state, or national forces. Although the resolution featured detailed instructions on how the commission should gather concise statements of loss, including the witnesses' affidavits, it contained no mention of payment of the claims.[32] The Indiana Morgan's Raid Claims Commission (IMRCC) was charged with recording and adjusting the claims, so that when the state legislature approved funds to pay them the proper records would be in order. Ohio's state legislature had gathered, assessed, and paid the claims in their state in one motion, but Indiana's combustible political atmosphere prevented such a swift resolution.

On July 10, 1867, four years and a day after the skirmish between townspeople and Morgan's cavalry, an attorney, three commissioners, and a clerk began taking affidavits and auditing claims in Corydon. Citizens swarmed to the courthouse to apply for compensation. On July 11, commission chair Thomas M. Browne wrote to Gov. Baker requesting additional staff, reporting that on the previous day the commission's single clerk had been able to process only 28 cases out of a total 458 filed for Harrison County alone. Browne pleaded that "the work before us is elephantine" and wrote that he was "hoping that we may live long enough to see the end of it."[33]

The commission's efforts, however slow, renewed citizens' hopes that they would receive payment for their losses. In December, the IMRCC finished its work and released a report, but its recommendations were of little worth without a bill from the state legislature to pay the claims. The commission's report noted the effort of Corydon's defenders and the raid's extensive toll: "The town, having been captured, was to a great extent despoiled."[34]

The 1869 session of the general assembly once again took up the matter of recompense for victims of the raid. The commission report was printed and distributed, and on January 25, Senator F. J. Bellamy, representing Ripley and Switzerland Counties, introduced S. 97, an appropriations bill that would make available $413,599.48 "to pay the Morgan raid claims." In spite of support from Gov. Baker and continued petitions from citizens of southern counties, too many politicians still opposed the bill. Extensive debate in the Senate revealed a general unwillingness for the state to assume the considerable cost of paying out the claims. Some senators argued that neither the nation nor the state was responsible for recompensing wartime damages; others agreed that the claims might be just but that the federal government, and not the state, should pay them, since "the damage done to property was not attributable to Morgan and his men alone, but in a great degree to the Federal troops." One supporter of the bill argued conversely, and correctly, that a large portion of the damage was done by rebel forces, and that the state had a responsibility to protect citizens and to compensate the losses of those who had rallied to defend Indiana.[35] In spite of all this debate, at the end of the year's session, no money had been allocated for those who had lost money and property—now six years earlier.

Through the 1870s and into the next decade, southern Indiana politicians continued to work to obtain payment for losses incurred during the raid. Strother Stockslager had been a lieutenant in the state Legion at the time of the raid. While serving in the state senate from 1874 to 1878 and as a representative to Congress from 1881 to 1885, he was among those who advocated for their constituents. In 1873, state representative William H. Pfrimmer wrote to the U.S. Quartermaster General asking for "a statement of the amount the government received for sales of horses and other property abandoned by and captured with Morgan."[36] Pfrimmer was still working on legislation to pay the claims and trying to determine how much property had been seized by the Union army and sold at auction. Because the army had confiscated all horses and equipment from the rebels, and auctioned off animals it could not use, the government had certainly kept some civilian horses or profited from their sale. In his response, the quartermaster general pointed out that although army quartermasters had recorded the number of horses confiscated and sold, the reports available through the U.S. Treasury would not differentiate between horses that Morgan's force had brought from Kentucky and horses seized in Indiana. The federal government had no policies that took into account the possibility of enemy forces using stolen horses, and under existing law, could only reimburse citizens for supplies taken or used by the Union army—and then only if army officers had left the civilians with receipts or vouchers.[37] The quartermaster general could, however, collect the IMRCC's claim records, review them, and be ready if Congress allowed for the repayment of claims; he could also pay the claims for items taken by Union troops (with proper receipts).

Not until 1879 did the quartermaster general's office request the IMRCC dockets in order to determine what property had been taken by Union forces. Federal law also restricted compensation to property included in the quartermaster's stores—including horses, saddles, and fodder, but excluding damaged property and items not normally supplied to troops. (One claim requesting payment for cakes consumed by Union cavalrymen was denied because the quartermaster did not regularly supply troops with confections of any kind.) A list of claims with affidavits and witness testimonies would have hastened federal efforts, but obtaining the state's records turned out to be difficult. In December 1879, the USQG's office asked Indiana's adjutant general to send the IMRCC records; the Hoosier official promised to send them as soon as he could have copies made. In March and again in May 1880, the USQG sent requests without receiving any reply. In July, the adjutant general claimed that the records had been "mislaid." Eventually, the quartermaster general concluded that the adjutant general was withholding the records for some reason, and he sent a letter to Indiana's governor, who replied that the adjutant general had already sent the appropriate records. Clerks in the quartermaster general's office noted that they had received only six ledgers listing claimants and amounts, not the dockets that IMRCC had collected. One clerk concluded in his report: "The whole thing is imperfect, being to a large extent written in lead pencil there is not 'abstract of evidence' in these books." By November 1880, the USQG had given up on receiving any additional information and ordered local agents to investigate only the 1st Class claims, i.e., property taken by Union troops. He took no immediate action on any other claims.[38]

Between 1880 and 1887, the U.S. Quartermaster General assessed and adjudged the claims as best he could, based on resubmitted information from the citizens of southern Indiana (including 468 claims from Harrison County). Most of the residents who lost property during the raid had kept copies of their 1867 claims; there were, however, several cases in which depositions had been lost or misplaced. All claims other than those for property lost to Union troops were marked "taking and use not proven" or "rebel." In 1884, the Senate Commission on Claims drafted Senate Bill 527, in an attempt to pay all Morgan's raid claims in Indiana and Ohio. Stockslager, a congressman at the time, worked in vain to gain sufficient support for the bill, which he believed did not pass because politicians from other states did not have any vested interest in compensating Hoosiers.[39]

Although Stockslager's criticism was surely accurate, the passage of over twenty years since the raid's occurrence likely factored into the resistance as well. By the 1880s, the nation was focused on industrialization, and the reconciliation between North and South was well under way. Those citizens who had lost property or money to the raiders must have shared Stockslager's cynicism—their sacrifices and losses were long forgotten and politically inconvenient.

The fate of Indiana's Morgan's raid claims, and specifically those from Harrison County, is obscured by the stories of Morgan's daring raid and the harrowing tales of civilians who witnessed it. Without help from state or federal authorities, citizens who suffered loss felt the true burden of war. For almost twenty years, many claimants continued to expect that they would be compensated. Governor Baker's appointment of a commission and the efforts of politicians such as Stockslager and Pfrimmer must have kept up the hopes of beleaguered residents, but the claims were never settled. The system failed the "losers" in Indiana, but the failure was more than just an example of the destructive partisanship of the state's Civil War–era politics—it demonstrates the true impact of Morgan's raid.

Popular books, reenactments, and even a musical have focused on the entertaining and sensational aspects of John Hunt Morgan's raid through southern Indiana. The victims of the raid may have felt excitement during the event, but its aftermath brought anxiety, uncertainty, destruction, and loss. This is the part of Morgan's raid that is easily forgotten and not often searched for. In 1923, eighty-year-old Strother Stockslager wrote a letter to the *Corydon Democrat*, criticizing both the state and federal governments' inability to redress the claims stemming from the raid. The commission's endeavor, he wrote, had been "a false hope" that "served to buoy up the loser who struggled on as best they could with this just hope of ultimate payment."[40] Stockslager would not be surprised that his words were soon forgotten and lost to history.

STEPHEN ROCKENBACH is Associate Professor of History at Virginia State University. This article originally appeared in volume 109, March 2013.

NOTES

1. File 435, box 605, Record Group 92, Office of the Quartermaster General, Claims branch 1861–1889, Quartermaster Stores (Act of July 4, 1864), Miscellaneous Claims, book 214, National Archives, Washington, D.C. (hereafter Record Group 92, OQG, Miscellaneous Claims, book 214, National Archives).

2. The literature pertaining to Morgan's July 1863 raid is vast, and ranges from voluminous collections of stories to short, county-specific descriptions of events. See the following books for various, and often conflicting, accounts of the raid, including some of the incidents that occurred in Corydon and Harrison County. Lester V. Horwitz, *The Longest Raid of the Civil War: Little-Known and Untold Stories of Morgan's Raid into Kentucky, Indiana, and Ohio*, rev. ed. (Cincinnati, Ohio, 2001); David L. Taylor, *With Bowie Knives and Pistols: Morgan's Raid in Indiana* (Lexington, Ind., 1993); Arville Funk, *The Morgan Raid in Indiana and Ohio* (Corydon, Ind., 1971); Scott Roller, "business as Usual: Indiana's Response to the Confederate Invasions of the Summer of 1863," *Indiana Magazine of History* 88 (March 1992), 1–25. For a sample of the countless unpublished accounts and memoirs, see folder 6, box 3 of the Don D. John Collection, Kentucky Historical Society, Frankfort, Kentucky. The collection also includes the only known original copy of the July 14, 1863, *Corydon Democrat* detailing the raid.

3. For mythology about farmers benefiting from superior horses left behind by Morgan and his men, see Horwitz, *The Longest Raid of the Civil War*, 377.

4. These totals were compiled from Claims 36–504, Record Group 92, OQG, Miscellaneous Claims, book 214, National Archives. The total of the claims submitted to the U.S. Quartermaster General differs from the Indiana Morgan's Raid Claims Commission ledger by only $152.83.

5. "Report of Morgan Raid Commission to the Governor," December 31, 1869, Record Group 92, OQG, Collective Correspondence File, Morgan's Raid, box 697, National Archives; U.S. Historical Census Data browser, online at http://mapserver.lib.virginia.edu/.

6. John P. Etter, *The Indiana Legion: A Civil War Militia* (Carmel, Ind., 2006); John Michael Foster Jr., "'For the Good of the Cause and the Protection of the border': The Services of the Indiana Legion in the Civil War, 1861–1865," *Civil War History* 55 (March 2009), 31–55.

7. H. S. Hisey to Gov. [Oliver] Morton, July 23, 1863, microfilm reel 6, Oliver P. Morton Papers, Indiana State Archives, Indianapolis, Indiana.

8. James Ramage considers the $690 in cash that raiders took from William Hisey to be "Union funds." James A. Ramage, *Rebel Raider: The Life of General*

John Hunt Morgan (Lexington, Ky., 1995), 172. The U.S. Quartermaster General denied Hisey's claim in 1886, and he was never reimbursed. File 248, box 603, Record Group 92, Miscellaneous Claims, book 214, National Archives.

9. In June, approximately 2,000 Legion troops assembled in the county over the course of two days to fend off a reported Confederate invasion. The supposed invaders turned out to be Kentucky Unionists patrolling the Ohio River in the aftermath of Capt. Thomas Hines's ill-fated raid into Harrison and Crawford Counties earlier that month. *New Albany Daily Ledger*, June 20, 22, 23, 1863; *Corydon Democrat*, June 30, 1863.

10. In the 1880s, the owners of the three mills applied for reimbursement for the ransom they had paid Morgan. Phillip Lopp also asked for $4,761 for his mill, which raiders burned on July 8, 1863. None of the claims fit the specifications of the U.S. Quartermaster General's office, and they refused payment.

11. Indiana Morgan Raid Claim Commission Records, microfilm, p. 37, Indiana Historical Society Library, Indianapolis, Indiana; *Corydon Weekly Union*, November 10, 1863, reprinted in "News of Long Ago: From Republicans of Another Century," scrapbook, Corydon Local History and Genealogy Library, Corydon, Indiana.

12. S. J. Wright to A. Stone, January 18, 1864, folder 5, box 10, Indiana Legion Records, Indiana State Archives.

13. Files 123, 147, 171, box 603; files 265, 342, 345, box 604; files 405, 424, 459, box 605; and file 503, box 606, Record Group 92, OQG, Miscellaneous Claims, book 214, National Archives.

14. J. Sanford Rikoon, *Threshing in the Midwest, 1820–1940: A Study of Traditional Culture and Technological Change* (Bloomington, Ind., 1988), 14–16, 30.

15. Henry Beebee Carrington to Gov. O. P. Morton, Filson Historical Society, Louisville, Kentucky.

16. *Indianapolis Daily Journal*, August 1, 1863; William Stuart Reminiscences, pp. 72–73, SC 2159, Indiana Historical Society.

17. File 434, box 605, Record Group 92, OQG, Miscellaneous Claims, book 214, National Archives. Pittman died in 1866, but his wife reported the loss of a sorrel mare worth $125 and a bay mare worth $200. In 1883, the U.S. Quartermaster General investigated and approved the claim, but adjusted the amounts to $100 and $130 respectively, to correspond to prices of cavalry horses at that time.

18. Ramage, *Rebel Raider*, 170–71.

19. Claims were not itemized, so cash is listed with other items in the quartermaster's records. The author estimates $3,126 in cash lost based on subtracting the common value of the other items listed. Files 56, 66, 113, 119, 150, 192, 231, 248, 267, 274, 360, 372, 462, boxes 602–606, Record Group 92, OQG, Miscellaneous Claims, book 214, National Archives.

20. Quote from file 454. Claims for destroyed or damaged boats are located in files 91, 106, 113, 114, 115, 185, 209, 264, 266, 272, boxes 602–604, Record Group 92, OQG, Miscellaneous Claims, book 214, National Archives.

21. Capt. Farquar commanded the "Mounted Hoosiers," a company of Legion cavalry from Mauckport. His name is misspelled in the official reports. "Report of Captain William Forquor," in *Operations of the Indiana Legion and Minute Men, 1863–4: Documents Presented to the General Assembly, with the Governor's Message, January 6, 1865* (Indianapolis, Ind., 1865), 42–43; Thomas Slaughter to "Sir," August 17, 1863, Indiana Legion Records, folder 5, box 10, Indiana State Archives; Journal entry for July 9, 1863, Curtis Burke Journal, Filson Historical Society. The text can be found in Pamela J. Bennett, ed., "Curtis R. Burke's Civil War Journal," *Indiana Magazine of History* 65 (December 1969), 283–327.

22. Horwitz, *The Longest Raid of the Civil War*, 61–62.

23. "Report of Colonel Lewis Jordan," *Operations of the Indiana Legion and Minute Men*, 33; Journal entry for July 9, 1863, Curtis Burke Journal; Muster rolls, Indiana Legion Records, folder 2, box 10, Indiana State Archives; Files 377, 453, box 605, Record Group 92, OQG, Miscellaneous Claims, book 214, National Archives. File 453 contains an affidavit from Glenn's neighbor, William Weaver, indicating that Peter Glenn chose to help the Legion cavalry oppose the Confederate raiders.

24. *New Albany Daily Ledger*, July 17, 1863; "Losses and Impressment of Property during the Morgan Raid: General Carrington Order," July 16, 1863, Oliver P. Morton Papers, microfilm reel 6, Indiana State Archives.

25. Files 435, 455, box 605, Record Group 92, OQG, Miscellaneous Claims, book 214, National Archives.

26. Horwitz, *The Longest Raid of the Civil War*, chaps. 12–13; Funk, *The Morgan Raid in Indiana and Ohio*; W. Fred Conway, *Corydon: The Forgotten Battle of the Civil War* (New Albany, Ind., 1991).

27. "Report of Morgan Raid Commissioner to the Governor," December 31, 1869, Record Group 92, OQG, Collective Correspondence File, Morgan's Raid, box 697, National Archives; U.S. Historical Census Data browser, online.

28. Emma Lou Thornbrough, *Indiana in the Civil War Era, 1850–1880* (Indianapolis, Ind., 1965), 185–87.

29. Ibid., 183–87; James M. McPherson, *Battle Cry of Freedom: The Civil War Era* (New York, 1989), 595–96.

30. Ariel E. and William H. Drapier, *Brevier Legislative Reports: Embracing Short-hand Sketches of the Journals and Debates of the General Assembly of the State of Indiana*, vol. 7 (South Bend, Ind., 1865), pp. 22, 34, 59, 86–90, 103–104, 199, 249–53, 266–70, 361–62, 369; vol. 8, 1866, pp. 170–71.

31. The "Morgan Raid Indemnity bill" would have allowed for claims up to a total of $370,000 to be paid out; if the total were higher, funds were "to be paid

pro rata." *Brevier Legislative Reports*, vol. 9, 1867, pp. 235–37, 396–97, 429–30, 435–37, 445–48.

32. "Concurrent Resolutions in Regard to the Appointment of Commissioners to adjust the Morgan Raid Claims," folder 5, box 2, Conrad Baker Papers, M0008, Indiana Historical Society.

33. Thomas M. Browne to Gov. Conrad Baker, July 11, 1867, folder 12, box 2, Conrad Baker Papers, M0008, Indiana Historical Society.

34. "Report of Morgan Raid Commissioner to the Governor," December 31, 1869, Record Group 92, OQG, Collective Correspondence File, Morgan's Raid, box 697, National Archives.

35. *Brevier Legislative Reports*, vol. 10, 1869, pp. 60, 203, 461–62, 555–57, 581, Suffix pp. 18–20; vol. 11, 1869, pp. 138, 172, 185–86, 199–200, 207–208, 217–19, 245.

36. William H. Pfrimmer to General Meigs, January 20, 1873, Record Group 92, OQG, Collective Correspondence File, Morgan's Raid, box 696, National Archives.

37. General Meigs to Willliam H. Pfrimmer, January 28, 1873, Record Group 92, OQG, Collective Correspondence File, Morgan's Raid, box 696, National Archives.

38. Report by M. J. Kinney, November 18, 1880, Quartermaster General's Office, Record Group 92, OQG, Collective Correspondence File, Morgan's Raid, box 696, National Archives. The other three classes of claims were property taken by state militia, rebel forces, or unknown parties. According to the report, the value of property taken by U.S. troops was $58,017.51, compared to $24,268.80 taken by state militia and $331,228.17 taken by Confederate troops. There were only 3 cases where claimants could not identify who took the property, and these claims totaled $35.

39. Hon. Secretary of War from Samuel B. Holabird, Quartermaster General, February 11, 1884, Record Group 92, OQG, Collective Correspondence File, Morgan's Raid, box 696, National Archives; *Corydon Democrat*, August 29, 1923.

40. *Corydon Democrat*, August 29, 1923, p. 7.

6

★ ★ ★

The Grand Army of the Republic, the Indianapolis 500, and the Struggle for Memorial Day in Indiana, 1868–1923

NICHOLAS W. SACCO

THE AMERICAN CIVIL WAR WAS the deadliest conflict in United States history, with upwards of 750,000 soldiers dead from 1861 to 1865.[1] The bloody consequences of this sectional strife shocked Americans, leaving survivors—veterans and those on the home front—with the challenge of remembering, interpreting, and grappling with what, exactly, the fighting had been all about.[2] In 1866, a group of Illinois Union veterans founded the Grand Army of the Republic (GAR), which eventually became the nation's largest Union Civil War veterans' fraternal organization, numbering more than 400,000 members nationwide by 1890.[3] As self-professed saviors of the Union, these GAR members took it upon themselves to act as gatekeepers of Civil War memory in the war's aftermath.

In 1868, as part of their strategy to preserve their memories of the war, the GAR declared May 30 as a day of solemn, public commemoration for the Union military's war dead. Challenges quickly arose, however, as to what the GAR deemed to be appropriate activities for Memorial Day.[4] By the turn of the twentieth century, GAR leaders across the country were taking issue with those who used Memorial Day to gamble on sports, consume copious amounts of alcohol, or run a business that stayed open during the holiday. In Indiana, the struggle centered around the running of the Indianapolis 500.

Beginning in 1911, the founders of the Indianapolis Motor Speedway held their annual five-hundred-mile automobile race on May 30, the same day as the GAR's Memorial Day holiday. This scheduling conflict motivated the GAR to lead a statewide movement against the Indianapolis 500, and in 1923,

State Senator Robert Moorhead introduced a bill before the Indiana General Assembly that called for banning the race on Memorial Day. GAR veterans throughout the state wrote letters to the editor and made speeches in their local communities advocating for the passage of the Moorhead Memorial Day Bill while criticizing the race as an insult to the memory of United States soldiers who died during the Civil War. The legislation, however, attracted both vehement support and opposition—the latter from many younger veterans of World War I and members of the newly formed American Legion. The Indiana GAR ultimately lost this battle when Governor Warren McCray vetoed the Moorhead Memorial Day Bill on March 5, 1923. The story of Indiana war veterans, Memorial Day, and the Indianapolis 500 raises questions about the nature of patriotism and the process of commemoration, and about who defines and regulates these practices.

Historian Jay Winter outlines a three-phase process by which public commemorative practices evolve as new generations replace old ones: the "creative" phase, the "institutional" phase, and the "transformational" phase.[5] This typology helps to explain the Indiana GAR's attempt to control Memorial Day and the historical memories of the Union dead. During the initial postwar period, memories of the dead triggered a creative phase, in which the GAR's collective desire for public commemoration led to the establishment of Memorial Day and the unveiling of its inaugural rituals in 1868. By 1900, repeated rituals institutionalized Memorial Day practices and solidified the holiday's place in America's commemorative landscape. The establishment of the Indianapolis 500 in 1911 finally ushered in the transformational phase, in which later generations inherited Memorial Day and used the holiday to convey their own interpretations, memories, and rituals onto society's collective past.[6]

THE GAR AND THE HISTORICAL ORIGINS OF MEMORIAL DAY

The Grand Army of the Republic observed Memorial Day as a time reserved to reflect on the past and meet the new demands of memory brought on by the war. The scope of death, destruction, and change to American society wrought by four years of bloodshed challenged Americans to contemplate the meaning of this massive loss of life and ensure, through commemoration and remembrance, that such suffering would never occur again. As one GAR handbook explained in 1884, Memorial Day was "the day of all days in the G.A.R. Calendar." "Comrades," according to the author, "should exercise great care" in ensuring that civilians understood that "the old soldier is capable of sober thoughts and earnest acts."[7] Union veterans believed that making the GAR "calendar" a part of every American citizen's calendar would perpetuate a proper remembrance of the Union dead and a stronger love of country.

The GAR officially acknowledged Memorial Day after National Commander John A. Logan issued General Orders Number 11 on May 5, 1868.[8] Logan defined the purpose behind the order as "preserving and strengthening those kind and fraternal feelings which have bound together the soldiers, sailors and marines who united to suppress the late rebellion." To enhance those feelings among veterans and the rest of society, Logan encouraged GAR members to use Memorial Day as a way to cherish "the memory of our heroic dead" by "guard[ing] their graves with sacred vigilance." By taking the time to observe Memorial Day and to remember those who died to save the Union, Americans would maintain the "solemn trust" between living veterans and the dead and perpetuate the memories of the fallen.[9] As sociologist Robert Bellah explains, the Civil War infused America's civil religion (the blending of religious themes with nationalist sentiments) with "a new theme of death, sacrifice, and rebirth."[10] Memorial Day ritualized these themes in an effort to foster an imagined community of citizens whose shared sufferings during the Civil War brought local communities across the nation together.[11] Through the commemoration of the Union dead, according to the GAR, Americans would forge a national identity as a reborn nation strengthened by the defeat of secession.

Thanks to Commander Logan's instructions to GAR posts to observe the day "in their own way," Memorial Day services at first took on a wide variety of incarnations. A one-thousand-page compilation of Memorial Day activities across the nation in 1869 (composed by Union veteran Ernest F. M. Faehtz to promote the day's observance) shows that while the general message of remembrance was almost universally embraced, different types of ritual services emerged. Indiana was no exception. That year, the Indiana GAR in South Bend enlisted the help of Republican vice president and Mishawaka, Indiana, resident Schuyler Colfax to boost awareness of Memorial Day in the area. After a large procession strewed flowers over all soldiers' graves in the area, Colfax argued in an impassioned speech that by honoring the dead, Memorial Day would "teach us to love our country more, to value its dearly-purchased institutions more, to prize its manifold blessings more, and to advance its greatness and true glory more." Colfax's comments held significance: prior to the Civil War, many Americans had viewed themselves as "present-minded people" who rejected "Old World" European notions of tradition and remembrance in favor of focusing on America's future. Now, through speeches and ritual, the Indiana GAR attempted to instill the importance of making Memorial Day a "tradition" in American society, one that emphasized the importance of looking back to the past for inspiration and examples of true patriotism.[12]

While Colfax's South Bend speech offered a somber reflection of the Union dead and their patriotic influence, the Memorial Day service in Indianapolis involved a lavish parade that included Republican governor Conrad Baker, officers of the Indianapolis police, and members of local Masonic orders and the Independent Order of Odd Fellows. Services in Fort Wayne, meanwhile, started with an afternoon march to Lindenwood Cemetery, where residents decorated soldiers' graves. During the subsequent ceremonies, GAR member R. S. Robertson spoke on the "appropriate and pleasant duty" of decorating the graves of those who had helped to defend "our free institutions." The rule of European kings, Robertson said, had a foundation based on "conquered provinces, of the millions who owe them the homage of serfs," but Union victory in the Civil War restored a republican form of government in America.[13]

Memorial Day services became more unified by the mid-1870s and early 1880s. The GAR began to provide "handbooks" that offered specific procedures, poems, and Bible verses for local post commanders to utilize.[14] According to historian Stuart McConnell, "on the day itself, the post assembled and marched to the local cemetery to decorate the graves of the fallen, an enterprise meticulously organized months in advance to assure that none were missed. Finally came a simple and subdued graveyard service involving prayers, short patriotic speeches, and music . . . and at the end perhaps a rifle salute."[15] As the ritual of Memorial Day gained importance within America's commemorative landscape, powerful individuals attempted to use the day's patriotic speeches to affirm their fealty to the dead. "The Decoration Day speech," David Blight asserts, "became an American genre that ministers, politicians, and countless former soldiers tried to master." Orators used Memorial Day to remind audiences that "their soldiers had died necessary deaths, they had saved the republic, and their blood had given the nation new life."[16] For many aging GAR veterans, in fact, Memorial Day became a commemorative centerpiece for instilling memories of the Civil War that embraced what historian Barbara A. Gannon describes as the Won Cause interpretation of the war, which argues that the fight to preserve the Union and end slavery were mutually laudable and co-existing goals of the United States government.[17] These speeches were addressed to all Americans—not just former Confederates—in an effort to curb what these veterans believed were serious violations of the spirit of Memorial

Day through apathy, frivolity, and rampant business interests and greed. At least one hundred published newspaper accounts of Memorial Day speeches in Indiana were recorded from 1868 to 1925, but a few examples provide a general outline of the ideas and themes invoked by Indiana GAR members on the importance of remembering the Civil War and the Won Cause.[18]

THE POLITICAL USES OF MEMORIAL DAY

In 1880, Comrade Henry H. Mathias addressed a Greencastle audience on the importance of virtue. Most wars, according to Mathias, stemmed from issues that "grew out of either lust, ambition or greed . . . the worst traits of man's nature." The Union war effort, however, had been an exercise in national virtue and sacrifice. "When the resources of diplomacy are exhausted, when national existence is at stake, when the freedom of the citizen is imperiled," argued Mathias, armed conflict could be justified. "Among nations as among men, there is a well defined rule of right"; those who had died defending the United States "fell in a righteous cause, in defense of those great principles set forth in that immortal instrument, the Declaration of Independence . . . they died that a Nation might live."[19] For Mathias, the Union dead had not perished in a vain, pointless conflict.

Similarly, former Republican congressman John Coburn addressed an audience in Martinsville in 1886 on the purpose of protecting the "sacred graves" of the fallen. "These men whose memories we honor to-day," asserted Coburn, "fell in no war of invasion or conquest; not in the strife for power, not to cramp and bind and tax their fellow men, but to give more rights, to uplift the downtrodden . . . And humanity shall sit down to an endless feast, generation after generation, prepared by these dying hands." GAR veterans did not "glory in war or take pride in its fearful consequences," but the thought of disunion and "national death" had horrified them more than war. National unification and the end of slavery established an "obedience to war" that recreated America as a "free, progressive, intelligent Nation in her own race of improvement, and in the uplifting of all men from the bonds of their oppressors." By the end of the war, Coburn argued, the entire human race emerged with an "enlargement of personal liberty."[20] These advances in human freedom were central to the meaning of Memorial Day, according to Coburn.

For S. R. Hornbrook—a clergyman appointed by Governor Oliver P. Morton as an agent of the wartime Indiana Sanitary Commission—the lesson of Memorial Day was peace. Who were "the men of 1861," he asked, and what did they represent? "They were men who loved peace and long strove to secure it," proclaimed Hornbrook. "This is the great lesson which Memorial days must teach the young," for the terrors of war should be feared by all. Hornbrook approved of "happy children bearing flowers for the dead heroes," and the opening of the "book of remembrance" by those who attended Memorial Day commemorations; he invoked Abraham Lincoln's Second Inaugural Address in wishing for future peace: "most fondly do we hope, most fervently do we pray . . . that the scourge of war may never come to this rising generation." But if war came, Hornbrook argued, "let them think upon the firmness of their fathers and shrink not from the trial." Indiana GAR veterans had passed the trial of war and transitioned into "active manhood."[21] Memorial Day would challenge younger generations to face future conflicts with an eye towards peace, but with another eye towards honor, bravery, and personal sacrifice if the nation were to face armed conflict again in the future.

Clearly, the Grand Army of the Republic intended to set aside Memorial Day as a day to reflect upon the memories of the Union dead, and many veterans argued that the day was created "for the dead." But Memorial Day, as it came to be practiced, was just as much about assuaging the concerns of the living. As Drew Gilpin Faust aptly described it, "without agendas, without politics, the Dead became what their survivors chose to make them."[22] Memorial Day services gained their cultural significance in American society because surviving veterans ascribed a particular meaning to the day. Decorating graves with flowers, reciting poems, singing patriotic songs, and making impassioned speeches all signified attempts by the living to mold the Union dead (and later the dead of other American wars) into their own vision of what it meant to be an American. The dead were incorporated into the mythology of the Union cause and promoted by the living as embodiments of honor, manliness, and American heroism.

Comrade John Coburn's 1886 speech in Martinsville outlined the importance of remembering the Union dead, but it also reflected on the meaning of the Civil War as viewed by the Republican party: Confederates had seceded because of their desire to maintain slavery, while Union supporters refused to comply with Confederate attempts to build "an empire of slavery, thus cutting us off from our great highways to the South by water and land." The thought of war was terrible, but "the doctrine that a dissatisfied State might, at any time, upon her own will, secede, [thus making] disunion legal" was worse. The results of the war proved that "the Nation is greater than the State and can compel obedience [to] war to hold together this vast, free, progressive, intelligent

Decoration Day, 1899. Photographer Frances Benjamin Johnston captured this image of young people preparing to decorate the graves of Civil War veterans. *Courtesy Library of Congress, Prints and Photographs Division.*

Nation."[23] Coburn asserted that the Won Cause of Union and emancipation was right, and that the use of military force to enact that cause was justified.

For Comrade George W. Spahr, the Civil War finally created a unified nation. In his 1893 Memorial Day oration in Cambridge City, Indiana, Spahr remarked that those who had been marked by the death and destruction of war were "consoled by the fact that we are no longer a doubtful confederation of States; that we are no longer a compact of colonies existing at the will and pleasure of the parties to the combine." The Civil War ensured that Americans would be governed by laws in a perpetual union, not by the whims of a few politically powerful men. Former supporters of the Confederacy, argued Spahr, were "more prosperous people than they would have been had they been successful in the establishment of human slavery and a slave oligarchy."[24] Based upon his claim regarding postwar economic success in the former Confederate states, Spahr believed that former secessionists should also embrace the Won Cause interpretation of the war.

For GAR members like Spahr, Memorial Day was also an appropriate space in which to advocate for political and financial concerns that benefitted living soldiers. Spahr used his Memorial Day speech to chastise the "class of ungrateful and unworthy citizens" who had opposed the expansion of pension benefits to Union veterans in 1890. These "unworthy citizens" were unpatriotic and had been "too cowardly to fight when the war was on." Union soldiers had demonstrated "unswerving patriotic devotion and self-sacrificing love of country" during the time of the nation's greatest need; paying a small monthly pension to disabled veterans through public funds after the conflict ended was but a small credit paid to the debt that could never be repaid.[25]

Veterans' Memorial Day speeches, however, were not monolithic. GAR veterans did not always agree with each other about the best path for the country's future and viewed questions of sectional reconciliation, states' rights, and public aid to African American freed people from a range of perspectives. Historian Nicole Etcheson demonstrates that the speeches varied in content based on the orator's political affiliation. Democratic GAR members sometimes complained when speakers like Republican Thomas Hanna (lieutenant governor at the time of his speech in 1881) focused too much on emancipation.[26] To counteract such orations, Democratic political leaders chose speakers who left out any mention of slavery as a cause of the war or emancipation as a positive consequence of its results.

Comrade Courtland C. Matson was one Indiana GAR member often selected by Democrats to make Memorial Day speeches. A Greencastle lawyer, Matson at first rejected the GAR in 1868 and formed a local political organization called the "Union White Boys in Blue" that opposed that year's election of Republican Ulysses S. Grant as president. At one point, as many as 120 veterans claimed membership in the organization. These men believed that Radical Republicans were to blame for strained relations between the sections, due in large part to their excessive protection of "hordes of unthrifty and indolent negroes" through their support of the Fourteenth and Fifteenth Amendments.[27]

Addressing an 1875 soldiers' Memorial Day convention in Indianapolis, Matson went so far as to call for the equal commemoration of the Union and Confederate dead during the day's services. In 1880, he gave speeches on both Memorial Day and the Fourth of July. While the Memorial Day speech was not published, his Fourth of July speech is telling. In it, he praised the Union war effort and the desire for political reunification between North and South. He mentioned how proud he was of his service as a Union soldier, but complained that he had been "[conscripted] by the strong arm of military power, dragged from his home, and deprived of his liberty without writ, warrant, hearing, or trial, and he feels that such an outrage yet calls for the most indignant expression of all just people."[28] By focusing on sectional reconciliation and the alleged abuses of the federal government in conscripting young men from their homes, Matson challenged the interpretations of Republican speakers like George Spahr who focused on the self-sacrifice of Union soldiers, and he questioned John Coburn's belief that the war established the federal government—over state governments—as the most qualified arbiter of the people's freedoms. Additionally, Matson typifies the blatant racism and whitewashing of emancipationist war memories that characterized some white Indiana veterans, both in and out of the GAR.

By 1900, Indiana GAR members and their supporters expressed with increasing frequency their desires to reconcile with former Confederates. Although the GAR and the United Confederate Veterans (UCV) never hosted a joint meeting during their years of active organization, members from both groups increasingly alluded to their mutual battlefield valor and to their wish to bury the political issues that the war had provoked.[29] In 1901, national GAR commander Leo Rassieur remarked at Indianapolis's Crown Hill Cemetery that the Union soldier had "fully appreciated that [his] service involved a bloody conflict with his fellow-citizens of the South"; the same year at Greenlawn Cemetery in Lafayette, Indiana, Rev. Frederick Matson suggested that the "issues" that had caused the Civil War "died on the day of Appomattox, and they are dead forever."[30] Meanwhile, the *Indianapolis Journal* proclaimed in 1899 that Memorial Day had become a "permanent institution . . . recognized throughout the country by all thoughtful people as a day set apart for the recalling of patriotic examples and the consideration of patriotic duties."[31]

The Indiana GAR, however, was not as positive about the status of their holiday in their home state. Even as the Indiana organization embraced reconciliation with Confederates to expand the meaning of Memorial Day, its members grew increasingly critical of how fellow Hoosiers observed the day.[32] Starting in the 1890s, the Indiana GAR complained that too many Hoosiers were allegedly using the holiday to engage in frivolous activities on the one day of the calendar reserved for reflection on the legacy of the heroic Union dead.[33] In 1913, Comrade George Scearce complained that younger people born during and after the war demonstrated a "tendency . . . to forget the purpose of Memorial Day and make it a day for games, races and revelry, instead of a day of memory and tears."[34] The "races" Scearce alluded to took place at the newly built Indianapolis Motor Speedway. When the Indianapolis 500 was held for the first time on Memorial Day in 1911, a new firestorm of controversy emerged over the meaning of the holiday in Indiana.

NEW MEMORIAL DAY TRADITIONS IN INDIANA

The leading figure behind the creation of the Indianapolis 500 was Carl Graham Fisher, a native of Greensburg, Indiana, who had a fascination with new vehicular technologies.[35] In 1891, at the age of seventeen, Fisher invested $600 in a bicycle repair shop in downtown Indianapolis, where his quirky publicity stunts gained him attention throughout the state. Within ten years he was selling motorcycles and appearing in automobile races around the Midwest.[36] What first appeared to be a risky investment in a gas headlight company with business partner James Allison in 1904 proved to be immediately profitable, and the two became multimillionaires when they sold their company in 1913. Thanks to the success of the Prest-O-Lite headlight battery company, Fisher and three business partners were able to invest in a tract of land five miles west of downtown Indianapolis to build a two-and-a-half-mile racing track in 1908.[37]

Fisher's success in the automotive industry reflected larger economic changes in Indiana. The Hoosier state (and Indianapolis in particular) experienced a considerable increase in its industrial capacities after the Civil War, and by 1880 Indianapolis had a larger percentage of workers in manufacturing occupations than did several northeastern cities, including Philadelphia. Both state investment in an extensive system of railroads and the discovery of a natural gas field in east-central Indiana in 1887 helped to attract new industries to the state. The first automobiles for sale came to the state in 1894, and by 1909 at least 67 Indiana automobile manufacturing companies employed 6,800 workers who produced $24 million worth of goods.[38]

Fisher hosted an inaugural balloon race that attracted a crowd of roughly 40,000 spectators at the Indianapolis Motor Speedway on June 5, 1909, and a three-day series of motorcycle and automobile races later that year during Labor Day weekend. Although serious issues with the racing surface led to several crashes and the deaths of three spectators, one mechanic, and one driver during the Labor Day races, the *Indianapolis Star* nevertheless extolled the benefits of the race and the entire automobile industry. Crowds were sparse for that year's races, however, prompting Fisher to change plans for future races.[39]

In 1911, to generate interest and boost attendance at the track, Fisher made the race a one-day event, lengthened it to 500 miles, and offered the winner a

Joe Dawson being flagged to victory at the 1913 Indianapolis 500 auto race. *Courtesy Library of Congress, Prints and Photographs Division.*

prize of $27,550—an unprecedented sum at the time. The date of the race was switched to Memorial Day. Newspaper accounts do not explain the reason for the change, although in 1923 Theodore E. Myers, manager of the Indianapolis Motor Speedway, explained that no other day would work because "the Fourth of July is very hot and the people are scattered in their vacations . . . We tried in 1919 to hold the race on the day after Memorial day and we know from experience that it is not successful." Former Indiana state legislator Robert L. Moorhead remarked in 1967 (at the age of 92) that the date was switched due to objections from labor unions who did not want the race on their day. Historian Mark S. Foster, Fisher's biographer, speculated that "Carl Fisher was very likely the inspiration for establishing the date."[40] Perhaps Fisher's sense of patriotism and personal business interests inspired the date change. At the inaugural balloon race in 1909, Fisher himself got into a balloon and unfurled six American flags, exemplifying an emerging trend of Indianapolis businesses using patriotic symbolism to support their commercial endeavors. Additionally, during the race's early years, Fisher frequently expressed his desire to have popular European drivers come to Indianapolis to race Americans. Perhaps

Fisher believed Memorial Day was an appropriate time to demonstrate the alleged superiority of American drivers and the Indianapolis automobile industry to the rest of the world.[41]

Whatever the reasons for the date change, Fisher's gamble paid off handsomely, as the Indianapolis 500 became wildly popular throughout the city and the state. "Undoubtedly a boon for city businesses of all types," argues historian Alexander Uribel, "the race was promoted as a unique event and the pride of the city." By 1913, at least 100,000 people were paying admittance fees each year to see the race on Memorial Day.[42] Rather than spending the day decorating the graves of Union Civil War veterans and quietly remembering those who had died in combat, many Hoosiers chose to spend their leisure time at the racetrack watching automobiles go upwards of 100 miles per hour.

THE INDIANAPOLIS 500 AND THE 1923 MOORHEAD MEMORIAL DAY BILL

Protests from veterans and religious groups against the Memorial Day race were immediate. The *Indianapolis Star* reported the day before the 1911 race that many churches in Indiana had argued for a "proper celebration in tribute to war heroes." Members of GAR George Thomas Post 17 in Indianapolis attended "a special Memorial Day service" at Central Avenue Methodist Episcopal Church, where the Reverend A. B. Storms proclaimed that "a nation must have conscience and memory" in order to meet its "destiny."[43] Days after the event, a member of the Sons of Veterans began circulating a petition—signed by many GAR members—calling for a law against races on Memorial Day. Fisher and other track leaders acknowledged these protests and made a public announcement that the 1912 race would be held on July 4 so as to not "overshadow the Memorial day tribute paid to the soldier dead." Nothing came of these plans, however, and the race continued to be held on Memorial Day.[44]

The protests continued throughout the 1910s. Speaking at the Indiana GAR's 1914 encampment, Senior Vice Commander John H. Hoffman reinforced his belief that it was "the duty of the Grand Army everywhere to use its influence in every legitimate way to discourage all sports and amusements that in any way detract from the interest in Memorial Day." In 1915, Spanish-American War veterans suggested switching Memorial Day to the first Sunday in June so that the race could continue to be held on May 30. GAR members refused to cede any ground. Former Indiana GAR commander Gil R. Stormont wrote to the *Indianapolis News* complaining about efforts to petition the Indiana General

Assembly to change the date. May 30, asserted Stormont, was "the one day of the 365 that the Grand Army has set apart as a memorial to the patriotic dead, and they claim to have earned the right to this one day of the year for the observance of this sacred duty. In the minds of GAR members, the speedway has become a national desecration and an offense to all who have a true regard for the sentiments of Memorial day."[45] If any event needed to be moved, argued Stormont, it was the Indianapolis 500.

Despite the GAR's loud complaints, the meaning of Memorial Day was changing in the minds of Hoosiers, becoming a celebration of forward "progress" and not a commemoration of past virtue. Uribel asserts that Memorial Day celebrations in Indiana evolved to be "based on leisure, auto-races, and a fascination with spectacle, speed, and technology that was loosely rationalized as a new form of patriotic commemoration."[46] The 1899 *Indianapolis Journal* editorial that had applauded Memorial Day as a "permanent institution" for recalling "patriotic examples and the consideration of patriotic duties" was replaced with editorials in Indianapolis papers cautioning against undue protests against the Indianapolis 500. The *Indianapolis News*, for example, complained that the 1911 petition to ban races on Memorial Day was "another example of the frenzy we have for regulating everything and everybody by law." While the values of "honor and good citizenship" were heartily endorsed by the *News*, education—not compulsory law—was the best method for promoting these values.[47]

A 1913 editorial in the *Indianapolis Star* took a similar stance by suggesting that the GAR was "perhaps a little unreasonable" in its protests against the race. Remembering the soldiers of the Civil War and decorating their graves was important, the editors wrote, but those who attended the race "are of the twentieth century; they are looking forward, not back as it is the nature of each generation to do." By attending the race, spectators actually "celebrate the triumph of invention and industry that of itself was made possible by the services of the veterans."[48] By spending money at the race and supporting Indianapolis businesses, the *Star* argued, race spectators actually honored the sacrifices of the Union dead by contributing to the economic success of the city.

The Indiana GAR's 1922 encampment sponsored a resolution protesting the "desecration of Memorial Day by automobile races heretofore held on our holy day." The GAR made a call to other military organizations including the veterans of the Spanish-American War (even though some members, including Stormont, distrusted them) and the recently created American Legion to protest the race. Realizing that "women [now] have equal rights with men," the

GAR also asked its own auxiliary, the Women's Relief Corps, to use its political voice to fight for a state law banning the running of the Indianapolis 500 race on Memorial Day.[49]

The GAR's ongoing effort at petitioning the Indiana General Assembly to take action against the race finally led to a new bill written for the 1923 legislative session. Authored by Indianapolis Republican senator Robert L. Moorhead—himself a veteran of the Spanish-American War and World War I—the Moorhead Memorial Day Bill aimed to ban all "commercialized sporting events," including the Indianapolis 500, on Memorial Day. If racetrack owners Fisher and Allison refused to switch the date of their race, legislators like Moorhead believed they had the constitutional power to control the types of events that took place on legal holidays and ban the race themselves. As Moorhead argued during the Senate debate on the bill, "the time is passed for the desecration of the one day in the year set aside for the honor of the soldier dead."[50]

The Moorhead bill appeared at a time when both Republicans and Democrats in Indiana embraced conservative social policies, low taxes, and limited government services. After years of progressive reform and strong government action, Hoosiers supported President Warren G. Harding's call for conservative "normalcy." According to historian James H. Madison, both parties avoided divisive issues, "whether they were raised by women, veterans, labor, farmers, Anti-Saloon Leaguers, or Klansmen."[51] Democrat Charles A. Greathouse lamented in 1924 that political consensus between the parties had grown so strong that "party lines and party affiliations are being lost sight of" in Indiana politics.[52] Yet political disagreements did emerge during the 1920s between and within each party over Prohibition, immigration, the Ku Klux Klan, and state tax code reform. The Moorhead Memorial Day Bill, too, provoked disagreements in the General Assembly by raising questions about the most conservative course of action for protecting Memorial Day: was it more prudent to enact legislation that regulated the holiday and promoted a patriotic, traditional commemorative observance, or was it more conservative to let Hoosiers decide for themselves how to observe the holiday? Opinions on the measure were strongly divided, and the bill was arguably the most contested piece of legislation during the 1923 session.

The bill initially enjoyed strong support in the Senate, with members voting 38 to 9 for its passage on January 18. All nine senators opposed to the bill were Republicans, however, exposing internal party disagreements between those like Moorhead who desired regulation and others like Senator A. H. Beardsley of Elkhart, who argued that "you can not legislate against irreverence. We can not regulate everything under the sun, even the holidays of the people. We are infringing too much on personal liberty."[53] Similar disagreements emerged in the House of Representatives, where the bill passed 62 to 32 on February 13, with a solid Republican minority dissenting.[54] Republicans who opposed the bill were also acutely aware of the economic concerns of many Indianapolis residents and businesses. One local resident who wrote a letter to the Republican-leaning *Indianapolis Star* under the name "A HOOSIER BOOSTER" remarked with concern that "this bill, if passed, would be the deadliest blow that could be struck at the city of Indianapolis and its industries." Indianapolis doctor J. S. Whitley concurred, arguing that "unwise legislation . . . retards the progress of our great commonwealth."[55]

The *Indianapolis News* also followed the debate proceedings closely, reporting that "the Statehouse was packed with lobbyists[,] and every means known to legislative procedure was used in efforts to advance or kill the measure." Religious groups like the Logansport Methodist Episcopal Church and the Indianapolis Church Federation passed resolutions in support of the bill, while Republican Indianapolis mayor Samuel Shank released a letter written on his official stationery in the *Indianapolis News* in favor of the bill, arguing that "the time has come when the American People can well afford to take one day off to worship at the Shrine of Patriotism."[56] By reflecting on the memories of "our soldier heroes of all wars," argued Shank, Hoosiers would "help checkmate radicals and anarchy in this country, and reestablish Memorial Day as it was originally intended."[57]

Shank's concerns about "radicals and anarchy" were particularly acute because of the rampant labor disputes that took place during his time in office; the two-term mayor had actually resigned from office during his first term in 1913 after continued labor strikes by streetcar and teamster workers in the city threatened to lead to his impeachment. Strikes were common in Indiana at the turn of the twentieth century, and as late as 1920 there were 99 strikes throughout the state, many in Indianapolis.[58] Shank believed that remembering the soldiers who had fought to preserve "law and order" against Confederate secession in the Civil War and German aggression in World War I would inspire Hoosiers—especially those in labor unions who may have embraced radical political beliefs—to eschew ideologies like communism, socialism, and anarchism.[59] Throughout its history, many Indiana GAR members—reflecting their allegiances to the Republican Party—vocalized their distrust of labor unions and socialism, and Shank's comments about the usefulness of Memorial Day as a "checkmate" against radicalism undoubtedly garnered support from GAR leadership. For example, in 1887, the Knights of Labor and the GAR in Terre Haute planned a series of Independence Day festivities, but a last-minute change led to Robert Schilling of Milwaukee, Wisconsin, serving as the keynote speaker. Schilling was a member of the Knights of Labor, but his speech was boycotted angrily by the GAR once it was discovered that he was a socialist. For the Indiana GAR, as Michael Kammen has written, "socialism was not merely un-American, but apparently antithetical to the principles for which battles on behalf of the Union had been fought."[60]

Likewise, news of the Pullman Strike in 1894 brought strong condemnation from Hoosier veterans. Department Commander Albert O. Marsh remarked that year that "dangerous and un-American doctrines" had nearly left "the entire country in disorder and bloodshed." Marsh stood in favor of "law and order," and he proudly proclaimed that the example of the Grand Army of the Republic had compelled Americans to "take a stand in favor of the enforcement of law, and the prevention by force of lawlessness and crime against life and property."[61] Finally, just a few weeks before Memorial Day in 1919, National Commander Clarendon E. Adams proclaimed in Elkhart that "the ideal of the Grand Army of the Republic is 'America—one country, one language, one flag,' and you must agree in this hour of unrest that we can not allow the red flag to prevail on American soil."[62] Apparently, quiet reflection on Memorial Day would also ensure that America stayed free of socialism, communism, and labor strife.

Indiana GAR members strongly advocated for passage of the Moorhead Memorial Day Bill and wrote many public letters explaining their views on the measure. Comrade Lewis King understood that there were two sides to the issue, "on the one side money, on the other sentiment." Thanks to the Indianapolis 500, "steam cars, interurban cars, and street cars will be filled to overflowing. Hotels, cafes and other eating places will handle many a dollar as a result." Making money was appropriate in its "proper place," King argued, but when the GAR established Memorial Day in 1868, "we expected the American people would use their [leisure time] joining with us in its observance . . . we never expected to see our own state disgraced by the spectacle of a mighty sport enterprise laying hands on the day. If money wins this game, it will be a deep sorrow to at least some of us who have not forgotten. If sentiment wins it will indicate that patriotism and affection survive."[63] For King, no less than the fate of American patriotism and a proper love of country hung in the balance with the Moorhead Memorial Day Bill.[64]

Despite vocal support from the Indiana GAR, the bill drew much criticism from other organizations and from many politicians. Powerful interest groups including the Indianapolis Federation of Community Civil Clubs voiced their resentment at the legislature's attempts to shut down the 500, which was arguably one of the city's largest money-making operations. The automobile industry and its boosters—including the Hoosier Motor Club, the Indianapolis Automobile Trade Association, and the Indianapolis Chamber of Commerce—passed a resolution against the measure at a joint meeting in late January 1923, decrying the bill as "an encroachment on the personal liberties of citizens." Trade Association president John R. Orman went even farther, telling the *Indianapolis Star* that "no one violates the sanctity of the day by enjoying himself, but on the contrary the holding of a great international event of this kind serves to mark the day as an outstanding holiday, a fitting tribute to those who fought."[65] Ten of the eleven House members from Indianapolis (again, mostly Republican) opposed the bill. Included in the opposition's ranks was Republican Russell B. Harrison, son of former U.S. president and Indiana GAR member Benjamin Harrison.[66]

In Harrison's opinion, the bill did not go far enough. "This bill is so grossly unfair," announced Harrison at one legislative session, "that it is unconstitutional. It should include all amusement or none." For many veterans in Indianapolis, it seemed as though the Indy 500 was nothing to be concerned about. Russell Harrison, a veteran of the Spanish-American War, and his comrades annually observed Memorial Day at the Soldiers and Sailors Monument, roughly five miles east of the racetrack. He informed the legislature that "we are not bothered by the speedway races. No! We are bothered by two theaters, one on each side of the Monument. Bands are out playing in front of theaters while our exercises are in progress." Harrison challenged his fellow legislators by asking them, "how many of you who are going to vote for this bill can truthfully say you go to the Memorial day exercises every Memorial Day?"[67] Those who planned to vote in support of the Moorhead bill, said many of its critics, needed to understand that the owners of the Indianapolis Motor Speedway were not the only offenders of the unwritten rules of Memorial Day. Effective legislation would need to prohibit more activities than just one race.

The Indiana GAR placed particular importance on enlisting the help of the American Legion in gaining support for a ban against the race. Following the end of World War I in 1918, Lt. Col. Theodore Roosevelt Jr., son of the former U.S. president, and a group of World War I military officers formed what would become the American Legion, a new fraternal organization for the veterans of that war. The American Legion was similar in some respects to the GAR; Lt. Col. George White, a leader during the organizations formative years, even referred to the Legion as "the new GAR." As the Civil War had done before it,

"World War I had given American soldiers a common experience and a sense of fraternity toward one another," helping to inspire the organizations formation, according to historian Dean J. Kotlowski.[68]

When it came to politics and the Moorhead bill, the Indiana GAR thought they had an ally in this new veterans' organization. Legion leaders shared similar concerns about the rise of communism in Russia and fears that "left-wing doctrines might infect the restless troops" once they arrived home. To combat these threats, Legion leaders promoted "Americanism," the idea of "continued service to the nation," and pension benefits for World War I veterans. Furthermore, delegates from southern and western states at the Legion's inaugural convention in 1919 banded together with Hoosiers to locate the Legion's national headquarters in Indianapolis—not Washington, D. C.—so that the "poorest man in the country can come to the headquarters."[69] Instead of an alliance, however, a war of words emerged between members of both organizations.

Upon hearing that the Moorhead Memorial Day Bill was passed by the House of Representatives in late February, members of sixteen posts of the American Legion in Indianapolis and surrounding Marion County signed a letter to be published in the *Indianapolis News*. The letter, addressed to Governor Warren McCray, asked him to veto the bill. According to these Legion members, Hoosiers "do not require legislative direction in their private observance of Memorial Day . . . We ex-soldiers of Indiana bitterly resent the imputation that we have no respect for our comrades killed in action, and [we] deny any man and any force the right to use this sacred sentiment for political bombast." How one observed Memorial Day was a private affair, according to the letter writers. Defining the terms of patriotism and imposing those terms upon the entire population through legislative fiat was decidedly un-American, something a despotic monarchy or authoritarian government in the "Old World" would do, but not "freedom-loving" America.[70]

An anonymous Civil War veteran sarcastically responded that he was surprised to see that the American Legion "now assume[d] to tell the Governor of the state what to do and to dictate to him as to where his duty lies" (apparently, the GAR had not done this through their support of the bill). According to the veteran, "honoring the memory of the men who made the American Legion possible" was now apparently considered "unAmerican and unpatriotic" by Legion members. The "egotism, arrogance and assumption[s]" of World War I veterans had led to a failed understanding of the "terms" of Memorial Day, according to the Civil War veteran, who signed his letter to the editor by describing himself as "A VETERAN OF THE (FROM THEIR STANDPOINT,

OBSOLETE, FORGOTTEN AND NOT TO BE CONSIDERED) WAR FOR THE SUPPRESSION OF THE REBELLION."[71]

Another ex-soldier named "G. L. M." (who most likely fought in World War I) responded with a biting attack on the supporters of the Moorhead Memorial Day Bill. Correctly noting that the members of the House of Representatives from Indianapolis opposed the bill, G. L. M. decried the bill as "class legislation" that unfairly targeted business interests seeking to earn a part of their living on Memorial Day. "I do not like the idea of the state legislature to point out to me what to do on Memorial day or any other day," the veteran complained. In plain language directed towards supporters of the bill in the General Assembly (and the GAR, ostensibly), G. L. M. asserted that "[the] bill was passed by a bunch of hicks, who were born and reared in some little jerk-water town, older than Indianapolis . . . these fellows are not accustomed to progress as we are." Supporters of the bill from rural areas in the state, argued the veteran, were ultimately "jealous of Indianapolis, our growing and prosperous city."[72] To have rural residents who lived far away from Indianapolis dictate the business activities of Indiana's most economically viable city was wrong.[73]

The term "class legislation" was used in the late nineteenth and early twentieth centuries to convey messages about legislation that was perceived as unfairly targeting certain groups in society; the term was frequently used in discussions regarding the legality and unfairness of legislation that favored tariff increases or labor regulations.[74] Some newspaper editors in cities outside of Indianapolis used similar cries of unfairness to criticize the Moorhead Memorial Day Bill. The *Evansville Courier* remarked that "if the only form of recreation to be penalized was the Memorial Day race at Indianapolis, then it would appear, from a commonsense viewpoint and without any appeal to legal technicality, that the bill was class legislation." Meanwhile, the *Lafayette Journal* stated that "the danger point is reached when attempts are made to legislate against the plain constitutional rights of the citizen and to set up rules by laws restricting this or that class."[75] On March 5, 1923, Governor Warren McCray vetoed the Moorhead Memorial Day Bill, citing the same "class legislation" argument that opponents of the bill had vocalized in the legislature and the press. When the bill was returned to the General Assembly, the Senate largely agreed with McCray's opposition to the measure and voted to uphold the governor's veto by a 35 to 5 vote. A political cartoon published in the *Indianapolis News* on March 7 ("Anti-Speed Way Bill") shows a race car flipped over on the track, its tires blown out and oil leaking from the engine, suggesting little possibility of another blowup over the race in future legislative sessions.[76] Meanwhile, in a move to punish opponents of the bill within the American Legion, Indiana State Commander Perry Faulkner, on the same day as the veto, suspended the charter of the Skidmore–Dean Post in Indianapolis, suggesting the possibility that Legion members were divided in their support of the bill.[77]

This vocal division in the American Legion most likely played a role in shaping Hoosiers' opinions about the bill. As GAR member George Scearce remarked in 1913, a barrier existed between those who had experienced the Civil War firsthand and those who had either learned about the war in history books or ignored it completely. For those born after the Civil War, World War I became the conflict from which shared memories of the U. S. in combat were created, and, as Barbara A. Gannon explains, "contemporary Americans understood that World War I soldiers and their tales of valor were displacing Civil War veterans."[78] As the few remaining Civil War veterans aged, American Legion members redefined what it meant to be a veteran in the United States, and a large part of this redefinition came in the form of new civic commemorations established by Legion members.

John Bodnar reminds us that the veterans of World War I, especially those who joined the American Legion, worked to create their own holiday on November 11, the day of Germany's surrender from the war. In the years after World War I, Armistice Day (now Veterans' Day) overtook Memorial Day as the major celebration of the American veteran in the nation's commemorative landscape. "People did not normally parade on the Fourth of July or Memorial Day," argues Bodnar, "but they always did so, between the [world] wars in Indianapolis, on November 11th."[79] Memorial Day was ultimately contested not only between veterans and non-veterans in Indiana, but between different veterans' groups as well. While veterans of the Civil War and World War I remembered war in a wide range of ways, the contrasting nature of Memorial Day and Armistice Day is significant. GAR veterans desired to remember the past by reflecting on the efforts of Union soldiers to save an imperiled nation from traitorous rebels within the country. In dealing with the shock and horror of Civil War death, these veterans determined that quiet and somber reflection was the most appropriate method for honoring the memories of the Union dead. American Legion veterans, in contrast, sought a more celebratory holiday that reflected the nation's collective joy in defeating a German enemy that was viewed by many Americans as despotic and undemocratic.

Two months after McCray's veto of the Moorhead Memorial Day Bill, the Indiana GAR held its annual state encampment in Muncie. Comrade F. M. Van Pelt announced: "I believe that I reflect the sentiment of the entire department when I say the greatest disappointment of the year was the lack of consideration given to Memorial Day . . . a protection which we think it deserves." Memorial Day was the "most sacred day of the entire year" and there was supposedly "universal appeal that came from the loyal law abiding people of the state" in support of the bill. Yet the "unfinished work" of ensuring that "sufficient safeguards are thrown around [Memorial Day]" would soon have to be left to the next generation. One could only hope that in the future, "the cry of class legislation will be consigned to the oblivion to which it belongs," argued Van Pelt.[80]

Seeking an opportunity to defend his patriotic reputation and explain his actions, Governor McCray traveled to Muncie to address the veterans. "I have a sacred reverence for the day designated as Memorial Day," announced McCray. "I always observe the proprieties of the occasion faithfully and reverently. To me the day revives certain distinct memories of my early boyhood."[81] The type of patriotism demonstrated by Civil War soldiers—"devotion to duty and not personal choice"—was needed "today in public service," the governor argued. "The patriotism of peace," according to McCray, required "courage to do what you believe to be right and not inclination to follow the lines of least resistance."[82] What constituted "right," argued McCray, was a devotion to the nation, the state of Indiana, and their respective constitutions.

What had been right in the eyes of Governor McCray also included a veto of the Memorial Day bill. Despite strong sympathy for the views of the Indiana GAR, the governor told his audience that he would not sign into law an "act in direct violation of [his] oath" to uphold the state constitution. McCray put several rhetorical questions to his audience: "Laws to be respected and observed must also be reasonable and fair. Is it right to single out a certain amusement and deny its right of existence, and at the same time permit other forms of amusement to operate without prejudice? Is there any reason why a circus, a theater, or a moving picture show should be permitted to give exhibitions without violating any law, and yet make it prohibitive under the law to hold a race of any kind?" McCray concluded by asking, "Is it justice for two to play golf in a tournament [one] for a prize and the other for amusement only and yet one be guilty of law violation under the act and the other not?"[83] Echoing Russell Harrison, McCray concluded that to ban the Indianapolis 500 while permitting other events on Memorial Day was discriminatory and illegal.

Following McCray's speech, Comrade Robert W. McBride rose to speak. An attorney and former Indiana Supreme Court justice, McBride argued that "the explanation by the Governor is wholly unsatisfactory and inadequate." The justice explained that there was a difference between "the consciousless [*sic*] profiteer who would rob us of the one day for the gratification of greed and a legitimate business with a theater or a motion picture show that operates day after day throughout the year." Such a difference, McBride believed, was akin to "piracy and honest business." To punish other "honest businesses" because of the Indianapolis 500's "desecration" of Memorial Day was not the intention of the Indiana GAR, and "the reason given by the Governor furnishes no excuse for denying the protection we ask." The proper observation of Memorial Day "testifies to the world that we as a people have not forgotten the cost of a great . . . undivided Republic nor have we forgotten the men who offered their lives that the Republic might be."[84] To the Indiana GAR, the Indianapolis 500 violated the sacred relationship between the Union dead and those who lived to reap the benefits of their victory over disunion and treason. Relegating Memorial Day to a day of trivial amusements would lead to a society unpatriotically forgetting about its past.

The Indiana GAR's efforts to ban the Indianapolis 500 on Memorial Day demonstrate the ways in which historical memories evolve and alter over time. During Memorial Day's transformational phase, the memories of Indiana GAR veterans were directly challenged by younger generations seeking to find their own methods for coming to terms with the past. Even as Governor McCray took pains in his 1923 encampment speech to assert his respect for Indiana's Civil War veterans, he did so by reflecting on nostalgic memories of seeing veterans during his boyhood more than fifty years earlier, essentially placing these veterans in a remote past detached from the present. Left unsaid in McCray's speech was any mention of whether or not the Indiana GAR's influence in creating Memorial Day in the first place gave them any right to continue setting the terms for an appropriate commemoration of their service as long they remained alive. The Indianapolis 500 helped to advance the transformational phase of Memorial Day from a day of quiet reflection to one of amusement, sport, and a showcase for civic pride and technological advancement. The Indiana GAR's efforts to turn back the clock and remove all "distractions" from Memorial Day failed partly because most of its members had died, but also because, by the 1910s and 1920s, those still living were seen as less significant to society's memories of its Civil War dead. Indeed, the Indiana GAR's failure alerts us to just how fragile and temporary our shared memories of the past really are.

NICHOLAS W. SACCO is a park guide with the National Park Service at the Ulysses S. Grant National Historic Site in St. Louis, Missouri. He holds a master's degree in History with a concentration in Public History from Indiana University–Purdue University Indianapolis. This article originally appeared in volume 111, December 2015.

NOTES

1. The most recent estimate of the Civil War death toll (750,000) is taken from J. David Hacker, "A Census-Based Count of the Civil War Dead," *Civil War History* 57 (December 2011), 307–348.

2. David Blight, "Decoration Days: The Origins of Memorial Day in North and South," in Alice Fahs and Joan Waugh, eds., *The Memory of the Civil War in American Culture* (Chapel Hill, N. C., 2004), 94.

3. For firsthand accounts of the GAR's origins, see Robert B. Beath, *History of the Grand Army of the Republic* (New York, 1888), 33–67; Oliver Morris Wilson, *The Grand Army of the Republic Under its First Constitution and Ritual: Its Birth and Organization* (Kansas City, Mo., 1905), 27–30. See also Mary R. Dearing, *Veterans in Politics: The Story of the G.A.R.* (Baton Rouge, La., 1952); Stuart McConnell, *Glorious Contentment: The Grand Army of the Republic, 1865–1900* (Chapel Hill, N. C., 1992). GAR membership statistics throughout the organization's existence are in Dennis Northcott, *Indiana Civil War Veterans: Transcription of the Death Rolls of the Department of Indiana, Grand Army of the Republic, 1882–1948* (St. Louis, Mo., 2005), 379–80.

4. Readers should note that the holiday was often referred to as "Decoration Day" in the late nineteenth century and early twentieth century. In this study I will use the term "Memorial Day," which is the common term for the holiday in the United States today. Memorial Day was switched to the last Monday in May through a 1968 federal law. See United States Congress, "Public Law 90–363" (PL, 28 June 1968).

5. Jay Winter, "Remembrance and Redemption: A Social Interpretation of War Memorials," *Harvard Design Magazine* (Fall 1999), 76–77; Karen E. Till, "Memory Studies," *History Workshop Journal*, no. 62 (Autumn 2006), 327.

6. For extended discussions on history and memory, see Till, "Memory Studies," 325–41; Avishai Margalit, *The Ethics of Memory* (Cambridge, Mass., 2002).

7. A. C. Leonard, *Grand Army of the Republic Hand Book* (Lancaster, Pa., 1884), 16.

8. For more information about commemorative practices on May 30 from 1865 through 1867, see Blight, "Decoration Days," 94–129; Michael Kammen, *Mystic Chords of Memory: The Transformation of Tradition in American Culture* (New York, 1991), 102–110; Caroline E. Janney, *Remembering the Civil War:*

Reunion and the Limits of Reconciliation (Chapel Hill, N. C., 2013), 98–99; John R. Neff, *Honoring the Civil War Dead: Commemoration and the Problem of Reconciliation* (Lawrence, Kan., 2005), 153–54.

9. The full text of General Logan's General Orders No. 11 is printed in Beath, *History of the Grand Army of the Republic*, 90–91.

10. Robert Bellah, "Civil Religion in America," *Daedalus* 96 (Winter 1967), 1–21.

11. Benedict Anderson defines "imagined community" as a socially constructed community that perceives itself as a cohesive group or nationality. Benedict Anderson, *Imagined Communities: Reflections on the Origin and Spread of Nationalism* (New York, 1983), 1–7.

12. Colfax quoted in Ernest F. M. Faehtz, *The National Memorial Day: A Record of Ceremonies Over the Graves of the Union Soldiers, May 29 and 30, 1869* (Washington, D.C., 1870), 167–68. Michael Kammen argues that antebellum Americans had an "indifference" about the past and believed that "government ought to bear little responsibility for the maintenance of collective memories." Historian Denise D. Meringolo similarly argues that "none of the amateur historians among the founding fathers or their successors argued that the study of history should be a function of government," and that Americans were ambivalent about "the notion of a national culture sponsored by the federal government." See Kammen, *Mystic Chords of Memory*, 40–61; Denise D. Meringolo, *Museums, Monuments, and National Parks: Towards a New Genealogy of Public History* (Amherst, Mass., 2012), 5–7. See also Earl J. Hess, *Liberty, Virtue, and Progress: Northerners and Their War for the Union* (New York, 1988), 27–28; Eric Hobsbawm, "Introduction: Inventing Traditions," in Eric Hobsbawm and Terence Ranger, eds., *The Invention of Tradition* (New York, 1983), 1–14.

13. Roberston quoted in Faehtz, *The National Memorial Day*, 160–73; Beath, *History of the Grand Army of the Republic*, 90.

14. Memorial Day rituals probably became more uniform as they evolved through years of experimenting with different practices and "General Order" directives from GAR leadership.

15. McConnell, *Glorious Contentment*, 184. New York was the first state to designate May 30 as a legal holiday for Memorial Day commemorations in 1873, and by 1890 all northern states had made the day a legal holiday. David W. Blight, *Race and Reunion: The Civil War in American Memory* (Cambridge, Mass., 2001), 71; Kammen, *Mystic Chords of Memory*, 103. For an example of a Memorial Day services handbook used in the twentieth century, see Grand Army of the Republic, *Services For the Use of the Grand Army of the Republic* (N. P., 1923).

16. Blight, "Decoration Days," 100.

17. Barbara A. Gannon, *The Won Cause: Black and White Comradeship in the Grand Army of the Republic* (Chapel Hill, N. C., 2011).

18. For example, see "The Union Dead," *Indianapolis Journal,* June 1, 1868; "Decoration Day," *Greencastle Banner,* June 3, 1880; "Memorial Day Parade," *Indianapolis News,* May 30, 1901; "Pays Tribute to Colored Race," *Indianapolis Star,* May 31, 1907. Indianapolis newspapers regularly published Memorial Day speeches in their papers between May 30 and June 3 on an annual basis. The *Indianapolis Journal* (1868–1903), the *Indianapolis Star* (starting in 1904), and the *Indianapolis News* are the best sources for analyzing Memorial Day speeches.

19. "Decoration Day," *Greencastle Banner,* June 3, 1880.

20. "The Union's Dead Soldiers," *Indianapolis Journal,* June 2, 1886.

21. "The Lessons of Memorial Day," *American Tribune,* May 30, 1890.

22. Drew Gilpin Faust, *This Republic of Suffering: Death and the American Civil War* (New York, 2008), 269.

23. *Indianapolis Journal,* June 2, 1886. For a similar speech on nationalism given by the Rev. A. B. Storms in 1914 at Crown Hill Cemetery, see "Tribute Paid to the Nation's Dead," *Indianapolis Star,* May 30, 1914.

24. "Memorial Oration," *American Tribune,* June 15, 1893.

25. Ibid. One critic of government pensions considered them acts of corrupt socialism. See William M. Sloane, "Pensions and Socialism," *Century* 42 (June 1891), 179–88. See also Theda Skocpol, *Protecting Soldiers and Mothers: The Political Origins of Social Policy in the United States* (Cambridge, Mass., 1992).

26. While an exact number of Democrats in the Indiana GAR is impossible to ascertain, Larry M. Logue estimates that roughly one-third of its members (31 percent) voted for Democrat Grover Cleveland in the 1888 Presidential election. Following the Indiana GAR's reorganization in 1879, the political allegiances of its membership may have remained consistent in a two-to-one ratio in support of the Republicans. See Larry M. Logue, "Union Veterans and Their Government: The Effects of Public Policies on Private Lives," *Journal of Interdisciplinary History* 22 (Winter 1992), 411–34; Nicole Etcheson, *A Generation at War: The Civil War Era in a Northern Community* (Lawrence, Kan., 2011), 195. The tactic of reviving negative memories of the war (and promoting memories of emancipation) was often referred to as "waving the bloody shirt," which Charles W. Calhoun defines as "inflaming the emotions of the war and Reconstruction for partisan purposes." Republicans attacked both former Confederates and Northern Democrats who they believed had engaged in treasonous wartime behavior. See Charles W. Calhoun, *From Bloody Shirt to Full Dinner Pail: The Transformation of Politics and Governance in the Gilded Age* (New York, 2010), 5.

27. Etcheson, *A Generation at War,* 174.

28. "An Address Delivered by Col. C. C. Matson, at Bloomington, July 4," *Greencastle Dollar Press,* July 23, 1879; Etcheson, *A Generation at War,* 193–94.

29. On Civil War memory and reconciliation, see Blight, *Race and Reunion,* 1–5; Cecilia O'Leary, "American All: Reforging a National Brotherhood,

1876–1917," *History Today* 44 (October 1994), 20–27; Thomas J. Brown, *The Public Art of Civil War Commemoration: A Brief History with Documents* (Boston, 2004), 1–14; Matthew Dennis, *Red, White, and Blue Letter Days: An American Calendar* (Ithaca, N. Y., 2002), 221–34; James H. Madison, "Civil War Memories and 'Pardnership Forgittin', 1865–1913," *Indiana Magazine of History* 99 (September 2003), 198–230.

30. In 1914, Indiana GAR member Newton M. Taylor shook hands with a former Confederate soldier at Greenlawn Cemetery in Franklin, although he stood by his premise that southern politicians brought on the Civil War. In contrast, Comrade Lew Wallace had warned in 1892 that "the Solid South is but another name for the Confederacy." See "In Memory of the Dead and Over Confederate Graves," *Indianapolis News*, May 30, 1901; "Blue and Gray Clasp Hands," *Indianapolis News*, May 30, 1914; "General Lew Wallace at the Annual Banquet of the Loyal Legion," *American Tribune*, June 2, 1892.

31. "A Grand Army Institution," *Indianapolis Journal*, May 30, 1899.

32. Many of these complaints were recorded in the GAR Encampment Records taken at the Indiana GAR's annual meeting. Hereafter I will use Gannon's format for citing GAR National and State Encampment records: "When GAR Encampments are cited, the entry will include the state, the meeting number, and the year the meeting took place." Gannon, *The Won Cause*, 223.

33. For example, veteran Ivan N. Walker warned in 1892 that Memorial Day was not "made a day of feasting, festivals and fairs," nor should it be "given over to base ball and other sports" because it was "set apart as a day sacred to the memory of our heroic dead . . . no day in the year is so important to us as a nation." In 1904, Indiana GAR commander George W. Grubbs asserted that "the increasing perversion of Memorial Day in many places to mere pleasure, amusement, and frivolity, is a national shame. The apathy which countenances it is a sign of the decline of national gratitude and conscience," while William Ketcham proclaimed in 1908 that Memorial Day was a "Holy day, on which we meet and pay tribute to our dead . . . For us this day is set apart and sacred to this and no other purpose whatsoever." See Indiana, *Thirteenth* (1892), 100; Indiana, *Twenty-Fifth* (1904), 102, 159; Indiana, *Twenty-Ninth* (1908), 94. Additionally, in 1907, some members of the GAR opposed the dedication of a statue to Indiana Civil War and Spanish American War veteran Henry Ware Lawton on Memorial Day, claiming it was an encroachment on the holiday. See Alexander Uribel, "The Making of Citizens: A History of Civic Education in Indianapolis, 1900–1950" (Ph.D. Diss., Indiana University, 1996), 135–39.

34. Indiana, *Thirty-Fourth* (1913), 102–103.

35. Later in life, Fisher moved to Florida, where his personal papers are housed at HistoryMiami Archives & Research Center. The other three founders of the Speedway—James A. Allison, Frank H. Wheeler, and Arthur C.

Newbury—have no known manuscript records. See Carl Fisher Papers, 1896–1958, HistoryMiami Archives & Research Center, online at http://historymiamiarchives.org/guides/?p=collections/findingaid&id=14&q=&rootcontentid=600.

36. For example, in the early 1890s Fisher had a friend make thousands of toy balloons with illuminating gas, fifty of which had "tags" with a redeemable coupon for a free bicycle in them. According to a Fisher relative, "some Hoosiers were so eager to get a free bike that they loaded rounds into their shotguns and shot at the balloons as though they were hunting geese." Quoted in Mark S. Foster, *Castles in the Sand: The Life and Times of Carl Graham Fisher* (Gainesville, Fl., 2000), 21–33.

37. Foster, *Castles in the Sand*, 45–59; D. Bruce Scott, *Indy: Racing Before the 500* (Batesville, Ind., 2005), 6–11.

38. Robert V. Robinson and Carl M. Briggs, "The Rise of Factories in Nineteenth-Century Indianapolis," *American Journal of Sociology* 97 (November 1991), 627–28; Scott, *Indy*, 3; Foster, *Castles in the Sand*, 43.

39. Foster, *Castles in the Sand*, 76–80; "Auto's Aid to Prosperity," *Indianapolis Star*, September 4, 1910.

40. There is no evidence from newspapers at the time to support Myers or Moorhead, and no known manuscript records exist for Moorhead. "Speedway Through if Bill Passes, Myers Says," *Indianapolis Star*, January 29, 1923; "May 30 Race Ban Fight Recalled," *Indianapolis News*, May 30, 1967; "World's Greatest Auto Race Planned," *Indianapolis News*, September 6, 1910; Foster, *Castles in the Sand*, 80; Terry Reed, *The Race and Ritual of the Indianapolis 500* (Dulles, Va., 2005), 5–13.

41. Alexander Uribel argues that "the commercialization of Memorial Day in the years before the Great War became rampant. Advertisements by local merchants, perhaps fearing less the wrath of aging soldiers, blatantly coopted [sic] the images of Memorial Day to sell flags, shoes, suits, and other goods. L.S. Ayres . . . advertised a wide assortment of flags for sale, for all budgets." Uribel, "The Making of Citizens," 146; Foster, *Castles in the Sand*, 76, 80.

42. Uribel, "The Making of Citizens," 141.

43. "Deplores Sports on Memorial Day," *Indianapolis Star*, May 29, 1911.

44. "To Bar Sports on May 30," *Indianapolis News*, June 1, 1911; "Would Bar Sports on Memorial Day," *Indianapolis Star*, June 1, 1911; "Speedway Picks July 4 Date," *Indianapolis Star*, June 3, 1911; Uribel, "The Making of Citizens," 143.

45. Indiana, *Thirty-Fifth* (1914), 71; "To Maintain Memorial Day," *Indianapolis News*, January 29, 1915.

46. Uribel, "The Making of Citizens," 146.

47. "A Better Memorial Day," *Indianapolis News*, June 1, 1911.

48. "No Disrespect to the Day," *Indianapolis Star*, May 31, 1913.

49. Indiana, *Forty-Third* (1922), 75.

50. "Way Sought to Save the Speedway Races," *Indianapolis News*, February 19, 1923; "38–9 Oppose 500-Mile Race," *Indianapolis Star*, January 19, 1923. If the Moorhead bill passed, Representative Asa Smith was prepared to submit a bill that would give the mayor of Indianapolis the right to declare any day of the year a legal holiday in the city. Smith explained that allowing the mayor to declare another day as a holiday for the purpose of holding the Indianapolis 500 would "protect the speedway in event the Moorhead bill passes."

51. James H. Madison, *Indiana Through Tradition and Change: A History of the Hoosier State and Its People, 1920–1945* (Indianapolis, Ind., 1982), 75.

52. Quoted in Madison, *Indiana Through Tradition and Change*, 63.

53. Indiana General Assembly, *Journal of the Indiana State Senate during the Seventy-Third Session of the General Assembly* (Indianapolis, Ind., 1923), 92; *Indianapolis Star*, January 19, 1923.

54. Indiana General Assembly, *Journal of the House of Representatives of the State of Indiana during the Seventy-Third Session of the General Assembly* (Indianapolis, Ind., 1923), 370.

55. "Keep Speedway Race," *Indianapolis Star*, February 5, 1923; "Would Save Speed Classic," *Indianapolis Star*, January 28, 1923; see also Homer McKee, "Keep Their Spirit Alive," *Indianapolis Star*, January 29, 1923.

56. "Memorial Day Bill," *Indianapolis News*, March 6, 1923; "Want State Censorship," *Indianapolis Star*, January 5, 1923; "Praise Race Bill Vote," *Indianapolis News*, March 1, 1923; "Shank on Record for Race Bill," *Indianapolis News*, March 5, 1923; "Mayor Shank Quits," *New York Times*, November 29, 1913; "Shank, Samuel Lewis (Lew)" in David J. Bodenhamer and Robert G. Barrows, eds., *The Encyclopedia of Indianapolis* (Bloomington, Ind., 1994), 1254–55.

57. *Indianapolis News*, March 1, 5, 6, 1923; *New York Times*, November 29, 1913; *Encyclopedia of Indianapolis*, 1254–55.

58. In 1881, there were eleven strikes in Indiana. By 1903, that number jumped to 172, with 22,678 employees going on strike. Clifton J. Phillips, *Indiana in Transition: The Emergence of an Industrial Commonwealth, 1880–1920* (Indianapolis, Ind., 1968), 346–60.

59. Working-class voting returns in Indiana during the first quarter of the twentieth century do not follow any simple pattern. Historian Julie Greene argues that regional party allegiances often shaped working-class preferences more than union leadership groups like the American Federation of Labor, although many laborers identified as Democrats or Socialists. Julie Greene, *Pure and Simple Politics: The American Federation of Labor and Political Activism, 1881–1917* (Cambridge, UK, 1999), 209.

60. "Couldn't Stand Schilling," *New York Times*, July 5, 1887; Kammen, *Mystic Chords of Memory*, 104.

61. To be sure, some Indiana GAR members did support labor unions and perhaps even the tenets of socialism. The *American Tribune* remarked in 1890 that "we believe in labor federations. Since labor began to organize, the intelligence and prosperity of those concerned in the movement has improved fifty per cent, and it has not disturbed the prosperity and happiness of the rich either." *American Tribune,* September 5, 1890; Indiana, *Sixteenth* (1895), 110–111.

62. Indiana, *Fortieth* (1919), 6–7; "G.A.R. Leader Scores Bolshevik Propaganda," *Indianapolis News,* May 7, 1919.

63. In his letter to the editor, King explained that he was in Florida, "Away Down South in Dixie." It is not clear if King had moved to Florida or was merely visiting the state at that time, but his use of the phrase "our own state disgraced" suggests that this may have been the Reverend Lewis King, who was a former state commander of the Indiana GAR and a member of the Isham Keith Post number 13, Columbus, Indiana. "Memorial Day Thoughts," *Indianapolis News,* February 20, 1923; Northcott, *Indiana Civil War Veterans,* 388.

64. The remainder of this essay will rely heavily upon primary sources, some of which were found with assistance from Chandler Lighty of the Indiana State Library. Secondary sources on the Indianapolis 500 and its relation to the Moorhead Memorial Day Bill are lacking. To my knowledge, this is the first analysis of the bill and the Grand Army of the Republic's support of it.

65. "Action Started to Prevent Passage of Anti-Race Bill," *Indianapolis Star,* January 22, 1923.

66. "Race Bill Wends Way to Governor," *Indianapolis News,* February 28, 1923; *Indianapolis News,* February 19, 1923.

67. "Memorial Bill is Passed by House," *Indianapolis News,* February 27, 1923.

68. Thomas R. Rumer, *The American Legion: An Official History, 1919–1989* (New York, 1990), 33; Dean J. Kotlowski, "Launching a Political Career: Paul V. McNutt and the American Legion, 1919–1932," *Indiana Magazine of History* 106 (June 2010), 124–25.

69. Kotlowski, "Launching a Political Career," 129; John Bodnar, *Remaking America: Public Memory, Commemoration, and Patriotism in the Twentieth Century* (Princeton, N.J., 1992), 86.

70. "McCray's Action on Race Bill Awaited," *Indianapolis News,* February 27, 1923.

71. "A Civil War Veteran's View," *Indianapolis News,* March 1, 1923.

72. "Disgusted With Memorial Day Bill," *Indianapolis News,* March 2, 1923.

73. Julie Greene cites the election of 1908 as an example of deep political differences between rural and urban Hoosiers. That year progressive Republican governor J. Frank Hanly helped advance a measure that gave all counties the right to prohibit alcohol with their boundaries, but "[the] proposal pitted rural against urban voters, allowing the mostly rural supporters of temperance to

outlaw liquor . . . despite the opposition of urban voters." Historian Leonard Moore, however, argues that Indianapolis was "more closely related to Indiana's smaller industrial cities and rural communities than to other large midwestern cities" thanks to a large native-born Protestant white population that reflected the state's demographics at the time. Greene, *Pure and Simple Politics*, 207; Leonard Moore, *Citizen Klansman: The Ku Klux Klan in Indiana, 1921–1928* (Chapel Hill, N. C., 1991), 82.

74. For example, in 1892 Democratic Indiana governor Isaac P. Gray criticized the 1890 McKinley Tariff which raised tariff duties on imported goods to the United States. Gray argued that this "extravagant . . . class legislation" would "enrich special private interests and protect special industries from competition." Likewise, former Indiana governor and vice president Thomas Marshall—also a Democrat—asserted in 1919: "I believe that every inequality which exists in the social and economic condition of the American people is traceable to the successful demands of interested classes for class legislation." "Gov. Gray's Speech," *Jasper* [Indiana] *Weekly Courier*, July 8, 1892; "Vice President Marshall's Creed of Americanism," *Washington Times*, February 8, 1919.

75. "Veto of the Memorial Day Bill," *Evansville Courier*, March 6, 1923; "The Speedway Bill," *Lafayette Journal*, March 6, 1923.

76. "The Last Lap," *Indianapolis News*, March 7, 1923.

77. "Governor Vetoes Memorial Day Bill," *Indianapolis News*, March 6, 1923.

78. Gannon, *The Won Cause*, 188.

79. Bodnar, *Remaking America*, 85.

80. Indiana, *Forty-Fourth* (1923), 48–49.

81. What sorts of memories McCray specifically refers to goes unstated, but it should be noted that McCray was born on February 4, 1865, three months before the official end of the American Civil War. Perhaps he is referring to the observation of Memorial Day services during his youth.

82. In this quote, McCray is referring to concerns about political radicalism. Indiana, *Forty-Fourth* (1923), 78–79.

83. Indiana, *Forty-Fourth* (1923), 78–79.

84. Indiana, *Forty-Fourth* (1923), 81; "Voices Criticisms of Governor's Veto of the Memorial Day Bill," *Indianapolis Star*, April 23, 1923. On McBride, see Linda C. Gugin and James E. St. Clair, eds., *Justices of the Indiana Supreme Court* (Indianapolis, Ind., 2011); Indiana Supreme Court, "Justice Biographies: Justice Robert Wesley McBride," at http://www.in.gov/judiciary/citc/2768.htm; Robert W. McBride, *Lincoln's Body Guard: The Union Light Guard of Ohio, With Some Personal Recollections of Abraham Lincoln* (Indianapolis, Ind., 1911).

7

The War against German-American Culture

The Removal of German-Language Instruction from the Indianapolis Schools, 1917–1919

PAUL J. RAMSEY

TRADITIONALLY, WAR HAS BEEN A "religious experience" for this nation; times of conflict have drawn from the American public a level of commitment to the cause that has at times bordered on the fanatical. Such zealotry was certainly apparent during World War I.[1] The United States declaration of war on Germany in April 1917 unleashed an era of what might be termed "superpatriotism," which led to the opening of a domestic theater of war against German-American culture.[2] This reaction, described by Carl Wittke as "a violent, hysterical, concerted movement to eradicate everything German from American civilization,"[3] manifested itself most clearly in a crusade against the German language, since it was through language that German-Americans in Indiana and elsewhere maintained part of their cultural heritage and "their different philosophy of life."[4] Through this "patriotic" war against German-American culture, nativists were able to halt the teaching of the German language in many schools throughout the country.

Although the superpatriots' cultural warfare was directed at a variety of institutions and organizations, it made sense that one of the primary institutions targeted for battle was the public school. Some Americans believed that public schools were quickly becoming instruments of imperial Germany; Gustavus Ohlinger, a leading American opponent of German culture, warned that German-language schooling was part of a policy of *Kulturpolitik* by which Germany had for years worked to pacify the world's citizens and to make them obedient to the *Vaterland*. This conspiracy in education was far-reaching, according to Ohlinger and other like-minded nativists, such as the western novelist Owen Wister, who warned of the peril of "Prussianized" education.[5] American scholars who had studied in Germany were said to be supporters of that country's policy, and German-born professors, some hinted, were using their positions to spread pro-German propaganda. More importantly, imperial Germany had loyal supporters in the "Prussianized" German Americans. These were the Germans who had emigrated not seeking religious or political freedom but only economic betterment; politically, nativists believed, they remained loyal to Germany.[6] These immigrants, Ohlinger suggested, worked through such organizations as the German-American Alliance—the leading German-American organization in the United States—to promote German-language instruction and pro-German textbooks in public schools so that the student's mind would become "so thoroughly saturated with ideas favorable to Germany that it [would be] ready to react to the crudest form of propaganda." If American education became imbued with German culture, Ohlinger feared, "there succumbs the nation."[7]

Schooling was significant in the cultural war for another reason as well. The school system in Germany was believed by some, notably American educators and school officials, to have been a direct cause of the war; that is, the German school had made the Great War possible.[8] Mary C. C. Bradford, president of the National Education Association (NEA), maintained in 1917 that "the teachings of the German schools . . . led just as inevitably to the present crisis as we know that sunrise follows sunset and night follows day." Central to the German school, as interpreted by American educators, was its emphasis on Nietzsche and his "cruel philosophy." Thomas H. Briggs, professor of education at Teachers College, Columbia University, told the members of the Indiana State Teachers Association (ISTA) in 1917 that the war had been "inevitable" because the German school inculcated militarism in its students. According to Briggs, German students repeatedly had to answer "What country is our natural enemy?" with "France," and "What must we do to the natural enemy of our country?" with "Destroy it."[9] Although the German school had in part caused the war, the American school could do its part by attacking any lingering expressions of German culture among immigrants. Following the advice of the World War I slogan, "If you can't fight over there, fight over here," an army of educators, officials, politicians, and concerned citizens fought for what Indiana University's James Woodburn described as a "*united* nation—with *one* people, *one* government . . . *one* allegiance, and, let us not be afraid to say, *one* language."[10]

This essay examines the campaign to eliminate German-language instruction from Indiana's, and especially Indianapolis's, schools. Before 1917,

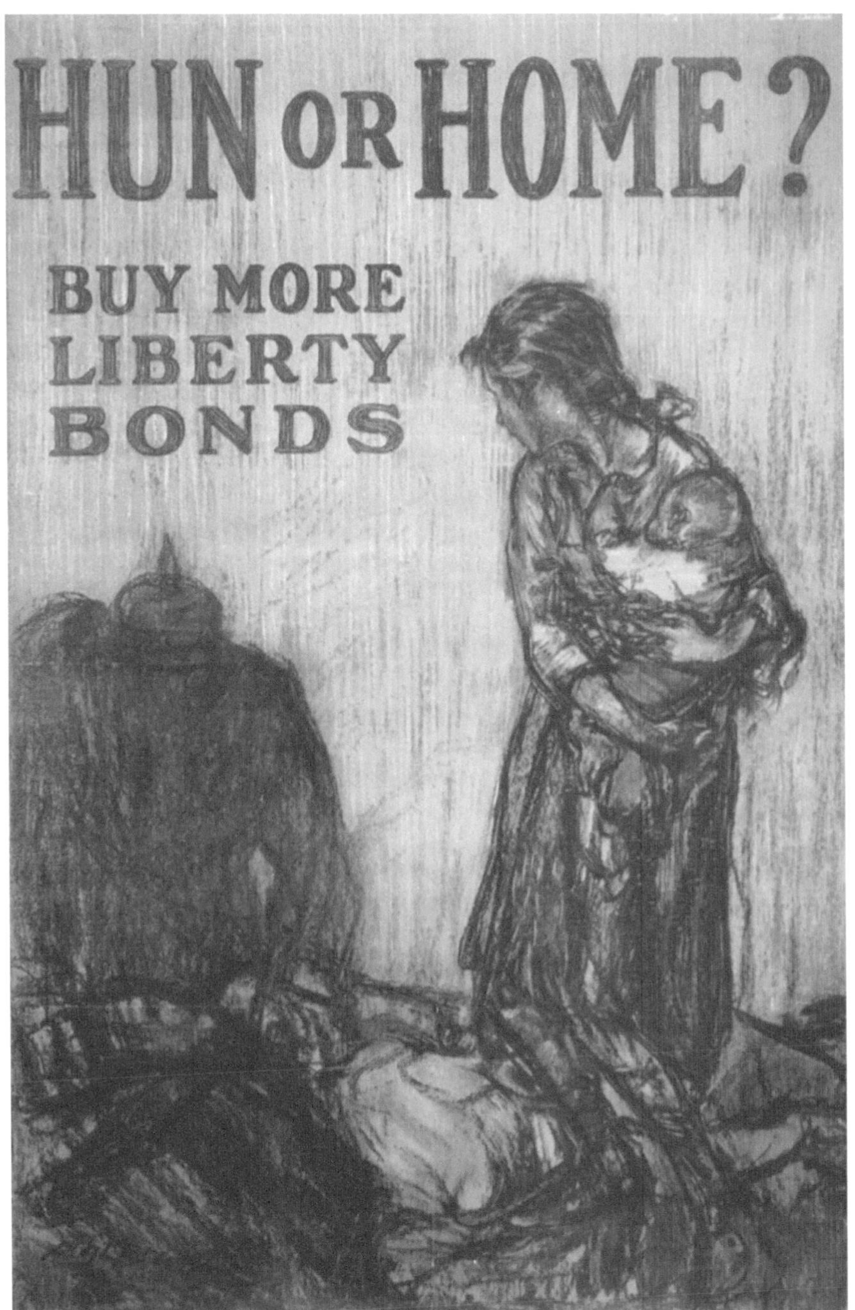

World War I propaganda posters frequently depicted German soldiers as murderous beasts, as in this 1918 poster promoting U.S. Liberty Bonds. *Courtesy Library of Congress, Prints and Photographs Division.*

German-Americans in Indianapolis had a thriving community and played an important role in the city's development, but that role was attacked and undermined after the United States entered the war. Superpatriotism, expressed by hysterical hatred of the German enemy, swept across the country during the war era, creating a demand for the removal of German-language instruction from the schools. That demand was at last met, in Indiana, by passage of the McCray Act in 1919.

In 1917 German-Americans were a sizable and visible segment of the Indiana population. The 1910 census reported that Indiana's population of 2,700,876 included more than a half-million people of "foreign white stock," i.e., either they or at least one of their parents had been born in a foreign country.[11] More than half of this group in Indiana listed German ancestry, while another 3.5 percent claimed Austrian heritage. In 1915, a leading German-American Hoosier, William A. Fritsch, estimated that more than half of Indiana's residents were of Teutonic lineage. The state's capital had a similarly large Germanic population. In 1910, statistics for Indianapolis resembled those for the state as a whole: nearly half of Indianapolis's citizens of "foreign birth or foreign parentage" had origins in Germany with another 2.8 percent having Austrian ancestry; taken together, Americans of German and Austrian parentage comprised some 30,938 of Indianapolis's 233,650 residents. The census reports did not reach beyond the second generation, but historian George Theodore Probst has estimated that in 1890 perhaps a third of Indianapolis's residents were of German ancestry.[12] One source reported that the typical German immigrant in the city was "Americanized in a political and economic sense" rather quickly but "maintained his customs and used his mother tongue," although the second generation was less likely to do so.[13]

German-Americans thrived in Indianapolis before the war. They maintained numerous institutions that supported and energized their culture, which many believed was greater than the dominant American culture. German-Americans established German churches, the Indianapolis Maennerchor (Men's Chorus), and a variety of other clubs and societies, including the Indianapolis Turnverein, a social and athletic club. Indianapolis also housed a chapter of the German-American Alliance. Just before the war, an Indianapolis man, Joseph Keller, served as president of the state chapter and first vice president of the national organization.[14] Indianapolis was also the home of several of Indiana's German-language newspapers, including the prominent *Telegraph und Tribune*, which ran six evenings a week with a circulation of 10,825 in 1915. In the same year, the newspaper's Sunday edition, *Spottvogel*, claimed a circulation of 11,979.[15] In addition to their own organizations, residents of Germanic heritage played key roles in local civic institutions as well. Shortly after the turn of the twentieth century, for instance, German-Americans in Indianapolis held the offices of mayor, chief of police, and sheriff.[16]

Indianapolis residents of German descent were also involved in another important institution: the school. Clearly, German-Americans exercised a great deal of control over German parochial schools, but they also held key positions in Indianapolis's public schools, among which were seats on the school board. Beginning in the 1860s, for instance, Clemens Vonnegut sat on the Board of School Commissioners for nearly thirty years, and Keller became the president of the board before World War I. German-Americans in Indianapolis were also heavily involved with manual training and physical education in the public schools. Frances Mueller, for example, became the first supervisor of physical education for Indianapolis's public schools, and, beginning in the 1890s, Charles E. Emmerich served as principal of the new Manual Training High School. Moreover, Indianapolis Public Schools (IPS) maintained an extensive German-language program before World War I, and the administrators who oversaw the program were also German-Americans. Emmerich was IPS's supervisor of German from 1873 until the early 1890s. Another German-American, Robert Nix, served in that role for sixteen years, until 1910, when Peter Scherer took over the position—the title was upgraded to director of modern languages in 1915—and held it until it was terminated in 1918.[17]

It was through the public school, along with the family, parochial schools, and the churches, that the German language was preserved for the generations of German-Americans with no firsthand knowledge of Germany and its language. Beginning in 1869 German-language instruction was required by law to be offered in many of Indiana's public schools. Indiana's Germans hoped the law would attract more immigrants to the state.[18] The law stated that "whenever the parents or guardians of twenty-five or more children in attendance at any school of a township, town or city, shall so demand, it shall be the duty of the School Trustee or Trustees of said township, town or city, to procure efficient teachers, and introduce the German language, as a branch of study, into such schools; and the tuition in said schools shall be without charge."[19] IPS began to experiment with German-language instruction within the city's heavily German wards even before this legislation had been formally proposed, but after the bill became a law the number of elementary schools offering the language steadily grew. By 1877, there were already ten schools offering German; six years later, sixteen schools provided German-language instruction to more than 2,400 students. Indianapolis's high school had been teaching German since 1868. In 1907, the practice was further encouraged by passage of a state law requiring either Latin or German to be offered to high-school students for foreign-language study.[20]

German-language instruction was by no means unique to Indiana. In 1839 Ohio had become the first midwestern state to provide for the teaching of German. Kansas enacted its German school law in 1867. In states without foreign-language laws, such as Missouri, some heavily German localities introduced German-language instruction into the public schools; without the backing of legislation, however, these bilingual programs often did not survive into the twentieth century. Nor was German instruction confined to the Midwest. Baltimore's public elementary schools offered German, as did schools in towns as diverse as New Braunfels, Texas, and Carlstadt, New Jersey. In all, more than two hundred public elementary schools in the United States offered German in 1900. In 1917, the U.S. Bureau of Education reported that foreign-language instruction in elementary schools was offered in nineteen of the American cities it surveyed, sixteen of which specifically included German in the curriculum.[21]

The IPS *Annual Reports* give some indication of the prominent role German-language instruction played in Indianapolis's public schools before World War I. During the 1908–1909 school year, for instance, German was offered in the city's two high schools as well as in thirty-eight of its "district" (elementary) schools. At the elementary and secondary levels, fifty teachers conducted 451 classes in German-language instruction, which, in the district schools, translated into daily half-hour lessons.[22] The district schools offered a seven-year German program beginning in the second grade, while the high schools offered both an advanced course of study, for those who had completed the district program, and a beginning German program for those who had no previous instruction. The second, third, and fourth grades enrolled the largest number of students, but the combined district and secondary programs offered German instruction to nearly 7,500 of the city's 28,342 white students. Most of those enrolled in German programs were neither immigrants nor first-generation German-Americans; no mention is made of second- or third-generation German students.[23]

Besides teaching the German language to large numbers of students, IPS, during the 1908–1909 school year, also sought to acquaint students "with Germany, with the nature and customs of the people, and with Germany's culture and intellectual life." To achieve that end, teachers in the fifth, sixth, and seventh grades taught "German fairy tales and legends"; IPS teachers were even offered advanced study in German legends through the school system. High school students in both the beginning and advanced programs learned about German culture through the works of Friedrich von Schiller and Johann

Wolfgang von Goethe, along with other classic and contemporary examples of German literature.[24]

In the period preceding America's entry into the First World War, the mission of the IPS German program was to give students not only language instruction but also a sense of *Kultur*. German was used as the language of instruction in order to develop students' *Sprachgefuehl* or understanding of spoken German, rather than their translation skills. During these years the German program continued to grow; by 1916, sixty-five instructors (six of whom were substitutes) taught more than 560 German classes containing nearly ten thousand elementary and secondary students.[25] A year later the U.S.'s entry into the war introduced a perverse form of patriotism that first threatened and ultimately destroyed German-language instruction throughout the city and state.

While Indianapolis's large German-American community had succeeded in sustaining a thriving culture before the war, conflict with other elements of the community was not an entirely new phenomenon. Early prohibition agitation had provided one source of tension.[26] The German-language education program itself had aroused resentment as early as the 1880s and 1890s, decades marked by nativist campaigns against immigrant education around the country.[27] In the mid-1880s, much of the opposition to German instruction in the public schools was disguised as fiscal concern; near the end of the decade, the attacks became serious. In 1890 the school board voted to end the German program. The surprise vote was taken when two board members who were supporters of German-language instruction were absent. However, the city's German-language press opposed the decision, and German-Americans organized and took the issue to court. The legality of the German program in the public schools was affirmed by the Indiana Supreme Court in 1891.[28]

Some scholars have argued that these historic areas of conflict are key to understanding the war against German-American culture that began in 1917. Historian Frederick C. Luebke, warning against a search for simple causes, writes that the war

> converted latent tensions into manifest hostility. For this reason, little understanding is gained by identifying scapegoats, either German-American extremists, who allegedly provoked the government to repressive measures, or superpatriots, who by their immoderate rhetoric may have incited Americans to riot.[29]

But Luebke's statement underestimates both the power of the superpatriots' harangues and the appeal of patriotism itself. Anti-German rhetoric resonated in the American mind during the war era and proved to be quite persuasive. For example, one of historian Erik Kirschbaum's sources noted that "'any audience . . . will cheer an attack on the German language more wildly than any other phase of a patriotic address.'" In addition to anti-German rhetoric, patriotism itself captured the minds of many Americans, particularly the young. Another Kirschbaum source remarked that college students who in the past had shown passion only for football now "'gave themselves wholeheartedly to the new master . . . they patrolled the armory, balking imagined plots of enemy spies.'"[30]

Although historic areas of conflict undeniably existed between German-Americans and the larger American society, the dominant fanatical patriotism and nativism of the war years manifested themselves on a scale hitherto unseen. These wartime emotions stemmed more from recent events—the sinking of the *Lusitania*, the exaggerated war reports from the British news monopoly, the Zimmermann telegram, and the alarming reports of Franz von Papen's encouragement of sabotage—than they did from any previous tension.[31] As a postwar writer noted of Indianapolis's German-Americans, only "a few years before these very 'enemies' had been praised highly for their accomplishments and contributions to the cultural life of the city."[32]

As the United States entered the war against Germany and its allies, professional conferences and journals of educators and school officials in Indiana began to reflect the increasingly reactionary mood of American society. Unsurprisingly, patriotic sentiment dominated the 1917 annual meeting of the ISTA. The NEA's Bradford noted the need to "keep alive in our communities and in our schools the old ideals of American life and patriotism." Indiana Senator James E. Watson told the audience that "you school teachers cannot impress these ideals of the American Republic, liberty, equality and fraternity too strongly upon the heart and conscience of the coming generation until they are filled with the holy doctrine."[33]

The senator's idea of fraternity did not seem to include the German-Americans. Watson was interrupted with applause when he stated that "there are no real German-Americans today; they all ought to be Americans." His patriotism was clear, but as Briggs noted in a talk otherwise marked by its anti-German sentiment, "patriotism often involves passion and hate and blinds us to reason, [and] may be used to advance the very ideals that we have entered the war to defeat."[34] Despite Briggs's caution, a detectable and growing paranoia informed the patriotism of Indiana educators. On November 1, 1917, Professor Woodburn told the history section of the ISTA that "[t]he German rulers and their hired agents in this country . . . have deliberately planned the invasion and partition of our territory . . . [and] have filled our lands with spies."[35] In 1919, the *Indianapolis News* assured its readers that, in fact, there had been a plot by some German-Americans to make the United States a "German country."[36] Reports of German propaganda caught the attention of Indiana educators during the war.[37] In one case, an Indiana school inspector came across a high school textbook that allegedly provided its readers with a favorable description of Germany's kaiser.[38]

In 1918 the frenzied atmosphere spread to other German-American institutions. Indianapolis's leading German-language daily, the *Telegraph und Tribune*, informed its readers throughout May 1918 of increasing pressures against the foreign-language press.[39] On May 31, the *Telegraph* abruptly announced that it would cease publication on Monday, June 3, because "a pronounced prejudice has arisen in this country against everything printed or written in the German language, regardless of the fact that the German language newspapers are the means of reaching thousands of persons who are reached in no other way."[40] The Indianapolis *Turnverein*, reflecting on the war era, stated in 1926 that "in Indianapolis hatred against the citizen of German extraction was artificially stimulated, and irresponsible hotheads even went so far as to threaten the societies composed of such of their fellow citizens."[41] This hatred of everything German compelled the gymnastic society to change the name of its club hall from *Das Deutsche Haus* to the Athenaeum.[42] Perhaps the most extreme manifestation of hatred occurred in neighboring Illinois, where in April 1918, a German immigrant was lynched by a nativist mob.[43]

Concern over German-Americans' loyalty to the U.S. was not entirely unwarranted. Some accusations of un-American activities contained a kernel of truth. Some German-Americans were Socialists, and many others acted out of a sense of loyalty to the *Vaterland*. For example, before the United States declared war, a handful of Germans in Indianapolis sought to join the German army, using *Das Deutsche Haus* as a headquarters. The city's German-language press, in this period, favored the Central Powers over the Allies. Some Americans expressed their suspicion of Germany's Delbrück Law, which allowed emigrants to keep their German citizenship even after being naturalized by another state. However, German-Americans were quick to point out that the dual citizenship law did not apply to German-born Americans, who were citizens of the United States only. Once America entered the war, most of the city's residents of Germanic background were in fact loyal to their new homeland.[44] In May 1917, the *Telegraph und Tribune* ran advertisements for liberty bonds that stated, "Uncle Sam needs your money! He has helped you. Now is the time to help him." A year later, the *Telegraph* was praised by the Liberty Loan campaign for the newspaper's "hearty, unselfish, patriotic co-operation in the publicity work incident to the Third Liberty Loan campaign."[45]

Despite evidence of their loyalty, German-Americans throughout the country—"hyphens" as they were sometimes derogatively called—were accused of everything from starting fires to putting broken glass in food and drink.[46] Although these accusations proved false, "Germanophobia" continued.[47] To be German was to be unAmerican and undemocratic. The history section of the ISTA, for instance, was quick to point out that "[t]he colonies had originally risen against George III, a German, because of his autocratic mood."[48] Ohlinger suggested that because the German language itself contained "no equivalents for such expressions as 'liberty,' 'pursuit of happiness,' [or] 'the consent of the governed,'" German speakers could never become truly American.[49]

The schools continued to serve as battlefields in this war of ideas. Teachers and administrators became, in Briggs's phrase, the "soldiers of the schools," attempting to counteract foreign notions through the process of Americanization.[50] The most obvious step in this process was the suppression of the "Hun Language."[51] Woodburn, for instance, hoped for a country in which only English was used. "Let us strive," he said, "to save America from being a polyglot nation—a conglomeration of tongues and nationalities, like a 'polyglot boardinghouse,' as Mr. Roosevelt has put it." The history section of the ISTA discussed this issue at its 1917 meeting. At ISTA's 1919 meeting, University of Washington President Henry Suzzallo announced that his immigrant father, who spoke five languages, wanted his children to hear only English.[52]

The assault on the IPS German-language program began the month after the declaration of war, when the American Rights Committee complained to the school board that the German language was being used in some German classes to sing patriotic songs such as the "Star Spangled Banner."[53] The organization's five hundred members demanded that the practice be investigated and, if confirmed, stopped immediately. On January 29, 1918, the board voted, over the objections of German-American member Theodore Stempfel, to end German-language instruction in the city's elementary schools immediately. The board justified the action by stating that "the public schools should teach our boys and girls the principle of one nation, one language, and one flag, and should not assist in perpetuating the language of an alien enemy in our homes and enemy viewpoints in the community." The German teachers were to be reassigned until their contracts ended.[54]

Facing, Indianapolis Star, March 13, 1918. The Indianapolis Public Schools board systematically eliminated study of the German language and German culture after the United States entered World War I.

CONDEMN ALL GERMAN VERSE

School Commissioners Take Further Steps to Clear Language From Books.

German poems and fables will not be studied in the future by the school children of Indianapolis. At the meeting of the board of school commissioners last night in the old Library Building it was unanimously decided to cut out all articles in the German language now appearing in local school textbooks.

This is the second step to be taken by the board in their plan to eliminate the German language from the local schools. The first plan went into effect several months ago when it was decided to forego the actual teaching of the language in the local schools. The plan of last night will go into effect immediately.

At this meeting it was decided to enforce the teaching of patriotic songs and poems to the extent that from now on the school children will be required to learn verbatim the words of such patriotic numbers as "The Star-Spangled Banner," "America," "Columbia, the Gem of the Ocean" and "The Battle Hymn of the Republic." Upon passing this resolution the members of the board contended that it would not only instill a deeper feeling of patriotism in the children, but would have a good moral effect on their elders whenever these songs are sung.

Some high school German classes were still offered, but their enrollment was seriously depleted, a trend that occurred throughout the country. At the beginning of the 1918–1919 school year, for example, only 112 students enrolled in German classes at Indianapolis's Technical High School, down from 1,178 during the 1916–1917 school year. For the most part, only students who had already begun the high schools' German program continued to take German courses; they did so in order to fulfill the foreign-language requirements needed to graduate. The position of director of modern languages was eliminated, but the former director, Scherer, became supervisor of German to oversee the remaining high school program.[55] Even the high school German textbooks came under attack. Max Walter and Carl A. Krause's text for beginners, used by order of a 1913 state law, was now said to be "pro-German in its tendencies."[56]

In 1918, Germanophobia was in full swing in Indianapolis's public schools. Teachers, who now had loyalty clauses written into their contracts, could be terminated if they spoke out against the U.S. or were found to "inculcate or aid in the support of, or admiration for the . . . Kultur of Germany." The school board, alarmed that IPS's elementary students might be harmed by lingering remnants of *Kultur,* banned one of the poems in the third reader, *Kaiserblumen,* and suggested that the pages on which the poem appeared could be glued together.[57] In the European theater of war, American troops helped defeat Germany and its allies by November 1918, but in the American theater of war, nativist soldiers believed they had not yet defeated German-American culture.[58] The Woman's Auxiliary of the Rainbow Regiment Cheer Association, consisting of female relatives of soldiers in the 150th Field Artillery, warned that "the German language in the elementary schools of the state will be a tool in the hands of German propagandists who are seeking to bring about a soft peace with Germany."[59] IPS had halted much of the German instruction in the city, but a stronger and farther-reaching measure was deemed necessary to stop the "enemy language" in Indianapolis: a statewide law banning German not only from public schools, but from private and parochial elementary schools as well. Supporters of Senate Bill 276, drafted by State Senator Franklin McCray and Lieutenant Governor Edgar D. Bush, reasoned that such a law would eliminate the next generation's need for newspapers and public information printed in a foreign language.[60]

Presented to the Indiana Senate on February 17, 1919, the first two sections of McCray's bill stated that English would be the only lawful language in which to teach subjects in Indiana's public, private, and parochial elementary schools. Section one further stated that "the German language shall not be taught in any of the elementary schools of this state." Another section of the bill included the provision that violators would be fined up to one hundred dollars and/or spend up to six months in jail. In mid-February 1919, a new measure was added to the bill that would repeal other laws that were inconsistent with it, such as the German school law of 1869.[61]

Only one senator, from South Bend, voted against the McCray bill. The following day, it was "favorably" reviewed by the house committee on education. The Indianapolis *Star* reported that "because of state-wide interest . . . [the bill] was easily identified by number" when it reached the floor of the house on February 25. The house suspended the constitutional regulation "requiring the bills be read on three separate days" and unanimously passed the bill in a quarter of an hour.[62] Shortly afterward, the governor signed the act, and it was taken to the secretary of state. Upon arrival, McCray's legislation became a state law "immediately," because it included a sixth section that stated that "an emergency exists for the immediate taking effect of this act." This process, from the time the bill was read in the house to the time it became a law, took just over an hour and a half.[63]

Indiana was one of the first states to pass such a law, and its German-Americans understood the mood of the country and adjusted to it. Some became self-conscious about their German ancestry. State Representative Sam Benz, for instance, stated, "I'm a German . . . but you can't make this bill too strong to suit me. Not only do I indorse the exclusion of German, but I would be in favor also of taking out all foreign languages." The Lutheran and Catholic schools in Indianapolis had halted German instruction during the war.[64] There was no longer a powerful German-language press to rally the protests of German-Americans and to protect German-language instruction as it had done in the nineteenth century; in fact, very few of Indiana's German-language newspapers, particularly secular papers, continued after the war.[65]

However, there were still those few lingering German classes in the high schools of Indianapolis and, presumably, throughout the rest of the state. Even before McCray's legislation was introduced, another bill appeared on the floor of the Indiana State Senate to address the remaining high school German courses. On February 5, 1919, State Senator Glenn Van Auken introduced Senate Bill 208, the purpose of which was to amend the 1907 state law that required German as a foreign-language option in the high schools of Indiana. Perhaps because the weakened high school programs seemed to lawmakers to pose less of a threat than those in the elementary schools, Van Auken's legislation did not have the same urgency as the McCray Bill. Senate Bill 208 was read three times, referred to committees twice, and amended once before passing the senate and moving on to the house.[66] After nearly a month in the house, the bill passed and was returned to the senate on March 10, 1919.[67] The amended school law stated that "Latin or any modem foreign language except German" was required to be taught in the state's high schools.[68] IPS's once-flourishing German-language program had come to an end, and German-American culture in the city had been irreparably damaged. Although the bill had eliminated the high school German classes, some German teachers managed to find new subjects to teach. At Shortridge High School, for instance, Louis H. Dirks switched to teaching English.[69]

What happened to Indianapolis's German-language program was not an anomaly. German instruction was severely restricted in many areas throughout the United States and Canada during and after the Great War. Even before the war, laws in Arizona and California, among other states, already mandated English-only schools. In the war era twenty-one states further restricted foreign-language education in the elementary grades, making English the only lawful language of instruction. There was a degree of variation among these restrictive state laws, however. Oklahoma, West Virginia, South Dakota, and Illinois all declared that teaching subjects in a foreign language was illegal in both public and private schools; by contrast, Indiana, as already noted, specifically outlawed the German language from its schools. In New Hampshire, children attending private schools were exempted from the state's mandatory attendance law only if they attended private schools where English was the language of instruction. Minnesota passed a law requiring English for the traditional school subjects and reducing the amount of time for foreign languages to one hour daily.[70] Nebraska, however, passed what the *Minnesota Law Review* called "the most far reaching legislation" regarding foreign-language instruction. The Nebraska law stated that "[n]o person individually or as a teacher, shall in any private, denominational, parochial or public school teach any subject to any person in any language [other] than the English language," and no foreign-language instruction would be permitted until the high school level.[71]

In many ways, the restrictive policies and nativism seen in Indiana and its capital city reflected those in the rest of the country, but, overall, Indianapolis's cultural war was rather mild. Some cities in the United States, for example, eliminated German programs without going through legal channels. Additionally, there were no public rallies against Germanic citizens in Indianapolis, as there were in other places, perhaps because the Germans in Indianapolis were not viewed as alien residents. Rather, the German-Americans were a large and integral part of the city's population; they were teachers, doctors, storekeepers, bankers, and laborers, as well as neighbors.[72]

Near the turn of the twentieth century, Stempfel characterized Indianapolis as "a peaceable city," where, at least in earlier decades, nativism "had a hard time taking hold."[73] Although many of Indianapolis's citizens were swept up in the patriotic and nativist fervor of the First World War, the tradition of primarily harmonious relations with their German-American neighbors may have held some of the more extreme fanatics at bay.

The American entry into the Great War did not end all aspects of the German-Americans' unique culture. The gymnastic clubs, churches, and the Maennerchor all survived the cultural persecution that occurred in Indianapolis.[74] German-language instruction, however, never fully recovered; it was still absent from the IPS curriculum in the early 1920s, but it found its way back into the high schools within a decade.[75] Senator McCray's legislation was eventually undermined when the United States Supreme Court decided in 1923 that the elimination of German from private and parochial schools was unconstitutional. In *Meyer* v. *Nebraska* and similar cases the court found that knowing, learning, and teaching a foreign language fall under the rights protected by the Fourteenth Amendment.[76]

Probst wrote in the closing section of his *The Germans in Indianapolis, 1840–1918* that "it is absurd to assume that use of a foreign language in an ethnic environment—be it German, Italian, or Polish—somehow makes a person an unpatriotic citizen."[77] It is perhaps equally absurd to assume that foreign-language instruction for elementary and secondary students undermines the American ideal. Yet in Indiana and other states, during and after World War I, patriotism, hysteria, and, at times, ethnic hatred fueled a campaign that allowed the German language to be seen as a threat rather than as an intellectual benefit.[78] When Ohlinger argued that France and, especially, England were America's "parent countries," he failed to note that those nations did not eliminate German instruction during the war; presumably, they recognized the value of knowing the language, especially while at war.[79] In many parts of the United States, the desire for English-only public elementary schools continues today. Activated for different reasons and affecting different groups of people, such sentiment nevertheless attests to the continued tendency of an anxious public to identify in foreign languages the threat of a "different philosophy" upon the American way of life.[80]

PAUL J. RAMSEY is Associate Professor at the College of Education, Eastern Michigan University. This article originally appeared in volume 98, December 2002.

NOTES

1. Erik Kirschbaum, *The Eradication of German Culture in the United States: 1917–1918* (Stuttgart, Germany, 1986), 45–46.

2. Frederick C. Luebke, *Bonds of Loyalty: German-Americans and World War I* (DeKalb, Ill., 1974), 225–59.

3. Carl Wittke, *German-Americans and the World War* (Columbus, Ohio, 1936), 163.

4. George Theodore Probst, *The Germans in Indianapolis, 1840–1918* (Indianapolis, 1989), 140.

5. Owen Wister, "Forward," in Gustavus Ohlinger, *Their True Faith and Allegiance* (New York, 1916), xii; Ohlinger, *The German Conspiracy in American Education* (New York, [1919?]), 11.

6. Ohlinger, *German Conspiracy*, 10–17, 29–32, 99–100; Wister, "Forward," viiix; Ohlinger, *Their True Faith*, 25–26, 32–34, 42.

7. Ohlinger, *German Conspiracy*, 11, 83; Ohlinger, *Their True Faith*, 37–38.

8. Indiana State Teachers Association, *Proceedings and Papers, 1917*, 43–44, 99–100, 286 (hereafter cited as ISTA, *Proceedings*).

9. *Ibid.*, 42–43, 99–100, 287–88.

10. Kirschbaum, *Eradication of German Culture*, 63; ISTA, *Proceedings, 1917*, 350.

11. U.S., Bureau of the Census, *Thirteenth Census, 1910:* Vol. II, *Population*, 518, 543.

12. *Ibid.*, 519, 543, 546; Frederick Franklin Schrader, *Handbook: Political, Statistical and Sociological for German Americans . . .* (New York, 1916–1917), 98; Albert Bernhardt Faust, *The German Element in the United States with Special Reference to Its Political, Moral, Social, and Educational Influences* (2 vols., Boston, 1909), I, 576–77, 582; Probst, *Germans in Indianapolis*, 90–91; William A. Fritsch, *German Settlers and German Settlements in Indiana* (Evansville, Ind., 1915), 4.

13. *Indianapolis Turnverein: Seventy-fifth Anniversary, 1851–1926* ([Indianapolis?], [1926?]), 21.

14. Probst, *Germans in Indianapolis*, 126–34, 140; *Indianapolis Turnverein*, 5; Schrader, *Handbook for German Americans*, 52; Ohlinger, *German Conspiracy*, 59–60.

15. James P. Ziegler, *The German-language Press in Indiana: A Bibliography* (Indianapolis, 1994), 15–19.

16. Probst, *Germans in Indianapolis*, 182–83.

17. *Indianapolis Turnverein*, 17–20; *Indianapolis Public Schools Annual Report, 1908–1909*, 4 (hereafter cited as IPS, *Annual Report*); Murray A. Dalman, "The Indianapolis Schools: A Brief History," in *Indianapolis Public Schools, 1853–1953* (Indianapolis, 1953), 93–96; Frances H. Ellis, "Historical Account of German Instruction in the Public Schools of Indianapolis 1869–1919," *Indiana Magazine of History*, L (June, September, December 1954), 119, 257, 357–58, 364–65, 368–69, 374–78; IPS, *Annual Report, 1916*, 2; Frederick K. Gale, *A Biographical Study of Persons for Whom Indianapolis Schools Are Named* (Indianapolis, 1965), see under "Clemens Vonnegut"; Probst, *Germans in Indianapolis*, 101, 140; Ohlinger, *German Conspiracy*, 59–60.

18. Indianapolis *Star*, February 26, 1919; Ellis, "Historical Account of German Instruction," 124–25.

19. Indiana, Superintendent of Public Instruction, *School Laws of Indiana*, (1877) 48–49.

20. Ellis, "Historical Account of German Instruction," 122–37, 252, 261, 363; IPS, *Annual Report, 1883*, 28; *ibid.*, *1908–1909*, 52–53.

21. Heinz Kloss, "German-American Language Maintenance Efforts," in *Language Loyalty in the United States: The Maintenance and Perpetuation of Non-English Mother Tongues by American Ethnic and Religious Groups*, Joshua Fishman (London, U.K., 1966), 233–35; La Vern J. Rippley, *The German Americans* (Boston, 1976), 120–22; L. Viereck, "German Instruction in American Schools," in U.S., Commissioner of Education, *Report, 1900–1901* (2 vols., Washington, D.C., 1902), I, 639–40; "Foreign Languages in the Elementary School," *School and Society*, VI, No. 151 (1917), 583; Frederick C. Luebke, "Legal Restrictions on Foreign Languages in the Great Plains States, 1917–1923," in *Germans in the New World: Essays in the History of Immigration*, ed. Luebke, (Urbana, Ill., 1990), 36.

22. In the 1880s and 1890s, IPS students studying German in the upper-elementary grades received language instruction that was similar to the "two-way" bilingual education method sometimes used today. That is, in the "German annexes" mixed classes of both native-English and native-German speakers were taught half of the day's subjects—including U.S. history—in German and the other half in English, enabling the two groups of students to gain proficiency in both languages. The German annexes did not continue into the twentieth century, but when nativists began to call for the elimination of German instruction in 1917, they suggested that the German language was used to sing patriotic songs such as "The Star Spangled Banner," which could suggest that some classes in Indianapolis used German as the language of instruction for nonforeign-language lessons. See IPS, *Annual Report, 1883*, 29–31; Ellis, "Historical Account of German Instruction," 258–61, 264, 357, 372.

23. IPS, *Annual Report, 1908–1909*, 28–30, 151–57.

24. *Ibid.*, 78–79, 128, 155–57.

25. *Ibid.*, 153–55; *ibid.*, *1916*, 92, 130–33; Ellis, "Historical Account of German Instruction," 369–71.

26. Probst, *Germans in Indianapolis*, 143.

27. For a detailed look at the nativist-led school attacks see Lloyd P. Jorgenson, *The State and the Non-Public School, 1825–1925* (Columbia, Mo., 1987).

28. Ellis, "Historical Account of German Instruction," 262–76.

29. Luebke, *Bonds of Loyalty*, xiii.

30. Kirschbaum, *Eradication of German Culture*, 94, 110.

31. *Ibid.*, 49–65.

32. *Indianapolis Turnverein*, 21.

33. ISTA, *Proceedings*, *1917*, 43, 290–91.

34. *Ibid.*, 105, 282.

35. *Ibid.*, 343–44.

36. *Indianapolis News*, February 26, 1919. These accusations were not entirely baseless. For example, in the early- and mid-nineteenth century, some German immigrants hoped to concentrate their settlement within the United States in order to form German states that might eventually separate; see Faust, *The German Element*, II, 184–85. But most of the reports of German machinations were grossly distorted; for the German-American response to the allegations of anti-American plots see Schrader, *Handbook for German Americans*, II, 60.

37. "How German Propaganda Worked in Respect to a School Text by an Indiana School Man," *Indiana Instructor*, II (May 1918), 32. According to this essay, in 1915 the German-American Alliance attempted to halt the publication of a book by an Indiana University history professor that commented on the war in Europe; the book proved to be offensive to some German-Americans, particularly to professors and teachers of German, presumably because of its anti-German sentiments. After the U.S. entered the war, the professor was called to testify against the Alliance before the U.S. Senate, when it was considering banning the organization.

38. "More Evidence of German Propaganda in the Schools," *Indiana Instructor*, II (July 1918), 15.

39. Indianapolis *Telegraph und Tribune*, May 8, 11, 17, 23, 1918.

40. *Ibid.*, May 31, 1918.

41. *Indianapolis Turnverein*, 21.

42. *Ibid.*; Probst, *Germans in Indianapolis*, 152–53.

43. Luebke, *Bonds of Loyalty*, 3–10. There was also a lesser-known murder that occurred in Indiana. Shortly after the sinking of the *Lusitania* in 1915, a pastor from Gary was killed by "*fantisierten Angloamerikanern*" for speaking out in favor of *Deutschtum* (Germanness). See Colin Ross, *Unser Amerika: Der deutsche Anteil an den Vereinigten Staaten* (Leipzig, Germany, 1936), 316; Schrader, *Handbook for German Americans*, 2.

44. Luebke, *Bonds of Loyalty*, 63; Probst, *Germans in Indianapolis*, 147–49, 151–52; Schrader, *Handbook for German Americans*, 22; Ohlinger, *German Conspiracy*, 18–19. While some German-Americans suggested that the Delbrück Law did not apply to U.S. citizens of Germanic origins, legal scholars during the war years were not so certain. David Jayne Hill, for instance, noted that the law certainly did not apply to all German-Americans because it required emigrants to obtain the "written consent" of the German government before it would restore their citizenship. He also suggested that the law became void if it was found to have "disturbed" a previously negotiated treaty with another nation. Hill argued that the treaties between the U.S. and Germany remained "undisturbed" by the Delbrück Law, so there was no reason to assume that Germany would not consider some Americans to be German citizens, particularly while at war. The American naturalization process, however, was the primary protection against dual citizenship because it demanded that new citizens renounce their previous citizenship "absolutely and forever." See David Jayne Hill, "Dual Citizenship in the German Imperial and State Citizenship Law," *American Journal of International Law*, XII (April 1918), 357–63.

45. Indianapolis *Telegraph und Tribune*, May 25, 1917, May 16, 1918 (author's translation).

46. Wister described German-Americans as the "Kaiser's helpful hyphens." See Ohlinger, *German Conspiracy*, xix.

47. Kirschbaum, *Eradication of German Culture*, 117–21.

48. ISTA, *Proceedings, 1917*, 337.

49. Ohlinger, *German Conspiracy*, 107–108.

50. ISTA, *Proceedings, 1919*, 104; Kirschbaum, *Eradication of German Culture*, 108. In general, educators around the country did not support the elimination of German-language instruction when the war first began. However, as the mood of the country became more radical regarding German-language instruction, educators revised their positions and often enthusiastically supported the nativist campaigns. See *ibid.*, 96–97, 108–11.

51. Indianapolis *Star*, February 26, 1919; Probst, *Germans in Indianapolis*, 153.

52. ISTA, *Proceedings, 1917*, 123, 335–36, 350.

53. Some educators resisted appeals to patriotism and instead promoted nativist designs by arguing that German instruction was simply not practical for American students because they would not have many opportunities to use the skill. See "Potent Reasons Why German Should Not be Taught in the Public Schools," *Indiana Instructor*, II (October 1917), 3–4. See also Kirschbaum, *Eradication of German Culture*, 106–107.

54. Ellis, "Historical Account of German Instruction," 371–75.

55. *Ibid.*, 378; Indianapolis *Star*, February 26, 1919; Luebke, "Legal Restrictions," 36.

56. Ellis, "Historical Account of German Instruction," 376; IPS, *Annual Report, 1916*, 133.

57. Ellis, "Historical Account of German Instruction," 375, 377–78.

58. Luebke, "Legal Restrictions," 42.

59. Indianapolis *Star*, February 26, 1919.

60. Probst, *Germans in Indianapolis*, 153; IPS, *Annual Report, 1909*, 154; *ibid., 1916*, 131; Indianapolis *News*, February 26, 1919; Indianapolis *Star*, February 26, 1919; Indiana, *House Journal* (1919), 519–20.

61. Indiana, *Laws* (1919), 50–51; Indianapolis *Star*, February 26, 1919.

62. Indianapolis *Star*, February 26, 1919; Indiana, *House Journal* (1919), 519.

63. Indianapolis *Star*, February 26, 1919; Indiana, *Laws* (1919), 51.

64. Indianapolis *Star*, February 26, 1919. Some parochial schools in Indiana protested against the McCray Bill and other similar types of legislation. For example, although it used English as the language of instruction for academic subjects, one Lutheran church—the First Evangelical Lutheran Immanuel Church of Seymour, Indiana—requested in a letter to the lieutenant governor that religious instruction be excluded from English-only legislation, such as House Bill No. 6, which was pending at the time the letter was written. Indiana, *Senate Journal* (1919), 156.

65. Ellis, "Historical Account of German Instruction," 375; Ziegler, *German-language Press*, 1–27.

66. Indiana, *Laws* (1919), 822–23; Indiana, *Senate Journal* (1919), 245, 969.

67. Indiana, *House Journal* (1919), 359–60, 828, 835, 1098.

68. Indiana, *Senate Journal* (1919), 823.

69. Laura Sheerin Gaus, *Shortridge High School, 1864–1981: In Retrospect* (Indianapolis, 1985), 109.

70. Wittke, *German-Americans and the World War*, 180–81; Jerrold B. Burnell, "The Decline of German Language and Culture in the North American Heartland, 1890–1923" (Paper delivered at the Annual Meeting of the Comparative and International Education Society, New York, March 18–21, 1982), 6; Luebke, "Legal Restrictions," 42; Henry J. Fletcher, ed., "Recent Legislation Forbidding Teaching of Foreign Languages in Public Schools," *Minnesota Law Review*, IV (May 1920), 449–50; Rippley, *German Americans*, 124.

71. "Recent Legislation," 450.

72. Probst, *Germans in Indianapolis*, 88–90, 153; Luebke, "Legal Restrictions," 36–42.

73. Theodore Stempfel, *Fifty Years of Unrelenting German Aspirations in Indianapolis*, eds. Giles R. Hoyt, Claudia Grossmann, Elfrieda Lang, and Eberhard Reichmann (Indianapolis, 1991), 21.

74. Probst, *Germans in Indianapolis*, 154.

75. Indianapolis Public Schools, *Survey Findings: Senior High School Division, Secondary Schools* (Indianapolis, 1934), 21–22; General Education Board, *Public Education in Indiana: Report of the Indiana Education Survey Commission* (New York, 1923), 102.

76. Wittke, *German-Americans and the World War*, 181–82; Luebke, "Legal Restrictions," 43–47; Rippley, *German Americans*, 125–26.

77. Probst, *Germans in Indianapolis*, 154.

78. Ellis, "Historical Account of German Instruction," 375.

79. Ohlinger, *German Conspiracy*, 113; Kirschbaum, *Eradication of German Culture*, 97–98.

80. For an interesting discussion of bilingual education and its opponents see David C. Berliner and Bruce J. Biddle, *The Manufactured Crisis: Myths, Fraud, and the Attack on America's Public Schools* (Reading, Mass., 1995), 202–207.

8

Draftee's Wife

A Memoir of World War II

VIRGINIA MAYBERRY

[ORIGINAL] EDITOR'S NOTE. THE FOLLOWING essay differs from the typical wartime reminiscence in at least two ways. While most such reminiscences deal with events in the more distant past—with the Civil War an especially popular topic—Virginia Mayberry's memoir is concerned with World War II, a conflict which occurred well within living memory. Also unusual is Mayberry's perspective. Most reminiscences deal with the experiences of members of the armed forces, a natural focus but one which overlooks the significant impact wars have on civilian populations. Mayberry's perspective is even more unusual because she was not just a civilian, but the wife of a serviceman. As she moved with her husband from one military base to another, she was exposed to both the civilian and the military worlds. Because of this she experienced such typical civilian situations as rationing, shortages, and transportation problems, as well as experiences peculiar to the families of servicemen, particularly the difficulties military families faced in attempting to build a relatively normal life and the frequent hostility such transient families faced from local residents when they moved into new towns. For those who lived through World War II, Mayberry's account should rekindle memories of life on the home front; for others, it provides an interesting view by a perceptive observer of what life was like during this critical period.[1]

MEMOIR

It takes all kinds of people to fight a war, even a popular war like World War II. There are soldiers and sailors. There are spies and nurses and aviators. And then there are those who only stand and wait. Service wives are like that; I was a draftee's wife.[2]

The rumblings of conflict reached me first at college on a September evening in 1938 with news of the Munich pact.[3] It was the second day of sorority rush. I, my mind weighted with the annual ceremony of choosing members for our sorority, nevertheless sensed drama taking place in Europe. My fraternal sisters sat on the floor of the drawing room, young faces tense, realizing not so much the seriousness of the international situation as the fact that our world, our inviolate collegiate sphere, was in danger of disruption. My mother had carefully explained to me when I was small that there would never be another war because American men had given their lives in 1918 to make the world safe for democracy.

Now our housemother attempted to prepare us. She was as well-equipped as any of her generation to foretell what was coming. In the four years of my undergraduate experience, even while upperclassmen left to enlist with the Canadians or tried their wings via CAA,[4] none of our learned professors held out to us a more than passing mention of the possibility of war in our time. Certain of them were at work right at Indiana University on the big bomb.[5] It may have been purposeful that the cyclotron there was presented to us more as a curiosity than as an instrument of warfare, but I think not.

The European situation abated as far as Yankee kids knew. To businessmen a favorite question college newspaper reporters asked, calculating to display precocity, was, "Do you think the European situation will have any effect on American business?" They replied yes, of course, nodding wisely, but never, never elucidated.

If we shook our heads over the Russo-Finnish entanglement,[6] a warning which no one seems to remember, it was assessed as just a far-off growl of thunder, rated far below the Great Depression as a matter for our concern. The Depression was something we understood. Allison Division of General Motors might be tooling up for airplane engines in Speedway City, just outside Indianapolis, but veterans in ragged coats still sold apples on Washington Street.

Germany *was* at war. The Selective Training and Service Act was passed in September and draft registration began in October, 1940. At school male students paraded in the Commons wearing grotesque costumes, large, flat-footed shoes and huge spectacles, carrying placards to the effect that there was a draft in here and would someone please close the door. Kitchen bands tootled "You're in the Army Now" and "Mademoiselle from Armentieres." The girls laughed, drank cokes, blew soda straw wrappers at the ceiling, and quipped at the snake dancers that we were going to get all the jobs now.

As June approached, seniors usually hunted jobs frantically, but business aspirations this year were limited to the feminine third of the class.

"Got a job yet?" I asked the telegraph editor at the *Indiana Daily Student*, the college paper.

"Hell no. What's the use? I'm going to have a good time 'til my number comes up."

"I'll Be Back in a Year Little Darling" they sang. That was how long a draftee was supposed to serve.

Commencement Day was sibyllic. It dawned a fair fifth of June. The speakers' platform was set up in Dunn Meadow, and visitors began to pour into the campus about noon. With them came black clouds. Gowned and mortarboarded, we sweated through a dull speech by a more than usually anonymous educator, which finally had to be cut short. Diplomas were handed down the rows in bundles. As soon as the coveted sheepskins were in hand, we new bachelors fled. Visitors already were scampering toward parked cars.

As I grasped my diploma in one hand the precious mortarboard (rented, and to be returned without fail to the comptroller's agent before five o'clock) in the other, I saw the lone university Reserve Officers' Training Corps representative mount the speakers' platform. In three minutes a hundred and fifty second lieutenants were sworn into the army reserve. The storm broke with a dramatic crash of thunder, and all those rented mortarboards wilted under a downpour.

My first job was just what journalism grads were taught to expect. The pay was nebulous. L.S. Ayres, a department store in Indianapolis, had acquired a new warehouse some distance from the main store. Also, the company was feeling the draft as one employee after another received "Greetings." I started a house organ to be mailed to warehouse workers, store personnel, and newly drafted stock boys to weld them into one big, happy family. I spent two weeks getting acquainted, riding furniture trucks, visiting alteration and furriers' departments, poking my head into the cooling system, shaking hands with the adjustment manager, and I met Joe.

"I want you to meet Joe," said the personnel director.

"Oh, you'll like him," whispered the switchboard operator. "He's a Beta from Wabash."

A view down Washington Street, downtown Indianapolis, 1937. After college, Virginia Mayberry worked for L. S. Ayres department store. *Courtesy Bass Photo Collection, Indiana Historical Society.*

"Hmm," I thought. School was three weeks behind me and I was fraternity-homesick in my new, non-collegiate surroundings. "He's been drafted and came to say goodbye," went on the personnel director.

"Oh damn," under my breath. But it would be a story for my paper.

He stood in the corner by the water cooler looking very uncomfortable in uniform.

"This is Joe. Talk to him. Get a story. Take his picture." And the personnel director vanished.

I gasped at the abrupt introduction, simpered, "How do you do? I'm the new house organ editor. Gee, you've got a bad sunburn, haven't you?" and felt stupid.

"Yeah," he laughed and got redder.

Papers and magazines were full of helpful hints on "How To Treat the New Draftee." He was a special person to be handled with Dresden-china care lest his delicate ego be shattered. The term "draftee" gradually was superseded by the more tactful "service man" to include volunteers.

I was cleaning dresser drawers the morning of Sunday, December 7, 1941, when a radio announcer interrupted a philharmonic concert to report the Pearl Harbor attack. I had been knitting Red Cross sweaters for several months. My first thought was that now I was sure they'd be used.

Because he was a college graduate and therefore presumably capable of leadership, Joe wasn't transferred away but stayed in the reception center at Fort Benjamin Harrison at Indianapolis. He never even took basic training. In November he had finally gotten around to asking me for a date and right after Pearl Harbor he made corporal. His pay increased from twenty-one dollars a month to what seemed like a magnificent figure, and he administered tests for placement to new inductees. Not that the results counted for much—"the army way" of assigning men to areas completely foreign to civilian experience was legend.

I got right into war projects. I rolled bandages for the Red Cross on my lunch hour and completed a first aid course. The government asked for volunteers to catalogue spellings of similar names for use by the services' mail delivery. I searched New York, Detroit, and Gary city directories and names like Moore, More, Mohr, and Mower rattled in long rows from my typewriter.

Then there was the United Service Organizations (USO). First I served as hostess to visitors at Fort Harrison. After Pearl Harbor the draft was stepped up, and hordes of volunteers swamped reception centers during December and January in a surge of national indignation. The mere location at a given time of any one inductee was a several-man job, but visitors still were allowed on the post. Fifth Corps Area included Ohio, Indiana, Kentucky, and West Virginia, and thence came bewildered families who still haunt me. Through bitter cold they drove with rationed gasoline in junk cars, whose motivation was a mystery, to arrive at an army post in turmoil. They didn't understand the war, they didn't comprehend the draft, they couldn't believe a son or brother had been snatched from the farm, where he was needed to milk cows and slop hogs, to fight Germans who supposedly had been taught their lesson thirty years ago. As for Japanese, most of them had never seen one.

It was my duty somehow to extract their soldier's full name from the family, fill out a form, and send a runner to search for the inductee. Sometimes I found him; but "I'm sorry. Private Beanblossom has been sent to another camp. I'm sure he'll write you his new address soon," was more frequent. After a month or so some higher-up got the idea that a twenty-two-year-old unmarried woman had not sufficient maturity for such close contact with so much raw humanity, and I was transferred to the canteen downtown.

The USO had humble beginnings. Ours was located in an abandoned interurban freight barn behind the bus terminal. It was not a nice neighborhood. A jovial old codger who went by the name of Snowball took care of the upper part of the building and supervised the showers, pool tables, and library on evenings when the complete contingent of girls was not present for dancing. Pairs of hostesses "received" downstairs and dispensed theater tickets, phonograph records, cards, cigarettes, information, or just conversation. I arranged for men to accept Sunday dinner invitations with volunteer families, find rooms at the YMCA, and get free tickets to a concert or roller rink. There were even weddings in that old brick shanty.

On Wednesday, Saturday, and Sunday nights whole "regiments" of service men's cadettes came to dance. We wore huge red, white, and blue pins, enamelled like jewelry with the letters SMC.

At the end of 1941 the novelty of house organ editing wore thin. I, like the whole country, suffered from war nerves. I needed to be needed. I had given blood for plasma and run myself ragged with local defense projects, and I felt totally useless. I applied for a civil service exam, and one rainy morning sat down with a hundred or so other youngsters to place my abilities on exhibition. Three girls were taking home economics tests, another and I academic ones. The rest were doing short mathematical problems and continually received oral instructions from the proctors. They clattered their protractors and asked five hundred questions during the two-hour work period. It was extremely distracting. I remember that I could not settle on a good definition for the word "enigma" but passed anyway.

Soon plans for the Women's Auxiliary Army Corps (WAAC) were aired.[7] Appointments for the first Officer Candidate School were to be made outright. I nearly burst an artery getting to the post office to register. This was something I really wanted. The first, or written, exam was similar to the civil service one I just had completed. An interview with the local selection board followed, then a physical at Fort Harrison. Then, oh joy, a call to Fort Hayes at Columbus, Ohio, for the final screening. I was screened. My short stature and lack of business experience did me in. I still appeared immature; furthermore, I was considering marriage.

Becoming a war bride in the popular sense was the farthest thing from my mind, but as winter wore into spring, I saw more and more of Joe. He picked me up after first aid class. We snatched time for a coke during office hours. We debated the pros and cons of wartime marriage. My parents were horrified and would not even discuss a wedding, but by August we hesitated no longer and began apartment hunting and a lot of paper and pencil budgeting. It was amazing how far a buck sergeant's pay and a house organ editor's eighteen dollars a week could be stretched theoretically.

Just when our plans seemed settled, my now-forgotten civil service appointment for the War Department in Washington, D.C., came through. I was to arrive not later than August 10. I wonder now if I would have made a successful government girl. For a time I argued that the fabulous pay would enable us to put aside a nice nest egg, but Joe took a dim view of long-distance marriage, particularly when he was sure to go overseas soon.

We obtained blood tests required by Indiana and on Thursday presented ourselves, trembling, at the license bureau.

Friday we called on Joe's cousin, Mary, at whose home our wedding was to take place since my parents still would not cooperate. Late in the evening someone remembered that a minister might be a useful person to be present, so an in-law of hers was summoned. Joe had been to the jeweler's that day.

The morning of Saturday, August 8, 1942, I took a new gingham suit I had bought for work to the alteration department at Ayres and told them my story. Something of a time record was set in making it a perfect fit. I also purchased a white satin nightgown. At five o'clock the minister sang "I Love You Truly," accompanied at the piano by Mary. Then we were married. Five adults and four babies were witnesses. We had a borrowed car and a lake cottage for the wonderful duration of Joe's three-day pass, and we had forty-five dollars cash.

Eight dollars a week, we thought, was the maximum rent our budget would bear, and after two discouraging weeks during which we lived at a hotel and counted nickels at restaurants we heard of a vacancy. There were others ahead of us, but I was determined to set up housekeeping in a certain yellow brick apartment house close to work. We pleaded with the custodian, a kindly old black man, who, bless Heaven, seemed to take a liking to us. His name was Bill. I phoned every day, and every evening we paid him a visit. At last he gave in.

"I'll show it to you," he said conspiratorially.

My hopes tobogganed as he opened the door and stepped back to exhibit a small living room, so empty it looked enormous. There was an equally vacant dinette and a huge bare closet into which swung a Murphy bed, devoid of fittings. Only the minute kitchenette was furnished.

"Uh, well—we thought this was furnished," I stammered.

"No ma'am," declared the black man. "It'll be unfurnished 'cept just what you see. This's thirty-five dollars."

"Thirty-five?" I dared not look at Joe. "Including utilities?"

"Yep."

"Well—," a pause. "Uh—what about a mattress?"

"No mattress. Just the bed, like you see."

"Oh," another pause. "And the dinette?"

"Well, some of these places used to be furnished. They's a dinette set down cellar maybe I could let you have 'til you got one."

"Oh yes, of course. Just until we can get one. Well—."

"Now lady, don't you take this place if you don't feel like you want it. You'll make a deposit, and I can keep it, but then if you don't take the apartment you'll be out that money. You go away and think about it. I ain't in no hurry to rent this place. You let me know."

Obviously Bill was well acquainted with the facts of newlyweds' poverty, but I had made up my mind.

We moved into the apartment at 306 North Pennsylvania with three pairs of window curtains and a studio couch. We had a set of dishes for two and several assorted collections of glasses given us as wedding gifts. That night we took home a pint of ice cream and some wooden forks, which served as our entire array of cutlery until I bought two paring knives next payday.

In September Joe made staff sergeant, and the following month the jingle of war money lured me into a defense plant. I was paid an unbelievable thirty-five dollars a week! The hours were longer, the work, in an X-ray photography laboratory, exhausting, and the daily drive to Speedway by car pool a long one. On the other hand we now had our tiny apartment adequately furnished, much to custodian Bill's satisfaction, we entertained occasionally, and we could afford Christmas gifts for our families. Mine had adjusted to the fact of our marriage once it was a *fait accompli.*

After the holidays I became aware that I was not well. Things in the lab annoyed me, mainly the flagrant waste of materials. I saw film thrown away and silver from X-rays washing down the drain while the war demand for both was forcing professional photographers to close shop. Resorting to the plant suggestion box to try to clear my own conscience, I was told politely but firmly to mind my own business. Allison's ran on a cost-plus basis.

I worried about ethics, had a cold, felt rotten, and finally went to our old family doctor who grinned and asked how I'd feel about having a baby. I said I felt as though I'd been hit by a falling elevator.

In February of 1943 married men were called up and others, formerly deferred for slight physical ailments, were being inducted for limited service. It became apparent that Joe's days at the reception center were numbered. Men working with him left for infantry and overseas assignment. Personnel non-commissioned officers routinely advanced to Adjutant General's Officer Candidate School. It was scheduled to close in June, so Joe slid in just under the wire and was assigned to Fort Washington, Maryland, for the last OCS class conducted there.

In February I came down with a strep throat and quit work, but I was secure in the knowledge that my defense plant insurance would just about pay for baby. By the time Joe left, sulfanilamide, a miraculous new drug, had controlled my violent cough and the miserable first three months of pregnancy were nearly over. We put our furniture into storage, and I went to wait with my parents.

Spring came early that year. By the first of June Washington was a weltering cauldron of humanity on concrete, but D.C. was good to service men. When Joe's parents and I arrived for OCS graduation, we were enfolded by the comfort of the well-ordered Wardman Park Hotel. I had seen a few other graduates, so I was spared the shock many wives experienced at their husbands' post-OCS appearance. A weight loss and the intensity of concentration aged a man years in those three months. A candidate ordered his new officer's pinks and greens as soon as it became apparent that his grades were adequate for graduation; consequently, six months later, as his body got back to normal, his wife had painstakingly to move buttons and let out seams as far as possibly consistent with regulations. Perhaps tight trousers were responsible for the traditional stuffy personalities of those second lieutenants, termed "90-day wonders" by regular army.

With the baby only three months away I was anxious about Joe's first assignment as an officer. Most new shavetails joined a pool and within six months went on foreign duty. Joe drew a classification assignment at Camp Crowder, a signal corps outfit near Joplin, Missouri. He left at once and within the week accomplished the impossible, a house, a whole house, a whole house furnished, ready and waiting! Fondly I set out dishes, kitchen utensils, linens, our precious photograph album. It took two barrels as big as me to pack them. They were shipped.

I left for St. Louis with a small bag and my knitting. I was making a dainty little blue and white bonnet. The coach I climbed on must have belonged to the *DeWitt Clinton*. The seats felt like petrified wood; it was dinerless and unair-conditioned; people hung, gasping, from the windows, through which soot and cinders poured. A young schoolteacher, returning from a wedding, shared my seat. From time to time she slanted a magazine out the window to engineer a bit of breeze in my direction. As the train creaked and jerked its agonized way across the sun-scorched fields of Indiana and Illinois, perspiration ran down my neck and into my new maternity girdle. After one particularly vicious wrench

Union Station, St. Louis, Missouri, ca. 1943. Union Station was one of the many places Virginia Mayberry traveled through during the war. *Courtesy Arthur Witman Collection, S0732-757, The State Historical Society of Missouri, Photograph Collection.*

a sailor in the seat ahead turned squarely around. "Doesn't that just kill you? It did my wife," he exclaimed.

That monstrous caterpillar was four hours late, and I missed my connection. As we pulled into St. Louis I saw my train heading west on another track. It was 1:00 a.m. Others also had missed out, and from the resulting scramble at the information desk I concluded there was no transportation to Kansas City, my next stop, until morning. The Travelers' Aid desk was empty, the Service Men's

Canteen closed. My now bosom friend, the schoolteacher, began to telephone hotels. After thirty minutes of rigorous toil with the Yellow Pages she came out of the sweaty phone booth with a look of doubtful triumph. "I got a room," she said, "at some kind of a hotel about a block from here. It's a dollar."

Giggling hysterically at the hotel we jammed a chair under the door knob, took sponge baths in the room wash basin and had a good night's rest.

Next day, failing even to approach two jammed trains for Kansas City, I hopped a trolley and hunted the railroad office, where some ingenious ticket agent discovered a pullman direct to Joplin, complete with diner and lower berth for me.

Seven out of eight houses in Joplin were white frame with chicken coops behind, and number 1414 on a street I can't remember was no exception. It caught what breeze there was. During our seven weeks there the thermometer was stuck in the upper nineties and finally hit 110.

We shared with a couple from Columbus, Georgia. He was an ex-schoolteacher, as lazy a fat man as ever came out of the Deep South, she a tall, good-looking woman in her early thirties with a soul devoid of humor. They did not choose to eat with us, so each evening our potatoes boiled in two pots side by side on the stove. They drank no coffee, tea, or milk, but at bedtime carried a gallon thermos of icewater to their room. I have no reason to believe that the contents were not entirely consumed during the night.

In Joplin I had no difficulty locating the office of the obstetrician. It was the one with the crowd around it. If the poor man had progeny of his own, they thought their daddy had gone to war. Certainly they could not have seen him for months. Only four weeks after I had made his acquaintance he fell victim to infantile paralysis. A general practitioner took up his practice, but, by the time I could get an appointment, Joe was transferred. Orders this time indicated attachment to the Army Air Force.

He was to report to Lunken Field, Cincinnati, headquarters of the Ferrying Division.[8]

So we bought Lizzybelle. She was a 1936 Plymouth with an acknowledged eighty thousand miles, and she looked every mile of it. "I'll sell her before the baby comes," I announced confidently. I didn't want to go anywhere by train again for a long time.

We piled everything we owned into Lizzybelle's dilapidated rear seat. The two of us and the knitting—I still was working on the blue and white bonnet—went in front. We drove fifty miles before the brakes gave out, but I remember Springfield, Missouri, with pleasure for the delicious chicken dinner we had in a converted mansion while awaiting repairs. Hot biscuits, rationed butter and iced tea appeared in a steady flow, borne by a small black genii, until we could eat no more. We spent the night in a tourist camp.

Next day we discovered Liz was an oil-eater and every fifty miles thereafter stopped to sustain her petroleum addiction.

We skirted St. Louis because I was sure the place would bring bad luck. After lunch Lizzybelle had a flat. Joe was anxious to make time, but I insisted on stopping to have it repaired immediately. Gut feeling told me not to trust Liz's one spare. I left myself open for a good razzing. Not ten miles farther, as we crossed the long Mississippi toll bridge, the same tire issued the familiar "phsss." Liz limped to the end of the span where Joe changed to the spare.

We reached Vandalia, Illinois, without further misadventure and spent the night at a hotel while Liz's rubber was overhauled. Across the street was the courthouse, from the window of which Abraham Lincoln is said to have jumped to avoid testifying at a trial. Next morning we fairly leaped along. At Terre Haute we pulled into a filling station.

"What's the matter?" I asked.

"Lizzybelle has a flat," announced Joe.

We reached Indianapolis about noon. Our pocketbook was flat, too.

Joe phoned from Cincinnati when he got there—by train. "I flipped a coin with another fellow," he explained. "He's going to Great Falls, Montana. We're going to Berry Field at Nashville, Tennessee."

I, who detest cold weather, rejoiced.

It was the middle of August now, and, since the baby was soon due, it seemed inadvisable for me to go to a strange town where chances of finding doctor, home, and hospital quickly were slim. I stayed with my parents and busied myself trying to sell Lizzybelle. As if in protest she had one final fling. I asked my father to run her around the block one evening, and during the spin she burned out a wire connecting battery and spark. After that repair she sulked in the drive for two weeks until a used car dealer offered me two-thirds of what we had paid for her. As much in demand as cars were during those years of nonmanufacture, prices depressed as one moved east. I parted with her reluctantly because of the money loss the day before our son was born.

Obstetrics being what they were then, I remember little of that day except fantastic dreams produced by total anesthesia. About 8:00 p.m. a nurse brought the baby to me. He was blond and blue-eyed, a miniature Joe. We already had decided to name him Richard but he soon became Blinky.

Joe sublet a furnished house in East Nashville. I applied to the ration board for extra gasoline for Dad's car. Late in October I packed his trailer with Blinky's bassinette and buggy. The trip south was uneventful until we reached

Hodgenville, Kentucky, where we missed a turn. The road became gravel and then a trail. At this point we came face to face with a black community funeral procession. There couldn't have been that many automobiles at the last rites of a movie star. Gasoline rations were liberal for funerals, and evidently all the deceased's friends and relations had obtained cars for the services. Our trailer, heavily loaded, couldn't be backed, so Dad recruited a brawny man from the crowd of mourners. As though it were a toy he unhitched the trailer, turned it, and held the tongue effortlessly until Dad maneuvered the car around in the opposite direction. Then we retraced the miles back into Hodgenville heading the longest funeral procession I ever have seen.

We sublet 1116 McChesney Street in East Nashville from Birmingham people. The furniture was tolerable, the house not so good. Joe, with the help of neighbors, had the place clean, but I was unprepared for rats. The foundation of the house was a hole in the ground, a few tree trunks for piling with some boards thrown up around them. The furnace sat squarely at the foot of the stairs and coal was dumped haphazardly in the window. Some previous tenant had used an unexcavated portion under the flooring as a dump.

The third day of our sojourn was a drenching one. As I went to the basement for a try at furnace stoking, I heard a scramble. A rat as big as a cat scampered through a hole in the siding. Shuddering, I paused at the window and outside saw another one carrying an ear of corn. I had visions of bubonic plague. Hastily I retreated to the kitchen and began to search frantically. Ah, just as I thought. "Electric Rat Paste," one box was labelled, and it was still fresh. So this was no new thing! I was afraid to leave the baby alone after that and flew out of bed when he made the slightest sound at night. I had the gruesome satisfaction of luring at least five rodents to their deaths with the "electric" concoction.

Never was there a more hospitable soul than our closest neighbor on McChesney Street. She insisted on caring for Blinky occasionally. One day I returned from the grocery to find her rocking him and crooning happily, "My little damnyankee. Oh my sweet little damnyankee."

When we had been in the house for two weeks, the owner and the Birmingham lessee began to bicker. We feared being caught in the crossfire. Besides, the rats really frightened me. Joe heard of a fellow officer who was transferring, so we snatched his place near the fairgrounds.

The Warfleigh subdivison house, a six-room brick, was much above the average rental. Its owner had been drafted. It sat atop a high hill and had a large garden in which a few flowers still bloomed. The maple furniture was similar to our own, stored so long ago. One bedroom was decorated as a nursery.

Moving day was a trauma. Army truckers carted groceries, baby furniture, and luggage. Then the wife of Joe's immediate superior, a wealthy young woman named Dodie, came to drive Blinky and me to our new home. This day Dodie was dressed in striking navy silk with white ruffles at wrist and throat. When we reached 1706 Stewart Place I expected my fashionable friend to say farewell at once. Instead she plunged into the house with enthusiasm, shouting, "Give me some linens. I'll make the bed. Where do you want these groceries moved? Heavens, here's the grandaddy of all dirts! Wait! I'll borrow a vacuum."

By the time I had my wraps off, she had dashed next door and was back with a vacuum, a pail, and an enormous scrub brush.

I never discovered what plans she had for the latter two items. The owner appeared to build a fire and show me how to regulate the thermostat. The poor soul was hardly in the door before Dodie had him by the arm.

"You'll help me with this mattress, won't you? I've got to clean under the springs."

Five minutes later she stood in the middle of the denuded bedstead, a broom in one hand, a dust rag in the other, a swirl of lint surrounding her.

"Would you think it just terrible if I skipped out now?" she asked apologetically. "I just happened to think of an appointment and I *am* getting dirty."

I waved goodbye to my impetuous benefactress and settled in. I saw no rats but did once invite a friendly tomcat in to dispose of a mouse in the attic.

Forsythia was blooming the day Joe called to say we were on our way to Great Falls, Montana, to be attached to the Air Force at Gore Field. It seemed the coin he'd flipped last August had turned over again. I hated leaving Nashville in springtime.

We were routed through Cincinnati to "Sunken Lunken" for army reasons, stopped one night in Indianapolis, then went on to Chicago. Travelling with a baby is no picnic, but we did very well until the fourth day. At seven, while Blinky was having a morning bottle, we pulled into a bare little mountain station and there were dumped from our pullman into an unlighted, unheated coach train headed north. After three hours' wait in below zero temperature, the train was made up and rolled. It took seven hours to complete two hundred miles to Great Falls, during which the baby whimpered incessantly. At one fork in the tracks we were informed there would be a ten-minute stop for lunch. There was a restaurant two blocks away. I tried to go, but a rising blizzard was too much for me carrying the wailing child, so Joe went alone and brought back sandwiches. One man bought bread and made his own.

"Do you know," he exclaimed, "bread costs fifteen cents here?"

It still was eight cents in Indiana.[9]

At the hotel we tucked Blinky, who obviously had pneumonia, into a makeshift bed of two chairs and several blankets. A maid came to check the room. I had used one hotel blanket under the baby which she jerked off the chair, announcing peevishly that she couldn't permit such use of hotel property.

Blinky was very sick, but after two weeks' warmth and nursing he once more laughed and regained his usual prodigious appetite. We began to house-hunt.

When, to a town of some 35,000, the personnel and dependents of two air bases are added, there must, of necessity, be a housing shortage. Great Falls was no exception. Some ranch families also wintered in town, and boarding houses were maintained for expectant mothers from ranches so they might be near the hospital for delivery. After almost a month of searching I arrived at the conclusion via slammed telephones and shaken heads that army couples generally were unwelcome and army couples with children were absolutely unclean. Finally a fellow officer rented a house and, for sake of economy, invited us to move in temporarily.

That month Joe made first lieutenant and went to Sacramento on temporary duty. By the time he returned I had found a two-room basement apartment on the south edge of Great Falls in view of the mountains. It consisted of a bedroom and a combination living-cooking room. In the family laundry section of the basement were a shower and stool. Laundry tubs served as a sink. In the Victory Garden I picked up an old beer can opener to use on Blinky's condensed milk cans.[10] It embarrassed me a bit but it worked. Before I had always used a hammer and a sterilized nail.

A month later another officer was transferred, and we sublet his house. A one-bedroom affair with a microscopic yard, 612 Fifth Street South nevertheless was a house, and there were neighbors our own age, Kia and "Spike" Schrader.

On the morning of June 6 Joe left for temporary duty in Denver and Cheyenne. I was in the midst of weekly ironing when news of D-day came. I think it affected me emotionally more than any other high point of the war. The kitchen woodwork and floor were scrubbed on adrenaline fed by the radio all day, and I mended socks until three in the morning to keep awake and listening to history a-making.

In August we had notice that the owners of our house were returning to town, so I began the hunt again. The most irritating situation in any military town was that, while government-subsidized apartments were open to families of "essential workers," this meant only factory people. Service personnel did not qualify as essential. Some argued that service wives ought to stay home instead of traipsing around hither and yon, dragging their brats into other peoples' towns. Most of us had no permanent homes anywhere and could only make them where our men were stationed. I feel a wife belongs by her husband's side, and a child should have his father's steadying influence so long as possible. I saw some men seek the company of cheap women simply because their wives would not endure the inconveniences of army following.

We found 517 Fifth Street South, another basement, this time in a dark brick building. It consisted of a long living room with closet and roll-away bed, a kitchen, a tiny bedroom for the baby, and, by some quirk of the architect's fancy, two baths. The place was a dungeon.

In September, when Blinky was a year old, Joe was assigned to temporary duty back at "Sunken Lunken" in Cincinnati. He had leave coming and agreed to take it for a visit in Indiana if I could obtain my own transportation. I called the two railroads. Twenty days at least. I called the one airline. Well . . .

The night before Joe was to leave there was a vacancy. As I was about to phone for a cab, it was cancelled. Next night they had one. Blinky and I caught up with Joe in Chicago and managed to ride the same commercial plane south, he going to Cincinnati, Blinky and I getting off at Indianapolis, where he joined us later.

The story of our return trip should be recorded in the annals of transportation under the heading, "If you've time to spare, go by air."

During the war travel was on a priority basis. On public transportation military personnel on duty and government personnel could "bump" civilians no matter how legitimate the citizens' travel needs were. Once "bumped" a nonpriority passenger then was bypassed even by other nonpriority travellers coming from greater distances. It was one huge parchesi game. One or more infants in tow, complete with blankets, toys, diaper bag, bottles, and many cans of condensed milk, simply added to the challenge which young mothers accepted as a way of life.

On a Thursday evening we all went to an Indianapolis airport together. We were reserved on American Airlines to Chicago and were to spend the night with my college roommate, who lived there. From Chicago Joe would take military transport back to Great Falls while I went via Northwest. As we waited, fog settled. Our plane appeared, circled twice, disappeared north. We returned to my parents. Two days later, Joe, at the very margin of his leave, took military transport west. I couldn't clear a reservation for a week.

Then, with Blinky swaddled in double diapers and two pairs of waterproofs, I tried again. This time American had a gas leak and was forced to bump a passenger, me, but an hour later I caught an Eastern on standby, arriving at Chicago about eight o'clock in a downpour. Northwest was due out at four in the morning.

In the chaos that was the tiny wartime Chicago terminal I concluded that I would do well to visit my old roommate after all, and give the sleepy child a few hours' nap. That decision was my undoing.

I propped Blinky up between an embarrassed major and an amused lieutenant and in an authoritative manner instructed them that he was in their care while I tried to telephone my friend. She was not in; nevertheless, after an hour's wait a well-tipped porter located a cab seat, and, packed in it with four officers, we made our rattling way across the dreary city. I have detested Chicago since that night.

At the apartment I learned my friend had left for New York, but I persuaded the desk man to give me her key. I put Blinky to bed while I dozed on the couch. At two I tried to call a cab. Poor little fool from the cornfields. I hadn't anticipated the independence of Windy City taxi men. None wanted to make the long run to the airport with only one passenger. At 2:30 I enlisted the aid of the hotel clerk, at 3:00 that of the airline office. At 4:00 I put the baby back to bed. Later in the morning considerable phoning elicited the information that in possibly a week I might get another air reservation. A train west would be two weeks.

Discouraged, I rummaged in my friend's refrigerator and found two oranges and a bottle of ginger ale. Blinky had the oranges for breakfast. At the desk I was told about a restaurant in the next building and hastened thence in hopes of coffee, only to find it closed on Wednesdays. This was Wednesday. I went back to the apartment and drank the ginger ale.

Tucking Blinky under one arm and his diaper bag under the other, I hailed one of the now-plentiful cruising taxis to the airport to give it one more try.

"We have a vacancy as far as Minneapolis right now," I was told. "Would you care to take that?"

"Yes," I shouted. It was in the right direction.

We almost set up housekeeping in the Minneapolis terminal. When we arrived I was informed there would be two planes that night on which there might possibly be room for us. By 6:00 at least fourteen persons awaited the same two planes. When these landed, priority passengers appeared to displace seven more.

Blinky's canned milk supply was exhausted, his diapers nearly so. The cafeteria had no milk, but an obliging taxi driver volunteered to buy several cans from an open-all-night grocery. "I got kids myself," he grinned. I wondered glumly if cab drivers in Chicago ever became fathers.

Harassed airport clerks arranged hotel rooms for the entire crowd of bumped passengers. Among them was a navy wife trying to reach her husband who had an unexpected three-day shore leave in Spokane. Her little boy was only a few months older than Blinky. We bathed the babies and spent a comfortable, if anxious, night in a shared room.

The following morning we were back at the terminal, joined by another army wife and her five-month-old. Also, a middle-aged hypochondriac was returning from having an operation in Boston. She must have been uncomfortable, but we with babies were nauseated by her constant complaining. She made thirty-seven dollars' worth of long distance calls trying to get some doctor to get her a priority. No one could.

Planes came and went. We mothers took turns hanging around the dispatch desk to heckle the clerks, who probably would have carried us piggy-back to our destinations just to get rid of us. Gradually the crowd thinned.

In the evening we were told hotel rooms were authorized for only one night, so, since we had used up that privilege, we simply staged a three-woman strike, commandeered the airport emergency room for our infants, and refused to budge. About midnight the oldest boy fell out of bed and bruised his forehead. He wailed, his mother wept, we others stormed the ticket desk demanding ice for his injury and, in general, someone to *do* something. Never underestimate the power of three women. The worn-out clerks wired Chicago to sell no more nonpriority tickets until Minneapolis could clear its waiting room.

About dawn a girl came to us with a cheerful, "Does anyone want to go to Billings, Montana?"

"I'll take that," I sang out. "We might get a bus to Great Falls from there."

"Oh, Great Falls?" She said it as if by then everyone in the whole terminal didn't know where we were bound.

"Oh, we can get you right through."

My seat companion was the chronic complainer who enthralled me with a stitch-by-stitch account of her operation all the way to Billings where, I thanked a merciful Heaven, she got off.

About a week after our return to Great Falls, the field housing bureau offered 2307 Sixth Avenue South to us. We lived there a year to the day. It was a five-room unit in the Villa, a privately owned but government-controlled housing project to which, by some loophole, service families were admitted. Rent was high. So were furnishings, which we leased, but we had a yard and two bedrooms once more.

Thanksgiving Day I was recovering from a heavy cold. We had two enlisted men for a duck dinner. I never had eaten, much less prepared, duck. The fact that we had no roaster added challenge to the project. I plopped the seasoned bird on a pie plate and turned on the gas oven. Soon we were staggering through a smoke barrage the like of which chemical warfare never achieved, emptying the pie plate every four minutes, my hollow hacking aggravated by smoke. They said the duck really was tasty, but I'll never eat one.

We came to the conclusion that Blinky was going to have a sister. Pregnancy was so much the fashion among army wives that I had felt indecently exposed wearing a flat tummy and was delighted to be one of the girls again. It was said that the high birth rate among service families in Great Falls was due to sub-zero weather. Then there was a popular little ditty to the tune of "Pretty Baby" which began:

"If you're nervous in the Service
And you don't know what to do,
Have a baby, have a baby—."

Insuring themselves against impassable roads, commercial Christmas tree cutters brought their first loads over the mountain from Kalispell on December 1. I paid a dollar for ours. Three strings of tree lights mistakenly shipped from Nashville now were happily unboxed. Replacement bulbs were unavailable, but, miraculously, none burned out.

Christmas Day two unmarried officers were our guests at noon. They were frequent visitors who considered a part of accepting an invitation that they should wash dishes, but the accumulation from the holiday meal was larger than usual. Late in the afternoon Joe's enlisted staff and their wives dropped in for eggnog. The two lieutenants still were elbow deep in suds battling a stubborn oyster pan. Their subordinates enjoyed that immensely and assumed a patronizing advisory role in burned pan logistics. They gave Blinky's new wooden train a workout too. There were no metal toys available. The big boys in the Pacific had all those.

There was an indefinable quality about parties at the officers' club at Gore Field that never will be equalled. Of course we had our celebrities. Leonard Pennario's[11] early concert piano career began at Gore Field. We all helped Captain Bob Crawford[12] render raucous versions of "The Army Air Corps" song and his lesser known composition entitled "Kill the Bastards." But it was not the entertainment I remember best. It had something to do with fraternity. Among people whose lives existed only from day to day there developed a keener sensitivity for pleasure that lent intensity to our brief joy. Man cannot own happiness, but he can borrow it almost anywhere.

Spring snowed itself right out of existence. Women tried to raise a few flowers in the barren gumbo of the Villa, despite the superstition that if a wife planted flowers it would surely bring about a transfer for her husband.

There were still chinooks. On nights when snow lay deep I awoke to hear the wind whining at the doorsills and burrowed deeper into the covers. What a surprise at daybreak to find the hot gale had melted a foot of snow in a few hours. I do not understand the physics of the chinook. Old-timers wove yarns about it. Cattle wandered afar in the sudden warmth to get caught in the next blizzard. The air force sometimes dropped dry feed to the cows when they could be located. Cattlemen hated chinooks, but I thanked Heaven for their respite in the long Montana winter. The same wind was no man's friend in summer. One night I awakened in discomfort. The corner street light was almost obliterated, and I was choking with dust. Half an inch of fine yellow dirt covered every surface in the house. It was piled in corners. It gritted between our teeth and was ingrained in our hair. Sandstorms blew in four times that summer.

As June wore on, I collected pink baby dresses. We planned for a girl. We were going to leave Blinky with Winifred, our neighbor to the east, while I was in hospital. I hoped I could have another officer's wife, a registered nurse, help me later at home. About the first of July Winifred came over, green-faced.

"I'm due about February tenth," she said. "I don't feel so well." I bargained with Dusty, the neighbor west, to take Blinky. While I was in the hospital, Dusty, a third neighbor, and the nurse all announced they were expecting; a fifth wife, who had been away on leave, returned wearing drawstring dresses; my old friend Kia from Fifth Street joined the club; and Ruth, our former neighbor at Nashville, wrote confidential news. I was nonplussed at the pattern we had set.

July turned hot for Montana, the natives suffering tremendously as the thermometer reached the upper nineties. The morning of the twenty-fifth I awoke at 5:30 and called Joe at 6:00. This was going to be harder on him than me. Having been away at the time of Blinky's birth, he only now would be initiated into the fraternity of waiting fathers. He didn't wait long. We dressed in a leisurely fashion, wakened Blinky to say goodbye, and drove to the hospital.

Suddenly everything became frenetic, like a speeded-up movie. It was a shoulder presentation. There was no soothing hypodermic. Anesthetic had no time to take effect. When the doctor appeared, I was engulfed by four black walls of pain and my own hysterical screaming. Before the epesiotomy I remember the doctor telling me once to *shut up*. I was shocked but never stopped protesting this unexpected indignity to my body. I suppose any mere man who earns his living listening to women yell themselves into motherhood frequently needs to express hostility. At the time I was angry and in agony.

Then someone asked, "What are you going to name this boy?"

I giggled weakly, "Go ask his father. What in the world am I going to do with all those pink dresses?"

It was three days before we settled on Douglas for a name. He became Dinky immediately. Truly, I think we both were a little relieved that the baby was a boy. Boys were easier to raise in army installations, and we expected to live that way a long time. Everybody thought the war had to be fought through all the islands to Japan.

Rumor flies fast in a military town. The commanding officer at Gore Field complained once that his wife could tell him what was going to happen at the base before he ordered it. So it was not surprising that, when a system of credit points was computed for length of service and dependents, many families began to pack. Most of them had quite a wait.

The women were impatient for discharge and would have moved mountains to speed it up. I really didn't think about it until V-J day. The complete surprise of the Bomb made the war's close, like its beginning, incomprehensible.

In the Villa wives ran in and out of each other's houses, hugging. Children went without baths. Meals were unprepared. The clinking of ice in tall glasses continued all day and far into the night. High school girls established fortunes minding babies while people celebrated. We couldn't find a girl, so an obliging little boy with a reputation for dependability was put in charge of five sleeping infants in our compound.

But while excitement mounted, while I chattered and laughed in the mardigras atmosphere of Victory night, I had an uneasy feeling of needing to retreat, to sort things out. Of course I was glad the war was over—wasn't I? Of course I wanted life to get back to normal, but what *was* normal? Our family knew nothing but the service. The foundations of our life, our wonderful, unpredictable, secure, military existence had crumbled with the Abomb.

In the days that followed I thrust gnawing fear back and back. Points for discharge, based on time of service, time overseas, and number of dependents, were recomputed. With the two boys Joe had seventy-five points, enough for immediate discharge.

The day before Blinky's second birthday Kia and her husband invited us to join them on a trip to Glacier Park. Their daughter and Blinky could go, too, but it was out of the question to take along little Dink, just five weeks old. At the same time it was unthinkable to forgo our only opportunity to visit the great park before leaving Montana.

Joe took a quick survey in his office and got information which led to the solution. A sergeant was just back from Europe. His wife had not yet joined him, and the entire field had a three-day pass for Labor Day. The sergeant said he could think of nothing more enjoyable than to spend his leave in a real-for-sure house, reading and writing letters. He knew all about babies. His sister had several.

I was dubious, but Joe brought the sergeant home, and while we packed, I talked. Formulas held no mystery for him. Dink's cod liver oil was an old acquaintance. Baths did not dismay. I felt pretty smug about my small hoard of disposable diapers, even though they weren't much heavier than paper towels. People to whom I divulged the identity of our sitter were anxious. "But is the baby *all right*?" I can't see why infant care should be regarded as a talent peculiar only to females.

Gore Field was scheduled to close in November. We would leave October 16. I felt sick. I had no heart for packing. We separated Blinky's wooden toys, crating the best, leaving broken ones for the last few days of play. His birthday tricycle was relegated to the garage where our boxes awaited army freighters. We sold houseplants to one neighbor, dime-store dishes to another, gave away groceries. In three and one-half years of marriage we had made twelve moves, and this was the first I had not looked at as an adventure.

We had dinner next door. During the meal Blinky painted his new white shoes with nail polish called *Red Badge of Courage* and drew pictures with a fountain pen on his clean, pink overalls, but, without other incident, we climbed on the 7:30 train. The large group of friends who saw us off at the station made me cry. I had never wept before.

Good connections at Minneapolis and Chicago sped us on our way. Miles clicked by steadily and all the guilty while I wanted to shout, "Stop, stop! Stop the train. Stop the clock. Let me think. Let me get used to this idea. I don't like it. God help me, I don't like it at all."

Out of Chicago a nurse with six overseas stripes handed Blinky a three-franc piece. She told me French women she had worked with had dry, coarse complexions from poor diet and brittle hair dyed pink, blue, and purple in celebration of peace. It sounded crazy, but the French always have known how to survive. Now I had to learn.

A sailor radiating an alcoholic glow kept giving Blinky water in those flimsy little paper cups they had on trains, the result being that every few jiggling rail miles necessitated a hasty trip for him to the gentlemen's end of the car.

We were in Indianapolis. Joe had three days at Baer Field, Fort Wayne, for debriefing and got a gold-colored "ruptured duck" pin to wear in his lapel.[13]

Our war was over and I was no longer a draftee's wife.[14]

VIRGINIA MAYBERRY was the author or editor of three articles that appeared in the *Indiana Magazine of History*, including "The Civil War Home Front: Diary of a Young Girl, 1862–1863," 87, March 1991. This article originally appeared in volume 79, December 1983.

NOTES

1. For discussions of the home front during World War II, see: Richard E. Lingeman, *Don't You Know There's a War On?* (New York, 1970); John Morton Blum, *V Was for Victory: Politics and American Culture during World War II* (New York, 1976); and Richard Polenberg, *War and Society: The United States, 1941–1945* (Philadelphia, 1972). The Indiana scene is discussed in James H. Madison, *Indiana through Tradition and Change: A History of the Hoosier State and Its People, 1920–1945* (Indianapolis, 1982), 370–407.

2. Virginia Mayberry was born in Cleveland, Ohio, on June 4, 1919, and reared in Indianapolis, where she attended Brookside Elementary and Shortridge High School. She graduated from the School of Journalism, Indiana University, Bloomington, in June, 1941. This account is written in the first person; in the interest of preserving this first person perspective, conversations are quoted verbatim, although it is recognized that such quotations may at times contain slight inaccuracies.

3. The Munich Pact, drawn up after an international conference in that city on September 29–30, 1938, ceded Czechoslovakia's Sudetenland region to Germany. The conference and cessions resulted when Germany complained about the treatment of the German minority in Czechoslovakia and threatened to attack the latter nation if the Czech area with the greatest concentration of Germans was not ceded. It was the Munich Conference which produced what British prime minister Neville Chamberlain proclaimed as "peace in our time."

4. The Civilian Air Army, a federal program to train pilots.

5. For a discussion of war-related activities at Indiana University, see Thomas D. Clark, *Indiana University: Midwestern Pioneer.* Volume III, *Years of Fulfillment* (4 vols., Bloomington, 1970–1977), 117–38. The first cyclotron at the university began operations in the spring of 1941; some data from early measurements made at the facility were used by researchers working on the nation's atom bomb project.

6. The Winter War between Finland and the Soviet Union broke out in November, 1939, when Finland refused to meet Soviet territorial demands. Fighting continued until the following March, when Finland was forced to seek peace. By the Treaty of Moscow the smaller nation made a number of territorial concessions.

7. The Women's Auxiliary Army Corps (WAAC) was created by Congress in May, 1942, and placed women in noncombat roles. Women's corps also were created for other branches of the armed forces during the war.

8. The Army Air Corps was created in 1926. It became the Army Air Force in June, 1941, and became co-equal with other forces of the army in February, 1942. The Ferrying Division of the Air Transport Command had the primary mission to deliver aircraft to allies and to United States forces. Berry Field delivered to India; Gore Field delivered to Alaska for pickup by the Soviet Union.

9. Money really was of minor concern. Ration points were important. Gasoline, heating oil, tires, shoes, sugar, meat, fats, coffee, and canned goods were closely controlled. Shortages in other commodities and foodstuffs developed, but we learned to substitute or do without.

10. During the war the government encouraged Americans to grow gardens, termed "Victory Gardens," to aid the war effort. Such gardens became very common and supplied a substantial proportion of the nation's fresh vegetables.

11. Leonard Pennario, noted pianist, was born in New York City in 1924. He appeared as a child prodigy with the Dallas Symphony and Los Angeles Philharmonic. After serving in the Air Corps he toured the United States and Europe in a trio with Jascha Heifetz, violinist, and Gregor Piatigorsky, cellist. See *International Cyclopedia of Music and Musicians* (10th ed., New York, 1975), 1645.

12. Robert M. Crawford, baritone and conductor, was born in the Yukon Territory in 1899 and died in New York in 1961. He studied at Juilliard and the American Conservatory at Fontainebleau, France, and was in charge of the Newark Symphony and a Chautauqua Orchestra in 1933. He composed several orchestral suites and songs, among them the "Army Air Corps Song." There is a memorial plaque in his honor inside the Cleveland, Ohio, airport. See Nicholas Slonimsky, *Baker's Biographical Dictionary of Musicians* (6th ed., New York, 1978), 360.

13. "Ruptured duck" was the irreverent term given by veterans to the eagle on the discharge pin they received. Probably it was one last attempt to camoflage serious emotions with a joke.

14. The family settled in Goshen, Indiana, Joe's hometown, where three more children were born. Virginia retired to freelancing from a variety of teaching and writing-related jobs. The couple lived in Middlebury, Indiana, where Joe ran a small advertising agency and was well known as an acrylic artist. Richard and Douglas both served in the army during the Vietnam conflict.

9

Education Denied

Indiana University's Japanese American Ban, 1942 to 1945

ERIC LANGOWSKI

ON OCTOBER 29, 1943, INDIANA UNIVERSITY'S (IU) Dean of Women Kate Hevner Mueller received an unusually frank plea for admission into the IU nursing school from Sumiko Itoi, a nineteen-year-old Japanese American working at Robert Long Hospital in Indianapolis. Itoi asked Mueller for "aid . . . in every possible way" to remain close to her sister, a student at Hanover College in southeast Indiana. Two weeks later, Itoi received her reply: a rejection letter based solely, unbeknownst to her, on a May 1942 decision from IU's Board of Trustees that "no Jap. be admitted to Indiana University."[1]

Itoi's frustrated pursuit of a college degree was indicative of the Nisei (second-generation Japanese American) experience during World War II. In 1942, about 7,500 of her peers—roughly 4,000 high school seniors and 3,500 enrolled college students—had found themselves unable to continue their educations after President Franklin D. Roosevelt's Executive Order 9066, which authorized the forced removal and incarceration of Japanese Americans from the West Coast.[2] During wartime, only one-quarter of American higher education institutions would enroll Japanese American students; their total enrollment numbers would never exceed their prewar peak.[3]

Indiana University administrators often cloaked their exclusionary policy in euphemistic language about limitations on out-of-state students or decisions based on military necessity. IU Director of Admissions Frank Elliott, for example, offered that accepting even a single Japanese American student "would mean the exclusion of some Indiana girl."[4] For the duration, and, inexplicably, beyond the end of the war, IU's ban on Japanese American attendance continued almost without exception despite policy changes at its peer institutions across Indiana and the Big Ten.

The choice to deny Japanese American students admission to IU was not foreordained. A review of the actions of IU administrators and trustees, and a deeper look at the campus community's response to their decisions, reveals the injustice of the school's approach to minority communities. The stories of the rejected applicants themselves offer further evidence of inequities faced by a generation of students as they sought to rebuild their lives at midwestern colleges. What remains is a need for institutional reconciliation and an effort to redress the public memory of Indiana University, deeply rooted in Indiana's history of white ethnocentrism.[5]

AMERICAN CONCENTRATION CAMPS & INDIANA'S JIM CROW

Anti-Japanese and anti-Asian sentiment began long before December 1941. Nativist ideology saw the Asian "other" as a danger to the white majority; during the nineteenth century, Chinese immigrants were gradually stripped of their legal rights and their ability to naturalize, and were persecuted or even murdered by white mobs.[6] In 1882, nativism was codified in the Chinese Exclusion Act, and Asians remained a small minority nationwide.[7] Public officials in California and along the West Coast, who now sought to exclude Japanese Americans as well, found common ground with southern politicians focused on forging a "white man's country."[8] In 1913 and 1920, California passed laws banning first-generation Japanese Americans (Issei) from owning land, and in 1924, Congress passed the Johnson-Reed Act, barring new immigration from Japan altogether.[9] By 1940, decades of anti-Japanese policies had left Issei—now barred from citizenship, immigration, land ownership, voting, and banking in California—and their young children vulnerable to persecution.[10]

Immediately after the attack on Pearl Harbor, government officials began responding to what they considered the potential threat posed by Japanese American communities on the West Coast.[11] Polling data showed that ninety-seven percent of West Coast Americans approved of the removal and incarceration of Japanese Americans in December 1942; with virtually universal support from the public and the press, President Roosevelt ordered the roundup of the 120,000 Japanese Americans living on the West Coast and sentenced them without trial to forcible incarceration under the guise of "military necessity." The U.S. Department of War, charged with carrying out the order, cited "the combination of spot raids revealing hidden caches of contraband, the attacks on

Japanese Americans at the Santa Anita, California, rail station, 1942. The station was one of the assembly points for Japanese Americans being removed to internment camps. *Courtesy Records of the War Relocation Authority, National Archives.*

coastwise shipping, the interception of illicit radio transmissions, the nightly observation of visual signal lamps from constantly changing locations, and the success of the enemy offensive in the Pacific." Military officials also argued that the public was "ready to take matters into its own hands" and that "while it was believed that some [Japanese Americans] were loyal, it was known that many were not."[12] As a result, Japanese American families languished in government custody for years as they gradually transitioned from temporary "assembly centers" to "internment camps," remembered by many today as America's concentration camps. Eventually, in late 1944, President Roosevelt, for the stated reason of maintaining "internal quiet," called for Japanese Americans to be "distributed—one or two families to each county as a start" as "75 thousand families scattered all around the United States is not going to upset anybody."[13] Government officials would euphemistically call this process "resettlement."

In the Hoosier State, where the pre-1940 Japanese population had never exceeded one hundred, this "resettlement" process permanently altered the state's Japanese American community.[14] After prominent Indiana politicians like Paul McNutt and Wendell Willkie declined to support the government's decision to incarcerate Japanese Americans, it seemed possible that the state might prove a hospitable destination. An editorial, reprinted in the *Muncie Evening Press*, however, suggested otherwise, calling for America to "clamp down now on our Japs" and to "put them all behind barbed wire and keep the sexes separate [to] not let them produce more Japanese-Americans."[15] Despite the efforts of Democratic congressman Louis Ludlow to keep resettlers out of Indiana, a War Relocation Authority (WRA) field office opened in Indianapolis in May 1943.[16] The head of the relocation office for Indiana, Edmond T. Cleary, responded to opposition by promising that Japanese Americans would be resettled only with community permission. As a result of what historian Nancy Nakano Connor has summarized as "prevailing prejudices in the community, in competition with contemporary job seekers, and . . . limited recruiting efforts on the part of the state's employers and universities," only 254 Japanese Americans settled in Indiana during the wartime period.[17]

Bloomington and Indiana University had their own history of racial segregation long before Executive Order 9066. IU largely excluded black students for the first century following its establishment. In the decades prior to World War II, that exclusion had come to be seen by many as a growing embarrassment. In November 1921, the Ku Klux Klan held a large public march through the heart of Bloomington; in at least one instance, university administrators had warned IU students of the damage their threats of racially motivated violence would do to the school's image.[18] Herman B Wells, receiving his initial appointment as IU President in 1937, inherited what his biographer James Capshew called "a system of segregation as rigid as any Jim Crow society in the Deep South."[19] In the first few years of his presidency, Wells worked to desegregate campus, but this task remained unfinished by the start of World War II.[20] Frank Beck and the Student Religious Cabinet (SRC) worked alongside President Wells to overcome religious and racial differences on campus. In a 1939 survey, the SRC found that black students were barred from R.O.T.C., the university band, the barbershop, and some honorary and professional societies within university departments. They were restricted from using the Union, attending campus dances, and taking part in some social programs. Black students were also forced into segregated housing and refused service in all but one local restaurant. Notably, Bloomington's racial hierarchy, in Beck's telling, often included "Chinese, Japanese, Indians, Africans, and South and

Central Americans" along with African Americans.[21] Change was slow and campus segregation did not officially end in Indiana until 1949.[22] One historian attributes Indiana's prejudices to a combination of Midwest provincialism, nativism, and "a Southern-influenced concept of the Negro as a separate and inferior being."[23]

Throughout this period of entrenched segregation, few Japanese or Japanese American students attended IU. University records show an average of twenty-eight students from all other countries combined in the five years before the war. Yet two students stand out in the records now maintained in the Indiana University Archives.[24] The first, Hero Ichinomiya of Tokyo, Japan, became vice president of his senior class in 1903. Ichinomiya wrote of his experience at IU in the student yearbook, the *Arbutus*, recalling that he had chosen the school for its reputation, rural location, and lack of a large Japanese population.[25] A second student, Masuji Miyakawa, who graduated from IU's law school in 1905, would become a pioneering Japanese American lawyer.[26] Unfortunately, the success of these pioneering students did not alter the racial realities which would, four decades later, bar admittance to those of Japanese ancestry.

EDUCATION OUT OF INCARCERATION

Incarceration only increased demand among Nisei for educational opportunities. Hundreds of college students were forcibly withdrawn from their studies to report to assembly centers; some wished to continue their interrupted degrees, while new high school graduates looked to begin their post-secondary education.[27] In May 1942, President Roosevelt assured California governor Culbert L. Olson of his tacit approval of Nisei students continuing their studies: "I am deeply concerned that the American born Japanese college students shall be impressed with the ability of the American people to distinguish between aliens and staunch supporters of the American system who happen to have Japanese ancestry."[28] Deemed "Jap Lovers" by conservative newspapers and "undercut" by the military, the War Relocation Agency, which largely oversaw incarceration, realized that they could not directly offer aid to the Nisei college students without creating a "public furor" and instead proposed that those students transfer to other non-West Coast institutions before incarceration.[29] The opposition of the army and the general desire of students to stay with their families made this proposal untenable.[30] Only 630 students—about one-fifth of the total 3,252 Nisei enrolled at West Coast institutions in 1941—were able to gain the sponsorship of a handful of college administrators and thus avoid the concentration camps altogether.[31]

After students were incarcerated, a government-sanctioned student resettlement organization was created to facilitate their acceptance into colleges and expedite "leave clearances" from the military.[32] The American Friends Service Committee (AFSC) became the primary sponsor for the National Japanese American Student Relocation Council (NJASRC) which took stewardship of higher education opportunities for Japanese Americans.[33] The NJASRC worked tirelessly on behalf of Nisei applicants, but military and government policy often presented insurmountable barriers to their success.

The plight of Nisei students received diverging responses from higher education institutions. Some West Coast educators, concerned about their former students and eager to assist their own East Coast counterparts in dealing with dramatic increases in the number of Nisei applicants, aggressively lobbied the government to allow Nisei to continue their education in 1942. Others withheld transcripts and rejected applications.[34] Approximately three-quarters of American institutions would deny admissions to Nisei students during the war.[35] Beginning in fall 1942, institutions could no longer admit incarcerated Japanese Americans without government leave clearance and NJASRC approval. The council required institutions to return a questionnaire which determined their willingness to cooperate.[36] These questionnaires asked for lists of available courses; information regarding the cost of attendance, scholarships, and work availability; and descriptions of the general local receptiveness toward Japanese Americans. Universities were also required to grant a student provisional admission before they could apply for military clearance in an arduous process.[37] For institutions willing to accept Japanese American students, the roadblocks set up by the government and the military, combined with the cautious approach of the NJASRC, required months of paperwork before a student could arrive on campus.[38] In some cases, people were left waiting for the duration of the war.

A few liberal arts schools—particularly some in Indiana, Michigan, Minnesota, Montana, North Carolina, Ohio, and Pennsylvania—were able to enroll Nisei students in fall 1942, thanks to their flexibility in quickly meeting government requirements.[39] The path from "concentration camp to campus" was so arduous that it was known as an "Underground Railroad." Students would only be considered for the fall 1942 term if they were in the "highest 15 percent of applicants." Institutions needed testimony from a public official vouching for community acceptance, institutional clearance from the Department of War, and a background check from the Federal Bureau of Investigations.[40] By the end of the academic year, only 890 Nisei students were successfully enrolled.[41] As the war progressed, the toll of incarceration wore on these young Nisei, resulting in a year-after-year decline in the number of graduating high school seniors applying for leave clearance.[42] Nisei often felt obligated to care for their families or chose to enlist in the armed forces instead. For other students, leaving for college in the Midwest could mean never seeing their parents again. As one father said: "I am old, someday you will hear that I am dying, perhaps while still in school. Forget about me. Make my dying days happy in the knowledge that you are studying and preparing yourself for service. My life is in the past, yours is in the future."[43] Looking to their futures, some Nisei continued their pursuit of a post-secondary education and, a year later, in spring 1944, an estimated 2,500 students had enrolled.[44]

By June 1944, government agencies determined that it was "now appropriate to repeal the exclusion order," and allow Japanese Americans to return to their West Coast homes.[45] Roosevelt opted to postpone the repeal until after that year's election. Meanwhile, the War Department removed all military restrictions on college attendance in September 1944, thus allowing any school to admit Japanese American students. Schools which had previously lacked clearance, such as the University of Minnesota and the University of Chicago, quickly moved to accept Nisei students, but others—including Indiana University and the University of Pennsylvania—failed to respond promptly.[46] By December 1944, more than 3,500 students had enrolled at over 550 institutions in 46 states, still falling short of annual pre-Pearl Harbor figures.[47]

NISEI WARTIME EDUCATION AT IU

In October 1941, Commander F.M. McWhirter of the Ninth Naval District wrote to IU Registrar Thomas A. Cookson asking for the names of any students of "Japanese descent enrolled with you."[48] Assistant Registrar Charles E. Harrell complied, naming one student, Sunao Miyabara.[49] Miyabara, an American citizen from Hawaii, had enrolled as a pre-medical student in September 1941, and would be IU's only Japanese American student during the war. A year later, he would withdraw to serve in the United States military as a Japanese language translator overseas.[50]

Weeks after Roosevelt's order to incarcerate Americans of Japanese ancestry, midwestern universities received a surge of applications from Japanese Americans desperate to find sanctuary. The University of Minnesota exceeded its Big Ten peers in the number of applications received. Minnesota President Walter C. Coffey, concerned with a possible "minor migration" of Nisei to his campus, wrote President Wells in March 1942 to ask for advice. Coffey asked Wells if he would "consider appointment of a refugee German" and also raised the matter of "Americans of Japanese extraction who may be forced to leave the restricted areas on the west coast."[51] Herman T. Briscoe, IU's first Dean of Faculties who assumed many of Wells's duties during his wartime absence, responded. Briscoe wrote that, while IU had "no Japanese students" and had not yet been approached by any, it did employ staff who were German refugees and would continue to do so unless "good reasons" for doing otherwise became evident.[52] This initial discussion, beyond overlooking Miyabara, highlighted a distinction that IU made between Japanese Americans and German refugees. With Wells's support, IU offered two scholarships for "German refugee students, for Spanish refugees, for Chinese Students, for the Czechoslovakian people" throughout the war; the school offered no aid for Japanese American students.[53] Now, the university weighed Coffey's query: Should IU admit Japanese Americans, wait for more information from the military, or ban them?

On April 29, 1942, the Administrative Council, a body set up by Wells consisting of unit managers, met to discuss "the question of admission of American-born Japanese who have been evacuated from the West Coast," specifically in relation to Coffey's inquiries from Minnesota. Finding that they could not agree, the Council decided to refer the matter to IU's Board of Trustees.[54] A day later, Sanford S. Elberg of the University of California wrote directly to L. S. McClung in the IU Department of Botany and Bacteriology, asking if IU could "help us out here" with two Nisei students he said were "definitely" going to be granted assistantships. The students were William Suyemoto and Robert Omata.[55] Their fate now rested with the Board of Trustees.

During their May 9 meeting, the trustees dealt with two issues related to Japanese Americans: first the general question of Japanese American admittance, and second, a set of four specific requests for admission, including Omata and Suyemoto.[56] Reading another letter from the University of California which requested that IU admit Japanese American students, Wells gave a general overview of "the question of admission of Japanese of American citizenship." Speaking of the other Big Ten universities, he explained that "some [had] no policy at all and others [did]." The only Big Ten school accepting Japanese Americans students at the time was, according to Wells, the University of Chicago, which admitted them only in "areas where there is [no] government research work." Wisconsin and Michigan would "admit them if proper military authority" gave clearance. In closing his introduction to the issue, Wells noted that the Administrative Council was split "about 50–50." Almost immediately after Wells finished his introduction, three trustees—Bloomington newspaper editor Paul L. Feltus, financier Uz McMurtrie, and banker William A. Kunkel Jr. —said they "would rather not take them for the duration." Trustee John Hastings, a lawyer, then added that, "aside from that, isn't there the point that our resources are pretty well strained now?" Wells responded, saying, "not particularly." Board president Ora L. Wildermuth then stated his opinion: "As I see it, there is a difference in Japanese and Germans or Italians—they are Aryans and can be assimilated but the Japanese can't—they are different racially. I can't believe that any Japanese, no matter where he was born, is anything but a Japanese." Kunkel and McMurtrie moved to vote "that no Jap. be admitted to Indiana University." With a majority of the trustees present having spoken against admitting Japanese Americans, the ban was sure to pass. However, one clarification question was asked: "Would you restrict the American born Japs, native of Ind[iana]?"[57]

On this topic, Wildermuth proposed a more tactful approach, suggesting that, "we might say that it is the recommendation of the Board that the Director of Admissions discourage the application of non-resident Jap applicants." Trustee J. Dwight Peterson suggested that a negative decision on the four Japanese American admission requests before the trustees would let the Director of Admissions "then just know by inference that we do not wish to do it." Wildermuth added that he was "afraid that any Jap would get into subversive activity whenever he would have a chance." Wells closed the discussion by suggesting that admitting Japanese Americans might make campus unsafe: "There is this to be said about the situation—when the casualty lists begin to come in—even though they might be loyal Americans as anybody, feeling is going to mount very high and you might have disturbances on the campus, particularly when you get this Navy here."[58] The trustees voted unanimously to adopt Kunkel's motion, as well as another by Hastings that the board deny the four requests from the University of California.

Indiana was the only university in the region to ban Japanese American students outright as of May 1942. None of the universities Wells cited had imposed a ban. The University of Minnesota voted to support any government-approved plan at the behest of President Coffey. Wildermuth's racism and reductive declaration that any Nisei applicant to the university would be nothing "but a Japanese" now seemed directly codified in a policy which indiscriminately banned Japanese Americans. An NJASRC official, hearing about IU's decision, expressed his disappointment in a university he had considered to be a "bigger and on the whole better" institution.[59] On May 12, Wells approved the following form letter to be sent to any Japanese American applicant:

Dear . . . . :

In view of the present uncertain military status of the southern Indiana geographical zone in which Indiana University is located, this University is not accepting Japanese students at the present time.

Yours very truly,

HBW

Camouflaging the Board of Trustees' anti-Japanese sentiment and the decision to enact an explicit ban, Wells offered little explanation to the recipients. IU mailed four copies of the form letter to the waiting students from the University of California.[60]

A week later Briscoe wrote to Frank R. Elliott, Director of Admissions, to clarify admissions policies. "The Board of Trustees took no action concerning the admission of American-born German and Italian students," he wrote, and there was "no reason why you should not consider . . . [scholarships] . . . from refugee students" on the same basis as the past.[61] Like Wildermuth, Briscoe apparently saw no contradiction in race-based policies that resulted in differential treatment between students of Asian and European descent. Japanese American students were potential subversives, while German American and Italian American students were to be treated as individuals.

THE BAN BEGINS AND CAMPUS RESPONDS

In June 1942, IU rejected three more Nisei admission requests, bringing the total number to seven. The unsuccessful applicants included two brothers from Oregon and a University of California, Berkeley medical student recommended by H.D. Bollinger, secretary of Wesley Foundation's college division.[62] Bollinger's local pastor, Merrill McFall, deferred to Wells: "I just want you to know that I would want you to handle it in any way you think best for the interests of Indiana University. There will be no pressure to bear from me."[63] In this particular case, Wells responded by citing IU's mandate to educate the people of Indiana but did not disclose IU's ban:

> We will be glad to consider his application, but because of the great number of students seeking admission to our School of Medicine it is necessary to limit the number of admissions from other states; therefore it is not likely that this young man could be admitted. As a state institution, it is necessary for

> the University to provide as much opportunity to study medicine as possible for students who are residents of the state.[64]

IU History professor C. Leonard Lundin attended the Conference of Foreign Student Advisers in late April 1942. His report on the conference, forwarded to President Wells in June, focused largely on Latin American students, but also included a section on the injustice faced by Japanese American students. "Since the United States Government has taken the unprecedented step of forcing a certain class of citizens to leave their homes for no fault of their own," he wrote,

> An obligation rests upon citizens living in other parts of the country to assist in reabsorbing into the national life those of the uprooted whose loyalty to our institutions can be proved and whose value to our civilization is evident . . . it is an injustice for universities in the central part of the country to refuse, as most of the great ones have done, to admit any considerable number of these deserving and often brilliant young Americans, whose only fault is their ancestry. It is obvious that, regardless of the military outcome of the war, we shall have lost it ideologically if we adopt racial theories and discriminations similar to those of the Axis Powers; and that is precisely what we are doing if we fail to make provision for the integration of Japanese-Americans.

Lundin recommended that IU should, in consultation with other universities, admit "a large number of Japanese-American students whose loyalty is certified" in the coming fall semester. If such arrangements could not be made, he continued, IU should "set an example of genuine Americanism by admitting some of the students by independent action." The positive experiences of Bloomington's one Japanese American student, he argued, "bears witness to the intelligence, the tolerance, and the friendliness" of campus and suggests IU's capacity to admit more Japanese Americans.[65]

Wells did not follow Lundin's recommendation. Two weeks later, the NJASRC wrote Wells with a request to "fill in and return to us at once the enclosed official questionnaire" to start the process of approving IU for Nisei students.[66] The Wells administration failed to respond.

In July, Frank Beck and the Student Religious Cabinet started a campus discussion. Beck had written the AFSC asking how IU could get on the organization's approved list of universities and have students "assigned to us," noting that "we have had an interesting and most worthwhile experience with Refugee students."[67] The NJASRC officials, wary of activist administrators who might upset the U.S. government, told Beck not to push "too hard" until the Council was able to establish a procedure for handling such requests.[68] Beck then turned his efforts towards campus itself and raised the issue of enrolling

Japanese American students in his meeting with the SRC.[69] After discussion, Beck arranged a meeting between the SRC and Wells on July 22. Chester Davis, a sophomore SRC member, reported: "Such an arrangement would not be contrary to University policy, according to President Wells, if the safety of the students enrolling could be ensured. The privilege for such students to enroll, however, would have to be procured from the U.S. Army."[70] The meeting generated coverage in the *Indiana Daily Student* (*IDS*), which reported Beck's faith that "the University would be willing to cooperate with . . . [the NJASRC] plan if it is agreed upon by the Army and the Association of State University Presidents."[71] Writing privately to Wells, Beck thanked the president for meeting with the religious cabinet "on the Japanese matter," adding that "they accepted one hundred percent your interpretation of the situation and will so report to their respective organizations. I thought that I knew the score but thought that there were great values to come from you giving it to them."[72]

Waiting for the national situation to change and unaware of the Trustees' ban, Beck asked the NJASRC for more information about their program and suggested that "Indiana University is interested in the program of education of the Japanese students in the United States." Despite that professed interest, Beck failed to secure the return of the Council's questionnaire by the IU administration.[73] After Beck failed to respond, the Council began to investigate other avenues. The NJASRC wrote to IU History professor Roger Shugg asking if he might "tactfully" secure the questionnaire's return and prepare administrators for "favorable acceptance."[74] Nestled within its extensive war coverage, the *IDS* featured a surprising call-to-action in its September 9 edition. Highlighting the challenges facing Japanese Americans and neighboring Earlham College's decision to admit Nisei, IU student Jean Johnson wrote that, "as yet, Indiana university has not taken action" and criticized the university's decision "to wait until called upon."[75]

By this time, outside organizations had begun to wonder how IU was dealing with the Nisei situation. Representatives of the University of Chicago's International House wrote Wells on July 22, inquiring about IU's policy.[76] Wells responded that "Indiana University, in common with most of the universities of the Middle West, can not adopt a policy . . . until an agency of the Federal Government is willing to be responsible for those students." He added that such students would require local police protection and that Bloomington would be unable to provide such protection.[77] In another instance, officials of the Indiana State Teachers College wrote IU's Registrar for more information; they received the original form letter drafted by Elliott in May, which had referred to the "uncertain military status of the southern Indiana geographical zone."[78]

Earlham College, a small, private, Quaker school 120 miles northeast of Bloomington, took a dramatically different approach to its Japanese American applicants, quickly accepting a half-dozen students over community protests. Earlham's president, W. C. Dennis, publicly advocated for Japanese Americans in an editorial that described the college's work as aligning "with the ideals for which we are fighting, and the principles of the religion which we profess." Dennis poignantly asked: "Is there any need to be forced to defend the enrollment of loyal American citizens in an American college?" Dennis later wrote directly to Wells about his work with the students.[79] In reply, Wells wrote that he "thoroughly agree[d]" with Earlham's actions and that "we want to have some of them here as soon as our local police officers are in a position to give them the protection demanded by the Federal Government." Historian Jenness Hall called this statement a "bald-faced lie" made only to be "politically correct" to keep IU on the "same moral high ground" as Earlham.[80]

The person most directly involved with the implementation of the ban was Frank Elliott, Director of Admissions since 1938. On September 14, 1942, a confused Elliott wrote Briscoe asking if the admission of Japanese students was still disapproved:

> You wrote me last April that we should admit them. Then on April 30 and May 6 you wrote that the Trustees would consider the question. Later I was advised that the Japs were not to be admitted. I so notified the various admitting offices on June 12. President Wells approved and initialed the following copy of a letter to go to Japanese applicants . . . We have sent this letter to all Japanese applicants since.
>
> Now Professor Cavanaugh writes that President Wells and you tell him that the barring of Japanese students must have been due to a "misunderstanding." He [Cavanaugh] has sent a "correction" to the Extension Center.
>
> . . .
>
> Beck wants the Japs here. He told me that he and a committee of students had been to see President Wells about changing the present regulation. This would seem good proof that *THERE IS A REGULATION* . . .
>
> Are we or are we not to continue to the regulation barring Japanese students?[81]

Although Wells had signed off on that rejection letter for Japanese American applicants, he had failed to inform Elliott of the Trustees' ban. Briscoe then met with Elliott and gave him the Board's specific action, but Elliott would continue to raise questions.[82] A month later, Elliott asked about "an epidemic of requests for admission by Japanese students" and requested "further specific instructions as to how these cases are to be handled" and asked if "the administration [had] something else to say to the Japanese students."[83]

On October 11, as part of a series of town hall discussions about various topics, the university community faced the issue of "Japanese in America." The event's organizers posed the question: "Should an American citizen of Japanese ancestry be deprived of his university education?" The *IDS* covered the issue in a handful of articles that appeared in the next week. On October 13, a news article described the "heated discussion" of the previous Sunday's town hall. The *IDS* reported that Sunao Miyabara had "described the democratic feeling prevailing among the Japanese in Hawaii" and that Frank Beck had argued that there "should be no discrimination against [Japanese Americans]." Few records of that meeting remain, but enough questions were left unanswered that the topic would be addressed again during the next town hall on October 18.[84] The *IDS* editorial board weighed in on October 14. They argued that students who thought that Japanese Americans should be excluded from IU were overlooking "a bulwark to democracy: logical thinking." The editorial continued to argue against anti-Japanese sentiment: "We cannot blame them for being Japanese. They were born with yellow skins, as we were born with white . . . we mustn't lose our heads in the case of hating our enemies. We should not exclude a chosen few from the periphery of the Japanese and condemn all that has any part of Japanese or any other aliens just because we happen to be warring with their patterns of living."[85] On Friday, the announcement for the upcoming Sunday town hall indicated that "Ernie Miyabara, sophomore, will explain the effect of the current problem of racial prejudice upon his people in Hawaii, and in the United States."[86]

During the October 18 event, the previous week's survey results were announced. Students who participated in the earlier town hall had polled members of the Bloomington community, the IU faculty, and the student body regarding the question: "Should an American citizen of Japanese ancestry be deprived of his university education?" The available results showed that thirty-six people believed that they should be allowed to continue their education, two were undecided, and fifteen believed they should be deprived. Students generally favored Japanese Americans' right to an education, reasoning that, "If it is ok with the F.B.I., it is ok with me" or simply that it was wrong to discriminate against a "racial group." On the other hand, some noted that they would not "want to live with them" or that Japanese Americans should wait until the war was over before trying to enroll. One felt that Nisei enrollment should be allowed in principle but that, because "you cannot absolutely know how a Japanese feels towards America," they should still be excluded. At least one student wrote that they wouldn't mind having a Japanese American for a roommate and others noted that it was a "constitutional right" and "they are as much American as us." Another argued, more pragmatically, that while it was a "swell idea," town opinion was too negative for it to work. One faculty member was "not in favor of granting them any privileges." Another, referring to the "apparent friendliness" of Japanese diplomats in the weeks leading up to the attack on Pearl Harbor, said students should be deprived of their educational privileges until after the war. Finally, a Bloomington housewife thought that the American government "ought to lock them all up."[87] The *IDS* concluded its series by noting that "a majority of the students polled answered 'yes' to the question of whether or not Japanese students who are American citizens should be deprived of their education."[88] The survey's aggregate results suggest that IU students were less open to their possible Japanese American peers than were midwestern college students at large. In a 1943 survey, 89 percent of midwestern college students reported that they would be happy to have occasional social contact with Nisei, 88 percent thought the Japanese Americans should be returned to prewar status, and 13 percent thought they should be excluded from the U.S. altogether.[89]

In December, History professor Albert Kohlmeier, a trusted faculty colleague of Wells, wrote to the NJASRC on the president's behalf explaining why IU would not participate:

> Inasmuch as our University is making an all-out effort to cooperate with the National Government in training and educating men and women for the armed forces, it would appear obvious that bringing some of these Japanese American students on to our campus would present us with a problem that would not be created in institutions that, because of their principles or for other reasons, would not have upon their campus men and women in uniform. Needless to say, we are in most hearty accord with your noble effort and we are sure that you appreciate our peculiar problem along with similar institutions. If, before the close of this academic year, we see any more favorable opportunity to assist you in the placing of some of these students, we will at once get in touch with you.[90]

Kohlmeier's "problem," that IU could not admit Japanese Americans while the campus also hosted military training programs, was a valid prima facie reason: IU did not have the necessary military clearance to do so.[91] Yet, as of the close of 1942, the Wells administration had not requested clearance nor replied to the NJASRC questionnaire. Even faced with what Admissions Director Elliott called "an epidemic" of Japanese American student applications, the administration failed to take any proactive steps to participate in the NJASRC program and gain military clearance.

In 1943, IU's trustees mentioned Japanese Americans only once.[92] Miyabara, IU's only Japanese American student, withdrew from his studies to serve in the military. Briscoe and Wells both accepted government assignments requiring them to spend extensive time off campus.[93] Finally, and perhaps most importantly to Wells and the trustees, roughly forty percent of the student body enrolled in Army and Navy training programs on campus in the fall.[94] The academic year was preoccupied with the war effort, not the cause of Japanese American students.

EDUCATION DENIED

In November 1943, Japanese Americans continued to apply to IU for admissions. By this time, some students who had independently secured leave clearances were able to apply to any institution they wished on the NJASRC's list of approved universities. Despite IU's absence from the list, one student—Sumiko Itoi—had her heart set on IU's nursing school. In April 1943, Itoi had received a gold badge in the nurses' aides program at the Minidoka (Idaho) Camp Hospital; she left for Indianapolis in July 1943.[95] In late October, Kate Hevner Mueller, IU's Dean of Women, received her plea for admission into IU's nursing school:

> I am a nineteen years old American of Japanese Ancestry who is greatly interested in applying for entrance into Indiana University for a year or so to take up a Pre-nursing Course. At the present, I am employed at the Medical Center, Robert Long Hospital in the Nursing Division. I am one of the millions of people who are engaged in an essential war industry and realize that I am contributing towards the welfare of those on the homefront. However, I feel as though I could do more if I could become trained for the profession that is so vital at this time. My parents are still at a War Relocation Authority Camp in Hunt, Idaho but are all for this plan of mine. I have a sister at Hanover College and a married brother who is a pre-med student in St. Louis, Missouri.
>
> I am residing at the home of Dr. and Mrs. John Ferguson of the Irvington Presbyterian church. You may write to him for any reference needed.
>
> Please understand that my father will provide financially but is very anxious to have me near my sister as possible. Therefore, I cannot look to other schools in the other states.
>
> I hope and trust in God that you will aid me in every possible way . . .
>
> P.S. I am pretty sure that I have all the academic subjects taken in high school which are required for College entrance.[96]

Itoi was IU's first known Hoosier Nisei applicant. Mueller wrote Wells asking for advice a few days later; he received the following response from the president's assistant, Robert Ittner: "We agree that nothing can be done at the present time about admitting this student to the University. We have not yet taken action to matriculate any AJA's [Americans of Japanese Ancestry]. I'll admit it does seem a bit strange that we employ such a person and yet do not permit her to become a student."[97]

Ittner encouraged Mueller to send a copy of Itoi's letter to Wells in the hopes the matter "would be again taken up." Mueller forwarded her response to Itoi's "very fine letter" to Wells, noting her "regret" at "our inability to take care of her request at present."[98] A penciled note, signed by Ittner, reads: "HBW thinks he told her that Jap Students from this state were admitted." Mueller's reply to Itoi was apologetic. She was, she wrote, "very sorry to send a discouraging reply to your very fine letter, and I am also sorry to have delayed in answering it." She noted that there were no arrangements for Japanese Americans to enroll at IU, stating that the university had "not received any applications" before Itoi's and encouraging her to look at other nursing schools.[99] The Wells administration would take no further action to admit Itoi.

After being denied admission from IU, Itoi joined the Cadet Nurse Corp at Adelphi College on Long Island, New York, on February 1, 1944, determined to "show the public that [Japanese Americans are] as much a part of the U.S. as anyone else." Isolated from her family, Itoi would not see her parents again until June 1944, when she visited her still incarcerated family in Minidoka, Idaho.[100] Itoi's separation from her sister and from her parents offers us a small glimpse of the personal impact of IU's exclusionary policies.

Writing on behalf of an unnamed "Japanese girl from Chicago," in December 1943, Mrs. Fred Scott of Jonesboro, Indiana, wrote IU asking for information on why a student who was qualified to enter IU with the intention of becoming a nurse was not allowed to do so, while "girls from Jonesboro are there." "Would it be too much trouble," Scott asked, "to explain this to me as the girl in question was so nice to me and looked in my own opinion so hurt. I have been unable to forget her."[101] Frank Elliott would respond on IU's behalf: "Since the outbreak of the war with Japan, Indiana University has not been accepting Japanese students . . . We are crowded for space for students of this state and for non-Japanese students from other states . . . to accept a Japanese girl from another state for nurses' training at this time would mean the exclusion of some Indiana girl."[102] This unnamed student would be at least the ninth rejected. The university would not find "space" for Japanese American girls—even those from Indiana—until after the end of the war.

The NJASRC had not forgotten about IU. Ruth Reimer, a graduate student representing the school's International Relations Club, wrote an update on the current campus climate, which was then forwarded to the NJASRC. Reimer had discovered that the Board of Trustees had "turned down the early applications of students for admission because such a 'flood' of them were received" at the beginning of the war. A dean she spoke with said that IU had "not taken any definite action to exclude students" and he thought that any applications received now would "be judged on the merits." Claiming inaccurately that "no applications have been received since the Spring of 1942," the dean suggested that the trustees might be willing to admit Japanese American students, but would not welcome them by asking the NJASRC for a favorable listing.[103] In his response, William Stevenson, who worked in the NJASRC Placement Department, informed Reimer that IU was listed as "uncleared," mentioning Kohlmeier's December 1942 explanation that IU was cooperating with the war effort and was unable to accept Japanese Americans. While Kohlmeier's reasoning had been valid at the time, Stevenson added, the "majority of the 410 colleges at which Japanese American students have been accepted are housing Army or Navy" units—units that even included, he pointed out, Japanese Americans. Finally, Stevenson mentioned a new clearance procedure with the Provost Marshal General's Office that would soon allow students to attend IU with only an extra background check instead of a broad institutional clearance.[104] With this letter, IU's claims of "military necessity"—so reminiscent of the government claims that had initially led to Japanese American incarceration—came under direct questioning by the NJASRC. By 1944, many IU officials were openly questioning why Japanese Americans could not be admitted. Ittner wrote to Wells about the "question of admission of a Japanese student to the extension center there in Indianapolis" and asked for a meeting:

> It seems . . . that the main reason for not granting such students admission to the campus, namely, their own protection, doesn't hold for Indianapolis. On the other hand, admission to the Extension Center should probably be interpreted as admission to the University; consequently, if the student would later wish to come to the campus, I do not see how he can be refused residence here. It seems to me that it is rather difficult from a logical point of view to designate the geographical portion of the University which such a student might attend. Even though the statement is made that the student knows he can not come to the campus it seems to me that some difficulty might arise. I might add that not so long ago we refused admission to our Nurses Training School to a Japanese girl.

In a handwritten note summarizing the resulting conversation with Wells on January 8, 1944, Ittner recounted: "Admission to a resident of Indiana cannot be denied. Policy referred to dealt only with those in relocation centers."[105] Wells had now revised the ban and created its first exception, but specifically banning all Japanese Americans in "relocation centers" raised new questions. Why were some Japanese Americans banned and others not? What justification did Wells see to deny education to incarcerated Japanese Americans?

Two weeks later, in response to a query from the Registrar of the University of Illinois, IU Registrar T. A. Cookson outlined exceptions to the university's exclusionary policies: one for Japanese Americans living in Indiana and the other for Extension Division students:

> On May 9, 1942 the Board of Trustees disapproved the admission of Japanese students. President Wells, I am told, believes we would have to make an exception of any Japanese who has qualified as a resident of the state, but no such case has come up. Our Extension Division will accept enrollments of Japanese Students. At present we do not have any Japanese students on campus.[106]

With IU now willing to admit Japanese Americans to its Extension Centers, the situation with the military continued to change rapidly. In January 1944, NJASRC officials informed IU that it was a listed institution. This new status meant that a "Personnel Security Questionnaire" (for American citizens) or "Alien Questionnaire" (for Japanese nationals) had to be filled out and approved by the Provost Marshal General before a Japanese American might attend or work at IU.[107] IU responded with an assurance that it would follow the regulations sent by NJASRC.[108] This process differed markedly from the situation beforehand. Instead of the military requiring institutional clearance, IU could seek approval for individual Japanese Americans after what amounted to a background check. The Provost Marshal General also created a procedure to lift these restrictions entirely if "certain classified activities" and Japanese American students could be kept separate on campus.[109] The NJASRC correspondingly asked IU for a map showing the location of these activities and inquired if this would be possible. Ittner responded simply by saying that it "is impossible to segregate some students from others."[110]

Wells brought the issue of Japanese American students before the trustees again in late January 1944. The trustees clarified their initial policy, ordering admissions officials not to exclude state residents and, in the case of one student wishing to re-enroll, to seek information "regarding his citizenship and recent history before making a decision."[111] When asked to clarify IU's policy by the

Indianapolis Rotary Club days later, university comptroller Ward Biddle wrote that only two non-Hoosier students per state could attend the School of Medicine and added that "the Board of Trustees has restricted citizens of Japanese descent living outside of the State. Any Japanese citizen of the State of Indiana, of course, has the right to come to Indiana University."[112]

In March, Admissions Director Elliott wrote all deans and administrative officers with an updated policy on applications:

> Applications from Japanese citizens of Indiana, former students of Indiana University, Extension students, and graduate students, should be considered on their individual merits. If a Japanese student, resident of the State of Indiana, is admissible or re-admissible under the normal regulations governing entrance to Indiana University, then he should be provided with a letter of provisional admission and should be referred to the office of the Provost Marshal General.[113]

Two weeks earlier, Elliott had met with Wells to discuss the case of "that Japanese student who requested re-admission." In response to the initial query (the identity of whose sender remains unclear), a penciled note reads: "Elliott to get together all of the data about the student . . . and then come in."[114] The confusion surrounding this policy was growing. Now, resident Nisei would be "considered on their individual merits" but non-residents would remain banned.

Ironically, that same week in March, President Wells gave a ringing endorsement to extend civil rights in his lay sermon at a local church:

> First we must prepare to renounce prejudice of color, class and race . . . Now this renunciation of class, color and race prejudice . . . where? In England? In China? In Palestine? No! We must renounce prejudice of color, class and race in Bloomington, Monroe County, Indiana. Our renunciation must be personally implemented by deeds. Our actions will be the measure of the sincerity of our words.[115]

The contradiction between Wells's ideals and the plight of Japanese American students is obvious. The campus administration, following the trustees' policy, would continue to exclude Japanese Americans from the opportunity to attend IU.

The updated policy did not help another crop of students who applied in May 1944. On May 9, 1944, Elliott wrote Wells about another "Japanese student whom [Earlham College] President Dennis is recommending for admission" and noted that before such a student could enroll that the NJASRC must be contacted to secure proper permissions.[116] Two other students applied through the NJASRC—meaning they were still incarcerated—to IU's School of Medicine and the School of Dentistry.[117] In one case, IU responded with the original denial letter drafted in May 1942.[118] On September 13, IU received a letter from the NJASRC stating it was no longer necessary to obtain approval for the employment or enrollment of Japanese Americans at IU.[119] With this act, in the NJASRC's words, Japanese American students were now to be accepted "on the same basis as any others . . . and all restrictions are now removed."[120] Two weeks later, Elliott confirmed his understanding that Indiana University no longer had to seek "approval from the Provost Marshal General for the employment or attendance of persons of Japanese ancestry at Indiana University." This letter was copied to a secretary who was asked to notify the employing heads of the university about the "removal of these restrictions on the employment of persons of Japanese ancestry." Elliott felt compelled to add, however, that despite the loosened restrictions on employment, "we are not admitting persons of Japanese ancestry as students."[121] With no further military justification or required approval from any outside agencies to enroll Nisei students at IU, Japanese Americans were now barred from enrollment due only to the trustees' action.

THE FIRST EXCEPTIONS

In May 1944, at the same time that IU's main campus was rejecting Nisei but before all restrictions were removed, R. E. Cavanaugh, Director of IU's Indianapolis Extension Center, wrote to the NJASRC that the center had tentatively accepted a married student living in Indianapolis and asked for approval subject to the Provost Marshal General regulation.[122] The NJASRC informed Cavanaugh that only the main campus of IU was on the "proscribed list" and the Extension Center required no such clearance. The NJASRC also gave Cavanaugh the name of another student who was interested in attending the Extension Center and offered any assistance to facilitate such an acceptance.[123] Cavanaugh responded to the NJASRC with a frank discussion of the situation at IU:

> It was the opinion of Dr. H. T. Briscoe, Dean of the Faculties of Indiana University, that there would be no objection to the admission of Japanese students to our extension centers since there were no student housing problems, no organizations of military groups and no special programs of instruction of military character under way. Your letter of May 9 seems to clear the situation completely according to present rulings and the result is confirmation of Dean Briscoe's opinion. We are glad to have your statement.

Cavanaugh also confirmed the enrollment of both students, noting that one was "a good student and a very satisfactory man" and both got "along well with other students."[124]

Still, Briscoe's idea that Japanese Americans and the military could not coexist was concerning. By mid-1944, the majority of colleges hosting Nisei also hosted military programs. In April, the trustees had even approved the establishment of a proposed Army Japanese-language training program, to be partially taught by Japanese Americans on campus.[125] Why did IU remain so reluctant to accept Japanese American students? Administrators certainly had a few theories. Elliott had previously written that a Nisei student would take the place of an "Indiana girl," a position seemingly reinforced by Briscoe's focus on "student" housing problems. In the abstract, this point seems at least plausible, but, in 1943, no more than twenty-five Nisei were enrolled at all Indiana colleges.[126] Briscoe and Elliott's argument, when IU could be expected to perhaps enroll at most twenty Japanese Americans, is especially strange given that some in Bloomington—including the YWCA and the International Relations Club—had even offered to help.[127]

As the war wound down, honorably discharged veterans began to apply or reapply to colleges. When two Japanese American veterans applied to IU in late 1944, IU faced a new challenge. Could IU reject veterans, who had honorably served their country, based only on their ancestry? On October 27, Pvt. James S. Nishimura, Company First Battalion, 442nd Infantry, of Honolulu, Hawaii, wrote IU seeking enrollment in the College of Arts and Sciences. Nishimura had been a student at the University of Hawaii until Pearl Harbor interrupted his studies and he joined the military. Nishimura was discharged at "Foster General Hospital, Jackson, Mississippi, as of June 22, 1944." Nishimura received a letter back from Elliott on November 20 which gave the following request: "Please be particular to state whether or not you are of Japanese nationality or ancestry."[128] A penciled note on his letter asks "Japanese?" and another note says "yes."[129] The second veteran, Motomu Musashi, who was still hospitalized, requested admission to IU under the "provisions of the G. I. Bill of Rights."[130]

On December 5, Briscoe wrote to Wells recommending that the issue of Japanese American veterans be presented to the Board of Trustees.[131] He attached a letter from Elliott which presented the cases of Musashi and Nishimura. Elliott also presented the case of Richard Doi, who was previously incarcerated with "the rest of people of Japanese Ancestry in my community" in Arkansas and had spent "more than two months" working in Cleveland. Doi noted that IU was "highly recommended to me by many of my friends and teachers."[132]

Elliott asked if the policy on Japanese Americans should be reconsidered "in view of the two new developments: (1) the fact that veterans are now among the Japanese applicants and (2) the fact that the Provost Marshal General has removed the former restrictions."[133]

On December 14, the Board of Trustees unanimously voted to approve the admission of Japanese American students who served and were honorably discharged from the armed forces. Present at the meeting were the same eight trustees who had voted for the ban in 1942.[134]

With this action, Doi was rejected, while Nishimura and Musashi were admitted; neither would enroll. Another student would soon be rejected. Donald Yamashiro, incarcerated at Heart Mountain, Wyoming, wrote IU asking for admission on January 30, 1945. The government had already rescinded the exclusion orders which prevented Japanese Americans from returning to the West Coast and began closing the camps, but Yamashiro was told that IU only admitted Japanese Americans who were legal residents of the state or honorably discharged veterans.[135] With all federal restrictions removed, these rejections were perhaps the worst. Why did Doi and Yamashiro's Japanese ancestry render them ineligible for admission? The ban remained in place and by the end of the 1945 spring term, at least thirteen students had been rejected—two veterans were admitted but did not enroll, and two Nisei were enrolled at IU's extension campus.

Japan surrendered on September 2, 1945. Three days later, Elliott wrote to Ittner asking "whether or not we should admit Japanese students." Elliott felt that IU should begin accepting students since "the war is over" and noted that an application was pending from Makoto Hayashi.[136] The next day, Ittner wrote to Wells and the Japanese American ban was added to the agenda for the next trustees meeting.[137] A few weeks later, Elliott consulted Wells about yet another applicant, Hiroshi Suzuki, who wanted to enroll at the School of Dentistry.[138]

The board met on September 20, 1945. Wells reopened the discussion of admissions, asking, "Shall American citizens of Japanese descent be admitted to Indiana University in any different manner than any other citizen of the United States?"[139] This time the Board of Trustees repealed its ban on Japanese American students, adding that "the admitting agencies of Indiana University are free to deal with the admission of American citizens of Japanese descent in the same manner and with the same safeguards as other students." Present at this meeting were five members who had voted for the ban in 1942.[140] Four days later, Wells passed the decision along to Elliott, writing simply that "The Board of Trustees . . . rescinded its action of May 9, 1942 to the effect that the Board disapproved the admission of Japanese students."[141] The ban that had lasted nearly three-and-a-half years had finally come to an end.[142]

Hayashi and Suzuki did not enroll at IU, and unfortunately the record is unclear regarding their decision; it was not until fall 1946—five years after Sunao Miyabara first enrolled at the university—that Japanese Americans again enrolled at Bloomington.[143]

REINTEGRATING THE UNIVERSITY: STUDENT STORIES

Ted Tsukiyama served with the U.S. Army's 442nd Regimental Combat Team and the Military Intelligence Service. In February 1946, he enrolled at the University of Hawaii, only to find that the campus's "hang-loose" lifestyle was holding back his studies. Looking towards the mainland, Tsukiyama befriended a professor at the University of Hawaii, Allan F. Saunders, who was a good friend of IU Professor of Government, Oliver P. Field. In his memoir, Tsukiyama described his acceptance as tenuous: "The IU Board of Regents was not ready to accept a student of Japanese ancestry, but Dr. Field interceded directly on my behalf with the university president."[144] With Field as his "unofficial guardian," Tsukiyama became, in his own words, the "only Japanese American in a student body of over fifteen thousand!" Living at Rogers Center, in what had been a cornfield, he noted that while he "never encountered discriminatory or unpleasant treatment," he noticed some anti-Jewish sentiment among other students. Ted found the "haole [white] people" to be the "nicest people in the world" once they got to know you and described his time at IU as "a most gratifying educational experience" in "sharp contrast to the backward South."[145] He was a member of the student body government and the YMCA, and participated in intramural sports.[146] Tsukiyama received his B.A. in Government in June 1947 before enrolling at Yale Law School.[147] He became a successful arbitration lawyer in Hawaii.

Kiyoshi Ota from Ogden, Utah, also enrolled in October 1946; Ota graduated in June 1948 with a B.A. in Psychology.[148] He was an active member of Photography Club, serving as the club's president in the 1947–1948 school year. Another veteran from the 442nd, Kiyoshi had received a Purple Heart in World War II and would go on to a long career with the U.S. Postal Service.[149]

Before admitting David Mitsugi Ohara, an IU official wrote to Graceland College, where Ohara was previously enrolled:

> We have received your transcript for David Mitsugi Ohara and note that he was born in Japan and is not yet an American citizen . . . The state of Indiana has practically no Japanese population . . . Indiana can accept only a few non-resident students and tries to select them very carefully. We wonder if you would be willing to give us your impression of Mr. Ohara and particularly indicate whether you think he would fit into our campus society.[150]

Ohara was admitted and he fit into "campus society" well, becoming the Campus Life Editor for the 1948 *Arbutus*. He graduated in June 1949 with a B.A. in English before receiving a Masters in English at the University of Pennsylvania in 1957.[151] Tsukiyama, Ota, and Ohara became the first Japanese American students at Bloomington after the ban alongside the two students at IU's extension campus.[152] Despite these signs of progress, not all was well for Nisei students at IU—in 1958, the trustees denied in-state status to a Japanese citizen who had previously lived in Indiana for six years.[153]

THE LEGACIES OF WILDERMUTH AND WELLS

The two administrators most responsible for IU's wartime policies regarding Japanese Americans were Board of Trustees president Ora L. Wildermuth and President Herman B Wells. Wildermuth's role in the Japanese American exclusion effort is particularly troubling. His white supremacist attitudes had shown themselves during the May 9, 1942, trustee meeting, when he argued that Germans and Italians could acceptably assimilate, while Japanese Americans were "different racially" and could not be "anything but a Japanese." Wildermuth's inability to see Japanese Americans as individuals heavily informed IU's policy, as his colleagues agreed to ban students of Japanese ancestry for three years. At the 1971 ceremony which renamed IU's fieldhouse as the Wildermuth Intramural Center (Wildermuth had been instrumental in the building's original construction), Wells, now serving as the first University Chancellor, spoke to the late judge's influence:

> An I.U. historian has pointed out that it was altogether fitting for the Board to be represented by Judge Wildermuth at the dedication of this fieldhouse, and it is particularly fitting now that the building be named for him. I knew Judge Wildermuth well . . . our close friendship continued as long as he lived.
>
> I am both pleased and gratified that from this day on the name of Wildermuth will be familiar to every student and that those who use this Center will pay tribute to its virtual founder through perpetuating his name.[154]

In 2007, a campus movement to rename the Wildermuth Intramural Center formed after an *IDS* editorial cited a 1945 letter to an IU administrator in which Wildermuth wrote: "I am and shall always remain absolutely and utterly opposed to social intermingling of the colored race with the white. I belong to the white race and shall remain loyal to it. It always has been the dominant and leading race."[155] IU trustees responded to the protest, first, by renaming the building the William L. Garrett-Ora L. Wildermuth Intramural Center in 2009.[156] Five days later, the trustees reversed their decision after learning of the Garrett family's opposition to the change.[157] The movement to recognize Garrett persisted with the dedication of an adjacent historical marker commemorating the athlete in 2017.[158] Then, on October 5, 2018, the Wildermuth Intramural Center was "de-named . . . [due to] historical documents linking the building's namesake to harmful attitudes regarding African-Americans, extraordinarily strong opposition to racial integration and animosity towards other groups including Japanese-Americans."[159]

Herman B Wells's attitudes, on the other hand, were characterized more by inaction than overt racism. Wells oversaw a bureaucracy that effectively executed a ban on Japanese Americans while also combating Indiana's Jim Crow policies and opening the campus to African American students. This incongruity seems like a bizarre oversight, but Wells's actions suggest otherwise. In 1942, whether unable to oppose Wildermuth or genuinely concerned with campus safety, Wells had worked to justify Wildermuth's racism. In May, speaking of "campus disturbances" and "the uncertain military status of the Southern Indiana geographical zone," Wells implied that IU would move to accept Japanese Americans once the situation improved—but Wells failed to act when presented with opportunities to improve the situation himself. In June, when the NJASRC asked Wells to return its questionnaire to meet the prerequisites for accepting Japanese Americans, he seems to have disregarded their request. That same month, when presented with a detailed report about the plight of Japanese Americans, Wells ignored the report's recommendations to "set an example of genuine Americanism by admitting some of the students by independent action."[160] Personally rejecting a Japanese American applicant in July, Wells wrote simply that "it is necessary to limit the number of admissions from other states," while he argued to another organization that IU could not accept Japanese Americans unless the federal government took responsibility for their safety. In August, when asked by a group of students to clarify IU's policy, Wells failed to mention the trustees' ban, arguing instead that the Army would have to give permission. In October, after being presented with neighboring Earlham College's acceptance of Nisei, Wells wrote: "We want to have some of them here as soon as our local police officers are in a position to give them the protection demanded by the Federal Government." Such protection was never secured.

As the war progressed and the national situation changed dramatically, Wells remained unwilling to act. In December 1943, when presented with an opportunity to admit a Japanese American applicant from Indianapolis, Wells allowed the rejection of the applicant although he suggested later that he thought he had said to admit the individual. In late January 1944, Wells explicitly asked the trustees to make an exception from their ban for Indiana Japanese Americans, but he stopped short of asking them to revoke the ban altogether. In September of that year, after receiving word that all military restrictions were removed from employment or enrollment, Wells still did not ask the trustees to end the campus ban. When presented with the applications of veterans in December 1944, Wells asked the trustees to make an exception only for honorably discharged Japanese Americans and explicitly rejected another pending application. It was not until the director of admissions called Wells, after the war ended in September 1945, that Wells asked the trustees to end this ban.

Perhaps Wells spent the war years trying to find a way to get around the ban without angering the trustees—his initial decision not to publicize the policy could have been a political one. But his administration failed to admit Japanese Americans during wartime and fell short of his own aspirations for civil rights.[161]

REDRESS ON COLLEGE CAMPUSES

In the 1980s, extensive lobbying from Japanese American political leaders motivated Congress to commission a report on wartime incarceration. In 1982, the report of the Commission on Wartime Relocation and Internment of Civilians, *Personal Justice Denied*, officially acknowledged the U.S. government's wrongdoing:

> All this was done despite the fact that not a single documented act of espionage, sabotage or fifth column activity was committed by an American citizen of Japanese ancestry or by a resident Japanese alien on the West Coast . . . The exclusion, removal and detention inflicted tremendous human cost . . . [including] the loss of liberty and the personal stigma of suspected disloyalty for thousands of people who knew themselves to be devoted to their country's cause and to its ideals but whose repeated protestations of loyalty were discounted . . . the wounds of the exclusion and detention have healed in some respects, but the scars of that experience remain, painfully real in the minds of those who lived through the suffering and deprivation of the camps . . . the promulgation of Executive Order 9066 was not justified by military necessity, and the decisions which followed from it—detention, ending detention and ending exclusion—were not driven by analysis of military conditions. The broad historical causes which shaped these decisions were race prejudice, war hysteria and a failure of political leadership.[162]

Based on the commission's findings, the federal government passed the Civil Liberties Act of 1988, granting reparations to surviving incarcerees as part of an official apology from the American people.[163] This apology allowed Japanese Americans to partially reclaim their place within American society and help in the healing process.[164] But the implicit charge that "they had not deserved their place in the educational system" remained part of the historical record both of West Coast institutions that denied them degrees and midwestern institutions that refused to admit them.[165]

In the 1990s, Nisei sought retroactive diplomas from the West Coast institutions from which they had been forced to withdraw in an effort to mitigate the injustice they suffered. Their stated goal was to "reclaim the ground from which they were expelled, to secure acknowledgement of their intellectual and social value as individuals," and, through an act which would bring the lessons of history alive, "imagine a different, more equitable future." They also hoped that the granting of retroactive degrees would require the participation of institutions and witnesses, thus acknowledging the work of Japanese Americans to prevent further injustice.[166]

The first institution to issue retroactive diplomas was the University of Washington (UW). In 2008, the university held an honorary ceremony which inducted Nisei into the university's class of 2008. The citation on the degree described the purpose of the ceremony and the meaning to its participants:

> Japanese American students at the University of Washington in 1941–42, whose lives were untimely interrupted, who were taken away, lifted from your homes and incarcerated for your Japanese ancestry, we come together this day to honor you and to confer upon you what rightly should have been yours decades ago.
>
> In the dim fog of war, the threads of fear and intolerance wove a clouded shroud. We gather to dissolve that shroud and enlighten.
>
> A trust was violated . . . We come together to restore. We acknowledge the injustice of the past, and we walk with you now into the future.
>
> For your courage, your grace, your magnanimity, for your remarkable achievements in the aftermath of what you endured, for your allegiance to your principles and your country, the University of Washington is proud to confer upon you the degree of Bachelor of Arts, honoris causa, nunc pro tunc.[167]

In the same year, the California State Assembly passed a bill sponsored by Assemblyman Warren Furutani which required public universities in California, including the University of California, to "confer an honorary degree upon each person. who was forced to leave his or her postsecondary studies" due to

Executive Order 9066.[168] The state of Oregon took the same approach.[169] As part of the retroactive diploma process, these institutions devoted, often for the first time, significant resources to identify former students and include them as alumni. These efforts at reconciliation and restoration chose a specific medium (retroactive diplomas to formally enrolled students) that made the extension of West Coast college redress to non-West Coast colleges difficult.

THE NISEI COLLEGE REDRESS PROJECT (NCRP)

For Nisei, post-secondary education represented both literal freedom from incarceration and, figuratively, the freedom to rejoin America. As one Nisei wrote of their experiences confined in the Santa Anita Assembly Center:

> Like the flickering flame of a candle my faith in this land of my birth almost dwindled after months of confinement . . . bitterness began to clutch my power of reasoning as I began to think that my Japanese face was the crime for which I was accused. How I prayed that somehow God would restore my faith in the nation that I loved . . . I was awarded a scholarship . . . which was the answer to my prayers.[170]

Few administrators answered these prayers. Instead they succumbed to military pressures, anti-Japanese community sentiment, and occasionally—as in the case of Wildermuth—their own base motivations. These non-West Coast institutions systematically denied education to Japanese Americans by retooling their bureaucracies to deny applications from all young Nisei. Administrators erased Japanese Americans from their deserved place in institutional archives and alumni rolls.

No large, non-West Coast institution has attempted to acknowledge or to apologize for its wartime actions excluding Japanese Americans. The stories of only a handful of non-West Coast institutions (primarily schools that accepted Nisei) have ever been told in detail.[171] Typically, institutions that denied education have failed to research their actions.[172] Universities could have followed another path. One public institution, the University of Nebraska, prominently admitted dozens of Nisei students during wartime with the strong backing of administrators and local religious leaders.[173]

The systematic denial of education to a class of people based only on their ancestors' place of birth is unjustifiable, and the cumulative denial of education to Japanese Americans was an injustice. To remedy these injustices, institutions ought to ask themselves a series of questions:

Does our institution understand how its past actions either challenged or perpetuated the racism Japanese Americans faced during wartime?

How would we respond today?

Should we act, as many West Coast institutions have, to seek reconciliation with the Japanese American community?

These questions are at the core of the mission of the Nisei College Redress Project (an initiative of the author) of which this paper is a part. By building contextualized institutional histories, and then drawing upon the lessons learned from the extension of redress to West Coast colleges, NCRP seeks to work directly with higher education administrators at eastern and midwestern colleges to understand how their institution's past actions affected the Japanese American community, to outline possible paths for reconciliation, and to invite reflection on how their processes may deny education to disadvantaged populations today.

In early 2018, Oberlin College in Ohio took on the challenge of addressing these questions head on. Oberlin hosted a travelling historical exhibit called "Courage and Compassion: Our Shared Story of the Japanese American World War II Experience" accompanied by "academic lectures, documentary film screenings, and talks by internment survivors." Interested alumni and students worked with Professor Renee Romano, as well as with the college archivist, an associate dean of Oberlin, and many others to create a project which contextualized the history of Oberlin and Japanese Americans as a unifying act. (For reference, Oberlin promptly accepted Nisei students during the Second World War, with one even serving as student body president in wartime.)[174] Beyond a simple factual remembering, Oberlin visibly worked to include Japanese American alumni.

—ʊʊ—

At Indiana University, Sumiko Itoi (who wanted to remain close to her sister), Richard Doi (who wanted to attend an institution highly recommended to him), and about a dozen others were denied admission not because of aptitude or academic qualifications, but because of their Japanese ancestry. Remembering this history perhaps is painful, but addressing it provides the foundation necessary for reconciliation. IU's *Golden Book*, an official registry of student veterans, now includes Sunao Miyabara, Ted Tsukiyama, and Kiyoshi Ota as a result of this research project.[175] A campus building named after Ora L. Wildermuth was recently renamed, in part due to the namesake's involvement in banning Japanese Americans, but the race-based rejections to IU's Japanese

American applicants stands uncorrected today. The next step should be the IU Board of Trustees' formal acknowledgement that their action of May 9, 1942, was an error.

Table 1 Enrollment of Nisei Students at Selected Universities

		1941	1943	1945
	Northwestern University	0	5	1
	University of Chicago	6	2	1
	University of Illinois	3	0	9
	Indiana University	2	0	0
Big Ten	Purdue University	4	4	5
	University of Iowa	5	0	2
	University of Michigan	15	3	22
	University of Minnesota	3	2	168
	Ohio State University	3	2	22
	University of Wisconsin	2	2	14
	DePauw University	0	2	0
	Earlham College	0	9	4
	Franklin College	0	0	1
	Hanover College	0	0	2
	Indiana Technical College	0	1	7
Indiana	Indiana Technological Institute	4	0	0
	Indiana University	2	0	0
	Manchester College	0	3	2
	Purdue University	4	4	5
	Saint Mary's College	0	2	3
	Tri-State College	3	1	0
	Valparaiso University	0	1	1

Statistics were compiled from a variety of sources and, while these are the most complete available, they do not include every student. For 1941, college registrars supplemented the Directory of Japanese and Nisei Students in the United States, Japanese Christian Association. For 1943, the Directory of American Students of Japanese Ancestry was compiled from the records of the National Japanese American Student Relocation Council. For 1945, the files of the Committee on Friendly Relations to Foreign Students was supplemented by information from community sponsors. See, Robert W. O'Brien, *The College Nisei* (1949).

ERIC LANGOWSKI is a 2018 graduate of Indiana University, graduate student at the University of Chicago, and board member of the Hoosier Chapter of the Japanese American Citizens League. This article originally appeared in volume 115, June 2019.

NOTES

1. Japanese Student Admission, Board of Trustees Transcript, May 10, 1942, Folder Japanese Students, 1941–1942, box 324, Indiana University President's Office Records, 1937–1962, C213, Indiana University Archives, Bloomington, Indiana. Editorial Note: Some of the primary sources regarding this topic contain racial epithets (i.e. "Jap") that we recognize as offensive today. We have included them in the context of this article to reflect the 1940s terminology used to refer to Nisei in the United States. The *Indiana Magazine of History* does not condone this language, but includes it in the interest of historical accuracy. For guidance on using primary sources of this period, see Japanese American Relocation Digital Archive at the University of California, online at https://calisphere.org/exhibitions/66/jarda-everyday-life/.

2. For high school figure see Thomas James, "'Life Begins with Freedom': The College Nisei, 1942–1945," *History of Education Quarterly* 25 (Spring-Summer 1985), 157. For college figure see Robert O'Brien, *The College Nisei* (Palo Alto, Cal., 1949), 135–37.

3. John H. Provinse, "Relocation of Japanese-American College Students: Acceptance of a Challenge," *Higher Education* 1 (April 16, 1945), 3. The best available figures suggest there were 3,530 students enrolled in college in 1941—1,493 students in 1943, and 2,870 in 1945. See O'Brien, *The College Nisei*, 135–49.

4. Frank Elliott to Mrs. Fred Scott, December 10, 1943, Folder Japanese Students, 1943–1944, box 324, Indiana University President's Office Records, 1937–1962, C213, Indiana University Archives.

5. John Bodnar defines the term "public memory" as "a body of beliefs and ideas about the past that help a public or society understand both its past, present, and by implication its future." John Bodnar, *Remaking America: Public Memory, Commemoration, and Patriotism in the Twentieth Century* (Princeton, N.J., 1992), 14–15.

6. "The Pacific coast must in time become either American or Mongolian. There is a vast hive from which Chinese immigrants may swarm . . . Upon the point of morals there is no Aryan or European race which is not far superior to the Chinese." *Report of the Joint Special Committee to Investigate Chinese Immigration* (Washington, D.C., 1877), v; Roger Daniels, *Concentration Camps U.S.A.: Japanese Americans and World War II* (New York, 1971), 4.

7. In California, home to the largest Japanese immigrant community, Americans of Japanese ancestry accounted for roughly two percent of state's residents. See Roger Daniels, *Asian America: Chinese and Japanese in the United States since 1850* (Seattle, Wash., 1990), 115.

8. Daniels, *Concentration Camps U.S.A.*, 5–7, 15; John Higham, *Strangers in the Land: Patterns of American Nativism, 1860–1925* (New Brunswick, N.J., 2002), 165.

9. Allan W. Austin, *From Concentration Camp to Campus: Japanese American Students and World War II* (Urbana, Ill., 2004), 5–6.

10. Most Nisei were born between 1918 and 1922 and came of legal age between 1939 and 1943. Daniels, *Asian America*, 155.

11. On December 15, 1941, Secretary of the Navy Frank Knox declared that Pearl Harbor was a result of "fifth column work." Greg Robinson, *A Tragedy of Democracy: Japanese Confinement in North America* (New York, 2009), 63.

12. *Final Report: Japanese Evacuation From the West Coast, 1942* (Washington D.C., 1943), 8–10; Arthur N. Feraru, "Public Opinion Polls on Japan," *Far Eastern Survey* 19, no. 10 (May 1950), 101–103.

13. Franklin D. Roosevelt, Press Conference Number 982, November 21,1944, in *Complete Presidential Press Conferences of Franklin D. Roosevelt*, vol. 24 (New York, 1973), 247–48.

14. The peak for Indiana was 81 residents in the 1920 Census. Nancy Nakano Conner, "Forming a Japanese American Community in Indiana, 1941–1990" (Master's thesis, Indiana University, Bloomington, 2005). In 1940, nearly half of Indiana counties had only white or black citizens; Japanese Americans were concentrated in larger cities like Gary, Indianapolis, and South Bend. Justin H. Libby, "Japanese," in *Peopling Indiana: The Ethnic Experience*, eds. Robert M. Taylor Jr. and Connie A. McBirney (Indianapolis, Ind., 1996), 301–302.

15. "Clamp Down Now on Our Japs," *Muncie Evening Press*, February 18, 1942.

16. Libby, *Peopling Indiana*, 302.

17. For a sense of the relative size of Indiana's resettlement effort, compare the statewide numbers to the 3,000 individuals who settled in the city of Cleveland, Ohio. For further discussion regarding efforts to keep Japanese American resettlement out of Indiana see Nancy Nakano Conner, "From Internment to Indiana: Japanese Americans, the War Relocation Authority, the Disciples of Christ, and Citizen Committees in Indianapolis," *Indiana Magazine of History* 102 (June 2006), 100–101, 108–109, 113.

18. Frank Orman Beck, *Some Aspects of Race Relations at Indiana University: My Alma Mater* (Bloomington, Ind., 1959), 31, online at Hathi Trust, https://babel.hathitrust.org/cgi/pt?id=uiug.30112117747904; James Capshew, *Herman B Wells: The Promise of the American University* (Bloomington, Ind., 2012), 16.

19. In Wells's inauguration speech, he quoted John Dewey ("Democracy has to be born anew every generation, and education is the midwife") and called on

IU to be a leader of democracy which derived its authority from reason instead of position. Capshew, *Herman B Wells*, 131, 138.

20. Ibid., 167–68, 171.

21. Beck, *Some Aspects of Race Relations at Indiana University*, 37, 49.

22. Robert Allen Lowe, "Racial Segregation in Indiana, 1920–1950," (PhD Dissertation, Ball State University, 1965), 9–10; Emma Lou Thornbrough, "African Americans," in *Peopling Indiana*, 21, 29–30.

23. Indiana was also the last state in the North to have a lynching (1930), end school segregation (1949), and repeal anti-miscegenation laws (1965). Lowe, "Racial segregation in Indiana, 1920–1950," 8.

24. Office of Admissions Report for the year ending September 30, 1942, Folder 1938–1944, box 1, Series: Admissions Reports 1938–1971, Indiana University Office of Records and Admissions Director's records, 1938–1971, C98, Indiana University Archives.

25. Ichinomiya had a poetic flare to his take of IU: "American air can be found in all the atmosphere where creature can penetrate; her influence her wonderful power the wonderful nation which I name, has full of wealth." *Arbutus* (1903), 194–96.

26. Miyakawa was the first Japanese American admitted to the bar of an unidentified state. This information could not be verified beyond unsubstantiated newspaper reports. "Masuji Miyakawa" (1870), *Notable Alumni*, 22, https://www.repository.law.indiana.edu/notablealumni/22.

27. Otis D. Richardson, "Nisei Evacuees—Their Challenge to Education," *Junior College Journal* 13 (1942–43), 6–12; "Relocating Japanese American Students," *Education for Victory* 1, no. 14 (1942), 2, 24.

28. President Franklin D. Roosevelt to Governor Culbert L. Olson, May 18, 1942, Japanese American Relocation Collection, Occidental College Library, Los Angeles, California, online at https://oac.cdlib.org/ark:/13030/kt8p30376q/?brand=oac4 (hereafter Japanese American Relocation Collection).

29. Jenness Evaline Hall, "Japanese American College Students during the Second World War" (PhD Dissertation, Indiana University, Bloomington, 1993), 73, 169.

30. Ibid., 76.

31. O'Brien, *The College Nisei*, 135–37; Robinson, *A Tragedy of Democracy*, 181.

32. Allan W. Austin, *From Concentration Camps: Japanese American Students and World War II* (Urbana, Ill., 2004), 26; Daniels, *Concentration Camps U.S.A.*, 97; Robinson, *A Tragedy of Democracy*, 181.

33. The NJASRC also "favored dispersal" and called on Nisei to serve as "ambassadors of goodwill" when resettled. Austin, *From Concentration Camps*, 2, 133.

34. Hall, "Japanese American College Students during the Second World War," 201–205.

35. Provinse, "Relocation of Japanese-American College Students," 3.

36. Austin, *From Concentration Camps*, 55.

37. Margaret Cosgrave, "Relocation of American-Japanese Students," *Journal of the American Association of Collegiate Registrars* 18 (April 1943), 222.

38. Austin, *From Concentration Camps*, 46.

39. The largest concentration of colleges in the Midwest was in Ohio and included Antioch College, Bluffton University, Denison University, Heidelberg University, Kenyon College, Oberlin College, Ohio Wesleyan, Otterbein University, and College of Wooster. Colleges in Indiana included DePauw, Earlham, and Manchester. Minnesota included Macalester and Carleton, while Missouri included Park University, and lastly Kalamazoo College in Michigan. Hall, "Japanese American College Students during the Second World War," 219.

40. James, "'Life Begins with Freedom': The College Nisei, 1942–1945," 160; Cosgrave, "Relocation of American-Japanese Students," 223.

41. Austin, *From Concentration Camps*, 96.

42. James, "'Life Begins with Freedom': The College Nisei, 1942–1945," 166.

43. Ibid., 170–71.

44. Austin, *From Concentration Camps*, 152.

45. Hall, "Japanese American College Students during the Second World War," 271.

46. Ibid., 276.

47. Provinse, "Relocation of Japanese-American College Students," 3; James, "'Life Begins with Freedom': The College Nisei, 1942–1945," 157.

48. F. M. McWhirter to Thomas A. Cookson, October 17, 1941, Folder United States Naval Intelligence Service, box 561, Indiana University President's Office Records, 1937–1962, C213, Indiana University Archives. In his letter, McWhirter also asked for "full name, date and place of birth, parents, previous schools attended, employment, date and place of entrance into this country, etc., and any personal knowledge or comment you can give regarding the student" and secrecy ("this information should be from your records and personal knowledge without contacting the student").

49. Charles E. Harrell to F. M. McWhirter, October 31, 1941, Folder United States Naval Intelligence Service, box 561, Indiana University President's Office Records, 1937–1962, C213, Indiana University Archives.

50. Sara Fox, Indiana University Office of the Registrar, email to John Summerlot, Director of the Center for Veteran and Military Students at Indiana University, May 31, 2018; "Sunao Miyabara," *Honolulu Star Advertiser*, August 27, 2010.

51. A month after Coffey's letter, the University of Minnesota decided to "not accept Japanese students pending formulation of a policy by the Federal government." Coffey wrote to officials in Washington and advocated for a federal

agency to formulate a nationwide plan—after which Minnesota would gladly participate—instead of a blanket ban on Japanese Americans. Walter C. Coffey to Herman B Wells, March 18, 1942, Folder Japanese Students, 1941–1942, box 324, Indiana University President's Office Records, 1937–1962, C213, Indiana University Archives; Walter Coffey to Fred J. Kelly April 8, 1942, Folder Japanese Students, 1941–1942, box 324, C213, Indiana University Archives; Associated Press, "Minnesota U. Refuses to Accept Jap Students," April 26, 1942; W. C. Coffey, *Minnesota Alumni Weekly,* June 6, 1942.

52. Briscoe also wrote that IU has "never been overly anxious to add enemy aliens to our staff . . . when United States' citizens of equal qualifications are available." Herman T. Briscoe to Walter Coffey, March 23, 1942, Folder Japanese Students, 1941–1942, box 324, Indiana University President's Office Records, 1937–1962, C213, Indiana University Archives.

53. Wells was "glad to aid" and had "three refugees" attending IU. Herman B Wells to Frank Beck, September 8, 1942, Folder Student Refugee Committee, 1942–1943, box 7, Frank O. and Daisy Beck Papers, 1890–1969, C168, Indiana University Archives; Admissions report for the year ending September 30, 1942, Folder 1938–1944, box 1, Indiana University Office of Records and Admissions Director's Records, 1938–1971, Indiana University Archives.

54. Administrative Council Meeting Minutes, April 29, 1942, Folder Administrative Council Minutes, 1942–1951, box 5, Indiana University President's Office Records, 1937–1962, C213, Indiana University Archives.

55. Sanford S. Elberg to Dr. McClung, April 30, 1942, Folder Japanese Students 1941–1942, box 324, Indiana University President's Office Records, 1937–1962, C213, Indiana University Archives; Frank Elliott to Herman T. Briscoe, Folder Elliott, Frank R. (Admissions), 1942–1943, box 4, Indiana University Vice President and Dean of the Faculties Records, 1940–1959, C26, Indiana University Archives.

56. The following were present at the meeting: Ora L. Wildermuth, President of the Board; Nellie Showers Teter, Trustee; Paul L. Feltus, Trustee; William A. Kunkel Jr., Trustee; John S. Hastings, Trustee; J. Dwight Peterson, Trustee; Uz McMurtrie, Trustee; Frank E. Allen, Trustee; Herman B Wells, President of Indiana University; Ward G. Biddle, Secretary of the Board; and Herman T. Briscoe, Dean of the Faculties.

57. Japanese Student Admission, Board of Trustees Transcript, May 10, 1942, Folder Japanese Students, 1941–1942, box 324, Indiana University President's Office Records, 1937–1962, C213, Indiana University Archives. For biographical information regarding the trustees, see Burton Dorr Myers, *Trustees and Officers of Indiana University, 1820 to 1950* (Bloomington, Ind., 1951), 375, 381–85, 421–27; Capshew, *Herman B Wells,* 95.

58. Japanese Student Admission, Board of Trustees Transcript, May 10, 1942, Folder Japanese Students, 1941–1942, box 324, Indiana University President's Office Records, 1937–1962, C213, Indiana University Archives.

59. Hall, "Japanese American College Students during the Second World War," 156–57; Austin, *From Concentration Camps*, 148.

60. Frank Elliott to Herman B Wells, May 11, 1942, Folder Elliott, Frank R., 1941–1942, box 182, Indiana University President's Office Records, 1937–1962, C213, Indiana University Archives.

61. Herman T. Briscoe to Frank Elliott, May 18, 1942, Folder Elliott, Frank R. (Admission), 1942–1943, box 4, Indiana University Vice President and Dean of the Faculties records, 1940–1959, C26, Indiana University Archives.

62. Clarence E. Oliver to Herman B Wells, June 5, 1942, Folder Ol-1941–1942, box 428, Indiana University President's Office Records, 1937–1962, C213, Indiana University Archives; H. D. Bollinger to Herman B Wells, June 29, 1942, Folder Methodist Church, 1942–1943, box 384, Indiana University President's Office Records, 1937–1962, C213, Indiana University Archives.

63. Merrill B. McFall to Herman B Wells, July 2, 1942, Folder Methodist Church, 1942–1943, box 384, Indiana University President's Office Records, 1937–1962, C213, Indiana University Archives.

64. Herman B Wells to H. D. Bollinger, July 20, 1942, Folder Methodist Church, 1942–1943, box 384, Indiana University President's Office Records, 1937–1962, C213, Indiana University Archives.

65. Charles L. Lundin to Herman B Wells, June 9, 1942, Folder Lundin, Charles L, 1937–1943, box 360, Indiana University President's Office Records, 1937–1962, C213, Indiana University Archives.

66. Robbins W. Barstow to Herman B Wells, June 17, 1942, Folder National Japanese American Student Relocation Council, 1942–1944, box 409, Indiana University President's Office Records, 1937–1962, C213, Indiana University Archives.

67. Frank Beck to American Friends Service Committee, July 6, 1942, Folder "Indiana University, Bloomington, Indiana," box 67, National Japanese American Student Relocation Council records, 1942–1946, Hoover Institution Archives, Stanford University, Stanford, California (hereafter, National Japanese American Student Relocation Council Records).

68. Naomi Binford to Frank Beck, July 7, 1942, Folder "Indiana University, Bloomington, Indiana," box 67, National Japanese American Student Relocation Council Records.

69. SRC Meeting Notes, July 12, 1942, Folder Bound Minute Book, 1940–1948, p. 2, box 1, Indiana University Student Religious Cabinet records, 1938–1951, C430, Indiana University Archives.

70. SRC Meeting Notes, August 9, 1942, Folder Bound Minute Book, 1940–1948, p. 1, box 1, Indiana University Student Religious Cabinet records, 1938–1951, C430, Indiana University Archives.

71. "I.U. Asked to Admit Evacuated Students," *Indiana Daily Student*, July 29, 1942.

72. Frank Beck to Herman B Wells, July 25, 1942, Folder Beck, Dr. Frank O., 1942–1943, box 66, Indiana University President's Office Records, 1937–1962, C213, Indiana University Archives.

73. Frank Beck to Dr. Smith, August 10, 1942; Barstow to Beck, August 14, 1942; Howard K. Beale to Frank Beck, September 25, 1942; all are located in Folder "Indiana University, Bloomington, Indiana," box 67, National Japanese American Student Relocation Council Records.

74. Howard K. Beale to Roger Shugg, September 25, 1942, Folder "Indiana University, Bloomington, Indiana," box 67, National Japanese American Student Relocation Council Records. One questionnaire was returned from IU, but it was from the General Secretary of IU's Young Women's Christian Association (YWCA), Joanne M. Fox. Citing the Trustees' ruling that Bloomington is in a "defense area," Fox stated that the YWCA would be willing to "cooperate if students can be admitted." The NJASRC classified IU as "unfavorable" based on this questionnaire and this classification would not change throughout the war. Questionnaire Japanese-American Student Relocation, May 13, 1942, Folder "Indiana University, Bloomington, Indiana," box 67, National Japanese American Student Relocation Council Records.

75. "Students Without School," *Indiana Daily Student*, September 9, 1942.

76. Charles A. Rovetta to Herman B Wells, July 22, 1942, Folder Ro-, 1942–1943, box 476, Indiana University President's Office Records, 1937–1962, C213, Indiana University Archives.

77. Herman B Wells to Charles Rovetta, July 28, 1942, Folder Ro-, 1942–1943, box 476, Indiana University President's Office Records, 1937–1962, C213, Indiana University Archives.

78. J. E. Grinnell to T. A. Cookson, November 11, 1942, Folder Indiana State Teachers College, 1942–43, box 304, Indiana University President's Office Records, 1937–1962, C213, Indiana University Archives; T. A. Cookson to J. E. Grinnell, November 18, 1942, Folder Indiana State Teachers College, 1942–43, box 304, Indiana University President's Office Records, 1937–1962, C213, Indiana University Archives.

79. William Cullen Dennis to Herman B Wells October 17, 1942, Folder Earlham College, 1942–1943, box 176, Indiana University President's Office Records, 1937–1962, C213, Indiana University Archives.

80. Herman B Wells to William Cullen Dennis, October 20, 1942, Folder Earlham College, 1942–1943, box 176, Indiana University President's Office Records,

1937–1962, C213, Indiana University Archives; Hall, "Japanese American College Students during the Second World War," 238–39.

81. Frank Elliott to Herman T. Briscoe, September 14, 1942, Folder Elliott, Frank R. (Admissions) (Restricted), box 4, Indiana University Vice President and Dean of the Faculties Records, 1940–1959, C26, Indiana University Archives.

82. Ibid.

83. Frank Elliott to Herman T. Briscoe, October 13, 1942, Folder Administrative Council Minutes, 1942–1943, box 5, Indiana University President's Office Records, 1937–1962, C213, Indiana University Archives.

84. "Situation of Japanese-Americans Considered at Town Hall Meeting," *Indiana Daily Student*, October 13, 1942.

85. "Japanese Controversy," *Indiana Daily Student*, October 14, 1942.

86. "'Japanese in America' Is Town Hall Subject," *Indiana Daily Student*, October 16, 1942.

87. Town Hall survey week of October 11, 1942, Folder Japanese Student Relocation, 1942, box 6, Frank O. and Daisy Beck Papers, 1890–1969, C168, Indiana University Archives.

88. "Town Hall Discusses 'Japanese in America,'" *Indiana Daily Student*, October 20, 1942.

89. Leonard Bloom and Ruth Riemer, "Attitudes of College Students Towards Japanese-Americans," *Sociometry* 8, no. 2 (1945), 157–73.

90. A. L. Kohlmeier to John W. Nason, December 16, 1942, Folder Japanese Students, 1942–1943, Box 324, Indiana University President's Office Records, 1937–1962, C213, Indiana University Archives.

91. Memo from War Relocation Authority, December 30, 1942, Folder "Indiana University, Bloomington, Indiana," box 67, National Japanese American Student Relocation Council Records.

92. Minutes of the Board of Trustees of Indiana University, 30 March 1943–31 March 1943, Folder 30–31 March 1943, box 13, Indiana University Board of Trustees Minutes, 1835–1859, 1883–2017, C218, Indiana University Archives.

93. Capshew, *Herman B Wells*, 152–53.

94. V. R. Cardozier, *College and Universities in World War II* (Westport, Conn., 1993), 116.

95. *Minidoka Irrigator*, April 17, July 17, and July 31, 1943.

96. Sumiko Itoi to Kate Hevner Mueller, October 29, 1943, Folder Japanese Students, 1943–1944, box 324, Indiana University President's Office Records, 1937–1962, C213, Indiana University Archives.

97. Kate Hevner Mueller to Herman B Wells, November 3, 1943, Folder Japanese Students, 1943–1944, box 324, Indiana University President's Office Records, 1937–1962, C213, Indiana University Archives.

98. Robert T. Ittner to Kate H. Mueller, November 6, 1943, Folder Japanese Students, 1943–1944, box 324, Indiana University President's Office Records, 1937–1962, C213, Indiana University Archives.

99. Kate Hevner Mueller to Herman B Wells, November 10, 1943, Folder Japanese Students, 1943–1944, box 324, Indiana University President's Office Records, 1937–1962, C213, Indiana University Archives.

100. "Cadet Sammy Itoi Here from NY on first leave," *Minidoka Irrigator*, June 10, 1944.

101. Mrs. Fred Scott to IU, December 6, 1943, Folder Japanese Students, 1943–1944, box 324, Indiana University President's Office Records, 1937–1962, C213, Indiana University Archives.

102. Frank Elliott to Mrs. Fred Scott, December 10, 1943, Folder Japanese Students, 1943–1944, box 324, Indiana University President's Office Records, 1937–1962, C213, Indiana University Archives.

103. Walt Godfrey to William C. Stevenson, November 29, 1943, Folder "Indiana University, Bloomington, Indiana," box 67, National Japanese American Student Relocation Council Records.

104. William C. Stevenson to Ruth Reimer, December 8, 1943, Folder "Indiana University, Bloomington, Indiana," box 67, National Japanese American Student Relocation Council Records.

105. Memo from Bob Ittner to Herman B Wells, January 7, 1944, Folder Japanese Students, 1943–1944, box 324, Indiana University President's Office Records, 1937–1962, C213, Indiana University Archives.

106. G. P. Tuttle to T. A. Cookson, January 8, 1944, Folder Illinois University, Urbana, 1943–1944, box 286, Indiana University President's Office Records, 1937–1962, C213, Indiana University Archives; T. A. Cookson to G. P. Tuttle, January 18, 1944, Folder Japanese Students, 1943–1944, box 324, Indiana University President's Office Records, 1937–1962, C213, Indiana University Archives.

107. C. V. Hibbard to Herman B Wells, January 19, 1944, Folder Japanese students, 1943–1944, box 324, Indiana University President's Office Records, 1937–1962, C213, Indiana University Archives; Memo from Alton C. Miller, January 3, 1944, Folder Japanese Students, 1943–1944, box 324, Indiana University President's Office Records, 1937–1962, C213, Indiana University Archives.

108. Robert T. Ittner to C. V. Hibbard, February 10, 1944, Folder Japanese Students, 1943–1944, box 324, Indiana University President's Office Records, 1937–1962, C213, Indiana University Archives.

109. C. V. Hibbard to Thomas A. Cookson, February 19, 1944, Folder "Indiana University, Bloomington, Indiana," box 67, National Japanese American Student Relocation Council Records.

110. Robert T. Ittner to C. V. Hibbard, March 31, 1944, Folder Japanese Students, 1943–1944, box 324, Indiana University President's Office Records, 1937–1962, C213, Indiana University Archives.

111. It is unclear what happened to the student's application, but as it is never mentioned again by the Trustees the student was likely denied admission. Minutes of the Board of Trustees of Indiana University, 28 January 1944–30 January 1944, Folder 28–30 January 1944, box 13, Indiana University Board of Trustees Minutes, 1835–1859, 1883–2017, C218, Indiana University Archives.

112. Wilbur T. Gruber to Ward G. Biddle, February 3, 1944, Folder Japanese Students, 1944–1945, box 324, Indiana University President's Office Records, 1937–1962, C213, Indiana University Archives; Ward G. Biddle to Wilbur T. Gruber, February 10, 1944, Folder Japanese Students, 1944–1945, box 324, Indiana University President's Office Records, 1937–1962, C213, Indiana University Archives.

113. Frank Elliott to Deans and Administrative Officers, March 25, 1944, Folder Elliott, Frank R. (Restricted), 1943–1944, box 7, Indiana University Vice President and Dean of the Faculties Records, 1940–1959, C26, Indiana University Archives.

114. Memo to Herman B Wells, March 10, 1944, Folder Japanese Students, 1943–1944, box 324, Indiana University President's Office Records, 1937–1962, C213, Indiana University Archives.

115. Memo to Herman B Wells, March 10, 1944, Folder Japanese Students, 1943–1944, box 324, Indiana University President's Office Records, 1937–1962, C213, Indiana University Archives.

116. Frank Elliott to Herman B Wells, May 9, 1944, Folder Japanese Students, 1943–1944, box 324, Indiana University President's Office Records, 1937–1962, C213, Indiana University Archives.

117. C. H. McCaskey to The National Japanese American Student Relocation Council, February 28, 1944, Folder "Indiana University, Bloomington, Indiana," box 67, National Japanese American Student Relocation Council Records; W. J. Emlen to William H. Crawford, March 24, 1944, Folder "Indiana University, Bloomington, Indiana," box 67, National Japanese American Student Relocation Council Records.

118. The Hoover Institution, home of the NJASRC archive, requires student's names to be redacted. William H. Crawford to redacted name, March 20, 1944, Folder "Indiana University, Bloomington, Indiana," box 67, National Japanese American Student Relocation Council Records.

119. Memo to Frank Elliott, September 13, 1944, Folder Japanese Students, 1944–1945, box 324, Indiana University President's Office Records, 1937–1962, C213, Indiana University Archives.

120. Austin, *From Concentration Camps*, 130.

121. Frank Elliott to Ann Hartley, September 25, 1944, Folder Japanese Students, 1944–1945, box 324, Indiana University President's Office Records, 1937–1962, C213, Indiana University Archives.

122. R. E. Cavanaugh to C. V. Hibbard, May 5, 1944, Folder "Indiana University, Bloomington, Indiana," box 67, National Japanese American Student Relocation Council Records.

123. W. J. Emlen to Gertrude Heberlein, May 9, 1944, Folder "Indiana University, Bloomington, Indiana," box 67, National Japanese American Student Relocation Council Records.

124. R. E. Cavanaugh to W. J. Emlen, May 15, 1944, Folder "Indiana University, Bloomington, Indiana," box 67, National Japanese American Student Relocation Council Records.

125. The April 1, 1944, trustees meeting included the proposal on the agenda. The Army proposed that a Japanese-language military training unit be established at IU to train 125 officers, with IU teachers alongside "eight Japanese-American informants." E. Ross Bartley, the director of university relations, felt that this would be permissible "from the standpoint of the state." The Trustees approved the Army proposal with Trustees Teter and Feltus voting against. The Army would eventually cancel its plan and the school would not be established. Minutes of the Board of Trustees of Indiana University, 01 April 1944, Folder 1 April 1944, box 13, Indiana University Board of Trustees Minutes, 1835–1859, 1883–2017, C218, Indiana University Archives.

126. See Table 1.

127. Questionnaire Japanese-American Student Relocation, May 13, 1942, Folder "Indiana University, Bloomington, Indiana," box 67, National Japanese American Student Relocation Council Records. For International Relations Club, see Walt Godfrey to William C. Stevenson, November 29, 1943, Folder "Indiana University, Bloomington, Indiana," box 67, National Japanese American Student Relocation Council Records.

128. Frank Elliott to James S. Nishimura, November 20, 1944, Folder Japanese Students, 1944–1945, box 324, Indiana University President's Office Records, 1937–1962, C213, Indiana University Archives.

129. James S. Nishimura to Director of Admissions, October 27, 1944, Folder Japanese Students, 1944–1945, box 324, Indiana University President's Office Records, 1937–1962, C213, Indiana University Archives.

130. Raymond D. Ewing to Indiana University, November 17, 1944, Folder Japanese Students, 1944–1945, box 324, Indiana University President's Office Records, 1937–1962, C213, Indiana University Archives.

131. Herman T. Briscoe to Herman B Wells, December 5, 1944, Folder Japanese Students, 1944–1945, box 324, Indiana University President's Office Records, 1937–1962, C213, Indiana University Archives.

132. Richard Doi to H. L. Smith, November 20, 1944, Folder Japanese Students, 1944–1945, box 324, Indiana University President's Office Records, 1937–1962, C213, Indiana University Archives.

133. Frank Elliott to Herman T. Briscoe, December 4, 1944, Folder Japanese Students, 1944–1945, box 324, Indiana University President's Office Records, 1937–1962, C213, Indiana University Archives.

134. Trustees at this meeting were Wildermuth, Feltus, Teter, Kunkel Jr., McMurtrie, Allen, Peterson, and Hastings, who all voted for the ban in 1942. Minutes of the Board of Trustees of Indiana University, 13 December 1944–14 December 1944, Folder 13–14 December 1944, box 14, Indiana University Board of Trustees Minutes, 1835–1859, 1883–2017, C218, Indiana University Archives.

135. William H. Strain to Donald Yamashiro, February 8, 1945, Folder Japanese Students, 1944–1945, box 324, Indiana University President's Office Records, 1937–1962, C213, Indiana University Archives.

136. Frank Elliott to Robert Ittner, September 5, 1945, Folder Japanese Students, 1945–1947, box 324, Indiana University President's Office Records, 1937–1962, C213, Indiana University Archives.

137. Robert Ittner to Herman B Wells, September 6, 1945, Folder Japanese Students, 1945–1947, box 324, Indiana University President's Office Records, 1937–1962, C213, Indiana University Archives.

138. President's Office Memo on Frank Elliott Phone Call, September 19, 1945, Folder Japanese Students, 1945–1947, box 324, Indiana University President's Office Records, 1937–1962, C213, Indiana University Archives.

139. President's Report to the Board of Trustees, Folder September 20–21, 1945, Box 16 President's Reports, Volume 43, 1945–1946, C654, Presidents' Reports to the Indiana University Board of Trustees, 1881–1947, Indiana University Archives.

140. Trustees at this meeting were Wildermuth, Feltus, Kunkel Jr., Allen, and Hastings (who had voted for the ban in 1942) and Trustees Mary Rieman. Trustees Mary Rieman Maurer, C. Walter McCarty, and George W. Henley (not on the board in 1942). Minutes of the Board of Trustees of Indiana University, 20 September 1945–21 September 1945, Folder 20–21 September 1945, box 14, Indiana University Board of Trustees Minutes, 1835–1859, 1883–2017, C218, Indiana University Archives.

141. Herman B Wells to Frank Elliott, September 24, 1945, Japanese Students, 1945–1947, box 324, Indiana University President's Office Records, 1937–1962, C213, Indiana University Archives.

142. Elliott would not receive the updated policy until September 24, 1945.

143. Sara Fox, Indiana University Office of the Registrar, email to John Summerlot, Director of the Center for Veteran and Military Students at Indiana University, May 31, 2018.

144. Field did directly write to Wells about Tsukiyama; Wells wrote back that he would be happy to meet with the student, but it is unclear if such a meeting ever took place. Oliver Fields to Herman B Wells, undated memo, Folder Field,

Oliver, 1946–1947, box 206, Indiana University President's Office Records, 1937–1962, C213, Indiana University Archives; Herman B Wells to Oliver Fields, September 13, 1946, Folder Field, Oliver, 1946–1947, box 206, Indiana University President's Office Records, 1937–1962, C213, Indiana University Archives.

145. Ted Tsukiyama, *My Life's Journey: A Memoir* (Honolulu, Hawaii, 2017), 94–98.

146. *Arbutus* (1946).

147. Sara Fox, Indiana University Office of the Registrar, email to John Summerlot, Director of the Center for Veteran and Military Students at Indiana University, May 31, 2018.

148. Sara Fox, Indiana University Office of the Registrar, email to John Summerlot, Director of the Center for Veteran and Military Students at Indiana University, July 10, 2018.

149. Obituaries, *Boston Globe*, March 8, 2015; *Arbutus* (1947).

150. William H. Strain to J. C. Bergman, May 15, 1947, Folder Oh-1946–1947, box 427, Indiana University President's Office Records, 1937–1962, C213, Indiana University Archives.

151. Sara Fox, Indiana University Office of the Registrar, email to John Summerlot, Director of the Center for Veteran and Military Students at Indiana University, May 31, 2018; Graduate English Alumni, University of Pennsylvania, online at https://www.english.upenn.edu/graduate/alumni/1950.

152. These students cannot be named due to archival restrictions.

153. Minutes of the Board of Trustees of Indiana University, 06 June 1958–09 June 1958, Folder 06–09 June 1958, box 23, Indiana University Board of Trustees Minutes, 1835–1859, 1883–2017, C218, Indiana University Archives.

154. Naming Ceremony, Ora L. Wildermuth Intramural Center, June 12, 1971, box 4, Indiana University Chancellor's Speeches, C548 Indiana University Archives.

155. "Analysis: IU building should not be named after a racist," *Indiana Daily Student*, April 10, 2007.

156. Minutes of the Board of Trustees of Indiana University, 19 February 2009–20 February 2009, Folder 19–20 February 2009, box 56, Indiana University Board of Trustees Minutes, 1835–1859, 1883–2017, C218, Indiana University Archives. Bill Garrett was IU's first black basketball player, who faced "open hostility from fans and players" as he desegregated the Big Ten. "Garrett-Wildermuth naming approved," February 20, 2009, Indiana University Media Relations, online at http://newsinfo.iu.edu/news-archive/10001.html.

157. "Wildermuth Center will not be renamed," February 24, 2009, Indiana University Media Relations, online at http://newsinfo.iu.edu/news-archive/10065.html; Minutes of the Board of Trustees of Indiana University, 23 May 2009, Folder 08 May 2009, box 56, Indiana University Board of Trustees Minutes, 1835–1859, 1883–2017, C218, Indiana University Archives.

158. "First black basketball player at IU, Bill Garrett honored with historic marker," *Indiana Daily Student*, April 5, 2017.

159. "IU Board of Trustees renames intramural center on the Bloomington campus," October 5, 2018, Indiana University Media Relations, online at https://news.iu.edu/stories/2018/10/iu/inside/05-trustees-rename-intramural-center.html.

160. Charles L. Lundin to Herman B Wells, June 9, 1942, Folder Lundin, Charles L, 1937–1943, box 360, Indiana University President's Office Records, 1937–1962, C213, Indiana University Archives.

161. There is no record that he ever discussed the matter after his September 1945 letter to Elliott announcing the end of the ban.

162. Commission on Wartime Relocation and Internment of Civilians, *Personal Justice Denied: Report of the Commission on Wartime Relocation and Internment of Civilians* (Washington, D.C., 1982), 3, 18.

163. Sharon Yamamoto, "Civil Liberties Act of 1988," Densho Encyclopedia, online at https:// encyclopedia.densho.org/.

164. Jane Naomi Iwamura, "Critical Faith: Japanese Americans and the Birth of a New Civil Religion," *American Quarterly* 59, no. 3 (2007); Karen M. Inouye, *The Long Afterlife of Nikkei Wartime Incarceration* (Stanford, Calif., 2016), 128–31; Donna K. Nagata, "Processing Cultural Trauma: Intergenerational Effects of the Japanese American Incarceration," *Journal of Social Issues* 71, no. 2 (2015).

165. Inouye, *The Long Afterlife of Nikkei Wartime Incarceration*, 150.

166. Ibid., 146–47, 151.

167. "Nunc pro tunc" is a Latin legal expression, translated "now for then," designed to correct an earlier ruling. Japanese American Students' Citation for the Honorary Degree, May 18, 2008, Office of Ceremonies, University of Washington, online at https://www.washington.edu/ceremony/files/2012/10/Nikkei-Insert-compiled.pdf.

168. Inouye, *The Long Afterlife of Nikkei Wartime Incarceration*, 154.

169. "World War II and the National Japanese American Student Relocation Council," by Zach Bigalke, in *Unbound*, a blog by the University of Oregon Special Collections and University Archives, January 23, 2015, online at https://blogs.uoregon.edu/scua/2015/01/23/world-war-ii-and-the-national-japanese-american-student-relocation-council/.

170. "Nisei Students Speak for Themselves," *Junior College Journal* 14 (1943–44), 244.

171. R. Todd Welker, "Utah Schools and the Japanese American Student Relocation Program," *Utah Historical Quarterly* 70, no. 1 (2002); Greg Robinson, "Admission Denied," *Pennsylvania Gazette*, January-February, 2000, online at http://www.upenn.edu/gazette/0100/robinson.html; *Courage and Compassion: Our Shared Story of the Japanese American World War II Experience*, exhibit,

February 17 to March 18, 2018, Oberlin College Baron Art Gallery, online exhibit at https://www.oberlin.edu/news-and-events/special-events/courage-and-compassion; "'Can't be done–This is war!': The Admission of Japanese Students During World War II," by Katie Martin, in *Blogging Hoosier History,* a blog by the Indiana University Archives, April 18, 2016, online at https://libraries.indiana.edu/%E2%80%9Ccan%E2%80%99t-be-done%E2%80%93-war%E2%80%9D-admission-japanese-students-during-world-war-ii; "The Effects of Pearl Harbor at IU Podcast," hosted by Ellen Glover on January 19, 2017 in the Voices from the IU Bicentennial podcast, online at http://blogs.iu.edu/bicentennialblogs/2017/01/17/bicentennial-podcast-outcasts-the-effects-of-pearl-harbor/; Samuel Gubernick, "The Lost Opportunity: The University of Arizona, 1941–1951" (B.A. thesis, University of Arizona, 2011); John J. Laukaitis, *Denominational Higher Education During World War II* (Cham, Switzerland, 2018); Hall, "Japanese American College Students during the Second World War;" Austin, *From Concentration Camps;* Gary Okihiro, *Storied Lives: Japanese American Students and World War II* (Seattle, Wash., 1999).

172. No detailed scholarship exists for many midwestern institutions. Ohio State University did not admit Nisei until August 1944. Gary Okihiro describes the University of Illinois as "reluctant to take on any more such responsibilities." On March 30, 1942, Purdue University's Executive Committee found it "not expedient, during the period of war, to admit, either as graduate or undergraduate students, any new students of Japanese origin, nor any non-citizen students of any other enemy race of nation." The University of Chicago found accepting Nisei students "inadvisable." DePauw University, in the words of historian Allan Austin, "surrendered" to community "prejudice against all people of Japanese blood." Austin, *From Concentration Camps,* 109, 144; Okihiro, *Storied Lives,* 31; Hall, "Japanese American," 150–54; Hans H. Jaffe to Luther Tucker, Folder "Purdue University, Lafayette, Ind.," box 77, National Japanese American Student Relocation Council Records.

173. Andrew B. Wertheimer, "Admitting Nebraska's Nisei: Japanese American Students at the University of Nebraska, 1942–1945," *Nebraska History* 83, no. 3 (2002).

174. *Courage and Compassion: Our Shared Story of the Japanese American World War II Experience,* online at https://www.oberlin.edu/news-and-events/special-events/courage-and-compassion.

175. The Golden Book of the Memorial Fund, Indiana University, online at https://goldenbook.iu.edu/.

10

★ ★ ★

"Patriotism May Require Opposing the Government at Certain Times"

Howard Zinn's Antiwar Speech at Indiana University, December 1, 1967

INTRODUCED, TRANSCRIBED, AND EDITED BY ALEX LICHTENSTEIN

> It was like the Lincoln-Douglas debate, except the controversy was over Vietnam instead of states' rights or slavery. But despite the time lapse, the battle was just as heated. A stolid man named Rusk stared impassively at hecklers, and a wiry man named Zinn from Boston University presented his case with fiery conviction. The rhetoric of both sides was irreconcilable. But so, it seems, is the problem.[1]

IN OCTOBER 1967, U.S. SECRETARY of State Dean Rusk visited Indiana University to address Convocation. Whatever the Convocations Committee had imagined when they invited him to speak earlier that month, his presence on campus as the Lyndon Johnson administration's key spokesperson on the war in Vietnam proved to be extraordinarily ill-timed.[2] By that fall, as his generally sympathetic biographer notes, "war protestors began to dog Rusk at all his public appearances."[3] With the number of U.S. troops in Vietnam approaching 500,000, October 1967 saw an appreciable escalation of the antiwar movement "from protest to resistance," especially on the nation's college campuses. IU was no exception. On October 21, a group of 300 antiwar students from Bloomington joined 100,000 protestors in the Washington, D.C., demonstration that culminated in a dramatic march on the Pentagon, violent clashes with U.S. marshals and military police, and 700 arrests. As historian Mary Ann Wynkoop remarks, "Those students from IU who had gone to . . . Washington realized that their resistance to the war was no longer a private, individual act."[4]

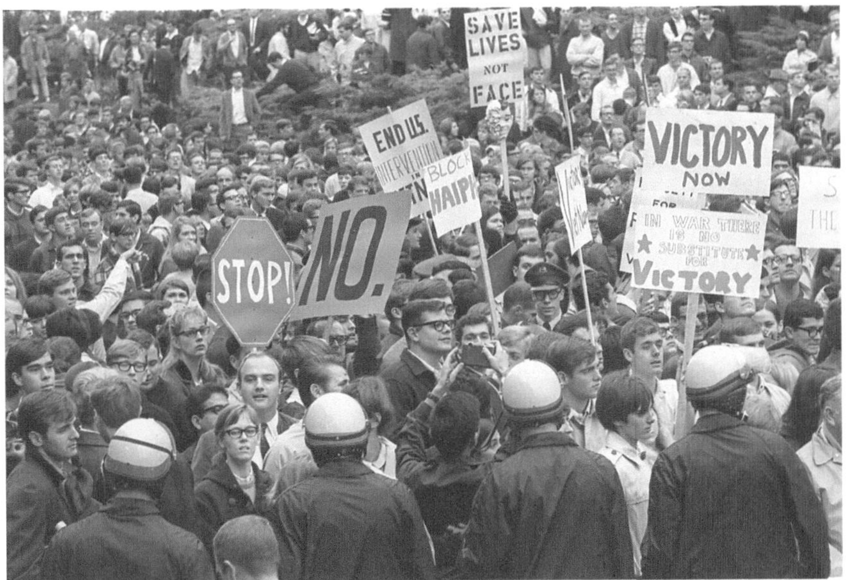

Pro-government and antiwar demonstrators greet Secretary of State Dean Rusk at Indiana University, Bloomington, October 31, 1967. *Courtesy IU News Bureau Photograph Collection, Indiana University Archives.*

When Rusk arrived on campus shortly after their return, these activists prepared to confront him. "We must show the warmakers that they can no longer come to the heartland of America and expect to find unthinking acceptance of America's current disastrous foreign policy," declared the impromptu "Dean Rusk Welcoming Committee" in a flyer that had circulated around the campus when Rusk's visit was announced.[5] Radical sociologist William Simon, one of the few IU faculty members who unequivocally supported the New Left activists, took to the pages of the alternative student paper, *The Spectator*, the week before Rusk's appearance to urge the university to rescind its invitation. "He comes to use the university platform to defend an administration policy on Vietnam that is widely opposed," Simon wrote in an open letter, and honoring him would be "applauding that policy." "There is a point," Simon concluded, "beyond which academic courtesy becomes complicity in the crimes of the Johnson administration."[6]

With the campus becoming increasingly polarized over the war and the limits of dissent and free speech, the Convocations Committee acceded to the demands of antiwar students and upset faculty that they invite an antiwar speaker to campus to "at least partially offset the 'imbalance' caused by a parade of pro-war spokesmen," or else rescind the secretary of state's invitation.[7] In the pages of *The Spectator*, campus antiwar leader Russell Block and student body president Guy Lofton published an open letter to the Convocations Committee. In the previous two years, they pointed out, the campus had hosted Gen. Maxwell Taylor, Richard Nixon, Lewis Hershey (head of the Selective Service System), and Vice President Hubert Humphrey, all prominent defenders of the war. Their suggestions for more dovish voices included journalist I. F. Stone, writers Mary McCarthy and Norman Mailer, New Left leader Carl Oglesby, and three prominent academics who opposed the war—the linguist Noam Chomsky and historians Staughton Lynd and Howard Zinn.[8]

On October 26, while insisting that it was not "giving into pressure or threats to stop Mr. Rusk's speech," the Convocations Committee announced its decision to invite Zinn to IU to speak on "Vietnam: The Logic of Withdrawal," the title of his recent book urging precisely that. The chair of the committee, law professor F. Reed Dickerson, confirmed in a letter that "after the announcement that . . . Rusk will speak at I.U. next week, a number of people pointed out that there was an imbalance in the views of the speakers" who had been invited to campus to speak about the war. Dickerson sought to defend committee members against the accusation that they had "taken a position on the Viet Nam war and are peddling it to the students," insisting that once critics asked for an antiwar speaker, "there was a quick and ungrudging agreement that a strong 'Dove' position needed an articulate spokesman" for a convocation address.[9] "If the university has a policy on the Viet Nam war," Dickerson claimed, "I have not heard what it is." He closed by expressing the hope that protestors would not be "rude or disruptive" during Rusk's appearance.[10]

Antiwar students, however, did believe the university had a Vietnam "policy," one displayed most obviously in its willingness to allow napalm manufacturer Dow Chemical Corporation to recruit on campus. In an unfortunate coincidence for the secretary of state, his campus visit was immediately preceded by an October 30 student protest against Dow. Following similar actions at the University of Wisconsin and other universities, several dozen students from Students for a Democratic Society and the local Committee to End the War in Vietnam (CEWV) occupied the placement office at IU's business school to prevent Dow from conducting recruitment. Bloomington police arrested thirty-five students.[11]

Speaking on the Indiana campus the following day, and just ten days after the massive Pentagon protest, Rusk took the opportunity to defend the

Johnson administration's policy in Vietnam. He insisted, for example, that the conflict was not a civil war internal to South Vietnam, but rather that U.S. "forces went in because of the increasing number of units moving from North Vietnam to the south."[12] Rusk repeated many other typical—and increasingly discredited—justifications for the war: the need to protect South Vietnam's supposedly freely elected regime; the strategic importance of the United States retaining its "credibility"; the desirability of a relentless bombing campaign to bring a supposedly recalcitrant Hanoi to the negotiating table.[13] At the same time, as one history of the antiwar movement notes, in the fall of 1967 "as the war escalated, so did anger and despair among protestors."[14] As graduate student W. Paul Vogt wrote in a letter to *The Spectator*, many activists felt that "if the voice of dissent is to be heard, it must speak more loudly."[15] Not surprisingly, then, Rusk's presence on campus generated well-attended, pro- and antiwar demonstrations. Opposing crowds, bristling with competing signs stating "Blockade Haiphong" and "End U.S. Intervention in Vietnam," jammed Showalter Plaza in front of the IU Auditorium. The *Indiana Daily Student* published a front-page editorial, entitled "Welcome Mr. Rusk," expressing pleasure at receiving such a "distinguished visitor" on the campus. In a carefully choreographed effort to soil this red carpet event, antiwar students attended the secretary's speech and heckled him from strategic positions around the hall, shouting "murderer" and "Eichmann" from the floor, much to the annoyance of the rest of the audience. "A breach of 'etiquette' is a moral act," insisted the head of IU's CEWV, in the pages of *The Spectator* prior to Rusk's visit. The alternative newspaper had already called for an "immediate withdrawal" from Vietnam in its "Special Vietnam Issue" a few weeks before.[16]

Although the CEWV and the Dean Rusk Welcoming Committee had explicitly "urge[d] that Rusk be allowed to make his speech," their disruptive tactics drew criticism from a range of sources. Some students in the audience shouted at the protestors to "grow up." Others, including the leaders of the Inter-Fraternity Council, the Student Athletic Council, and the Association of Women Students, circulated a petition apologizing to Rusk. Within a week, it had garnered nearly 14,000 student signatures. Many of the letters from faculty—and most from the public—to IU President Elvis Stahr in the wake of the Dow protest and the Rusk disruption denounced antiwar students for their violation of decorum and the precepts of "free speech," and urged Stahr to discipline them.[17]

In this overheated atmosphere, with faculty and university administration caught between the contending views of anti- and prowar students—not to mention those of concerned parents, state legislators, university trustees, and citizens around the state—Howard Zinn arrived on campus to present his own controversial views on the Vietnam War. Zinn, a professor at Boston University, had been one of the first academics to speak out against the war, as early as 1965.[18] His own horror of war derived from his experience as a World War II bombardier, "caught up in a fanaticism which let me participate unquestioningly in atrocious acts," as he recalled in his 1994 autobiography. In particular, his participation in the firebombing of the French village of Royan, where a contingent of German soldiers had holed up in the war's waning days, led Zinn later to reject the logic that demanded, in his words, "the acceptance of any means, however horrible, once you have entered a war with a belief in the total nobility of your cause."[19]

By 1967, Zinn's antiwar profile had reached its zenith. Frustrated by the unwillingness of liberal opponents of the war to say openly what he thought imperative, he published a small and widely popular book—almost a pamphlet—urging immediate and unconditional withdrawal of U.S. troops from Vietnam, regardless of the consequences.[20] *Vietnam: The Logic of Withdrawal,* which appeared in March, was praised by the *New York Times* as a "closely reasoned" brief against the war that offered both "a compact, accurate history of the United States' involvement in Vietnam" going back to 1950 and a "powerful moral argument" against the war based on the high numbers of Vietnamese civilian casualties. In it, Zinn proclaimed that "the sanity of unilateral withdrawal is that it makes the end of the war independent of anyone's consent but our own."[21]

Zinn's book was widely reviewed, and it made him a popular and sought-after speaker at antiwar events throughout 1967. In the months following the book's appearance, he spoke to church groups, women's groups, and high schools. He also spoke, of course, on the campuses of many American colleges and universities, including Carleton, Duke, Rochester, Western Reserve, and Wichita State. Invitations from antiwar students and faculty also came from Rutgers, the University of Illinois, the University of California Santa Barbara, Brown, and Vassar. But the opportunity that the Indiana University visit offered him—to "debate" Rusk, even indirectly—must have been irresistible.[22]

Zinn had attended the October 21 demonstrations in Washington, although he departed before the evening's violent confrontations at the Pentagon. He had also spoken at a major anti-draft rally that month on the Boston Common, at which dozens of young men had publicly burnt their draft cards.[23] By the time he arrived at IU, he had developed a well-honed message about the immorality of the war; the mendacity of President Johnson, Rusk, and Secretary of Defense Robert McNamara; and the necessity of immediate U.S. withdrawal as the only path to peace. A few days before his talk, he took to the pages of *The Spectator* to applaud the efforts of student protestors across the country (and at IU) to halt Dow recruitment on campuses, actions that he lauded as fully justified civil disobedience against complicity with an unjust war.[24]

The following transcription comes from a tape recording of Zinn's December 1, 1967, remarks given at the IU Auditorium. Made by WFIU, the university's radio station, the tape was digitized for me by the Tamiment Library at New York University, where Zinn's papers are held.[25] By the time of Zinn's visit, the title of his address had changed to "Vietnam: A Reply to Dean Rusk," and his speech served as the keynote for a full weekend of discussion of the war sponsored by a group calling itself the Faculty Committee for Peace in Vietnam.[26] That evening, Zinn spoke for about an hour, from notes, to a large, respectful, and apparently sympathetic audience (there was no jeering or heckling). He had taken the time to listen carefully to a recording of Rusk's convocation speech and used most of his time to "address [him]self to some of the things that Dean Rusk spoke about"—which for him meant challenging what he regarded as the secretary of state's dishonesty in defense of an indefensible war. I have transcribed about twenty minutes of Zinn's speech, focusing as much as possible on his articulation of a broad antiwar philosophy that went beyond the specifics of Vietnam.

"VIETNAM: A REPLY TO DEAN RUSK": EXCERPTS FROM HOWARD ZINN'S SPEECH AT INDIANA UNIVERSITY, DECEMBER 1, 1967[27]

Zinn began by talking about the limits of the "Munich analogy," one of the favorite rhetorical tools of the hawks of the day, who insisted that stopping Ho Chi Minh in Southeast Asia was akin to stopping Hitler in Europe in the 1930s. Rusk had resorted to such an argument when he appeared at IU in October. Indeed, a favorable review of Zinn's book in the Cleveland Plain Dealer *had noted that Zinn "explodes the Munich analogy on which our State department so heavily relies for our presence in Asia."*[28]

Dean Rusk took pains, I noticed, to remind us very close to the beginning of his talk, of the Second World War, which we constantly need to be reminded of. And of Munich, and Churchill, and Hitler, and all of those names from that period—the well-known Munich analogy. I think it's a false and a shallow analogy to use to defend the administration position in Vietnam. After all, what bothered us in World War II was that Hitler was trying to take over other countries by force. What bothers us about Vietnam is that the Vietnamese want to take over their own country by force. And that seems to me more like a civil war, or a revolution, than the kind of situation that obtained in World War II. So that it doesn't take much investigation to begin to see a difference. Now it's true that there's a lot more to it than that. The Vietnamese may be trying to take over their own country, but they're Communists. And Communists who are trying to take over their own country are a different sort of people than anybody else who would try to take over their own country. And this creates problems for us, because they are Communists and yet they're Vietnamese. And this is very hard to grasp, because Communists must be Russians or Chinese, but they can't really be Vietnamese. And this creates difficult problems of perception, sort of identity problems, which we have to deal with. And, well, one of the problems is that it's not only Communists that we wouldn't like to take over in Vietnam. Because, occasionally, when somebody who is not a Communist, or some group that is not Communist, decides it would like to have power or share power in Vietnam, we somehow come down hard on them too.... It seems that anybody who wants to take over Vietnam, other than the people we want to be in charge in Vietnam, is in some way reprehensible, and in some way gets tied up with Communism and the Communists....

We're very fortunate that every once in a while we have a war that has a little bit of a stamp of decency about it, and then we can go on parading for centuries under the slogans of that war. We fortunately have World War II, and Hitler, and the Nazis, and good facing evil, and everything is clean-cut and we can apply it to every other situation that comes up. And it makes things easier for us. At the time of the Spanish-American War they could point to the Civil War. That didn't really fit too well, but who cares? It was the handiest thing we had around. And we use whatever is handy in sophisticated diplomacy. Now, I think therefore that we somehow need to broaden our historical perspective. Perhaps think not about any particular war, any particular catastrophe, but think in the large about man's experience over a very long period of time. And it seems to me that looking at it this way, throughout history, for as long as we can remember—historically speaking—the rulers of nations have sent young men to war. This is a broad and sweeping statement, and there are these exceptions that come up just often enough to deter us from a very clean-cut judgment about war. But throughout history, as long as we can remember, it seems to me rulers have sent young men to war, and for no good reason except their own power, their own wealth, their own pride. And they've always used two methods. One was compulsion, and the other was words. The words were frightening words usually, about how the Muslims, or the Huns, or the Jews, or the Communists, or the Catholics were about to take over the world. Or inspiring words, about how the world would be made safe for democracy, or Christianity, or the Motherland, or Western Civilization. And almost always the men who went to war most often and died most frequently were the people who had nothing to gain. Eugene Debs was sentenced to ten years in jail in this democratic country, in 1918, for telling a crowd in Canton, Ohio, that—and I am quoting him now, so that I will now fit the terms of the Espionage Act also—"The master class has always started the wars, and the working class has always fought in them."[29] And so he was sent to jail for ten years. You may remember, Woodrow Wilson insisted on keeping him there. He was one of our great liberals. Debs was finally released by Warren Harding! It tells you a lot about liberalism and conservatism. Now, Debs's language is very old-fashioned. Master class, working class . . . it's almost embarrassing. But, of course, he was right. And in this war the largest percentage of the dead will be black- and brown-skinned people and the sons of poor families of all colors. The statistics already show that. Negroes are maybe 23 or 24 percent of the dead in the Vietnam War. And they're 11 percent of the population. Of course, this is as it should be. It's *traditional.* And they've always done the menial jobs, and this is the latest one. And, I have a feeling that these are the same people in all countries who go to war. These people are dutiful, obedient, they very often even believe in what they are fighting for, or whatever it is they're told they're fighting for. They believe in God and country and king; they're brought up on the flag, and the pledges of allegiance and the Boy Scouts and all of that. And not to reason why, but to do and die, and so on. They believe their leaders, because their leaders know best.

And I was thinking about this as I was reading the transcript of Dean Rusk's talk, and listening to him on tape. Because I had the feeling suddenly that he was talking to these people; he wasn't talking to a university audience. It suddenly occurred to me . . . that the administration has stopped talking to the universities. It doesn't matter that they stand on university stages; they're not talking to the universities anymore. They know they don't have the universities anymore. They're talking for the television audiences, and they're talking for the people out in the "boondocks." They're talking for the people about whom they're really worried, the people who are the cannon fodder of the war. And you can tell who they are talking to by the way they reason out the case for the war. And that's what Dean Rusk was doing; these are the people that he was talking to. They're the people who don't have time to check up on facts, the people who don't have time to look into the history books, the people who haven't read the newspapers too carefully, who haven't read any books on Vietnam, whose memory is short—most of our memories are short.

That's the only explanation I can give for some of the statements that the secretary of state made that night. He referred to the UN Charter. He hoped that no one would go and read the UN Charter. Because it doesn't take much reading of the UN Charter to see that there is—I don't want to make an extreme statement, of course. We want to make all of our statements moderate because this is an academic environment. But it doesn't take too much looking at the UN Charter to see that there's some discrepancy between the way the U.S. has behaved in the Vietnam War and what the UN Charter says about how nations should behave in the civilized, peaceful community that they hoped they would erect after World War II. The preamble talks about obligations, and that armed forces should not be used save in the *common* interest. It doesn't say armed forces may be used in the *national* interest. Remember, we've had a lot of talk recently about fighting for our national interest. But the purpose of the UN was to say that from now on nations should no longer fight for some national and parochial interest. If there is some common interest that the people of the world share, then perhaps—and if there's some threat to that common interest—then perhaps there may be some police action that members of the UN should take in concert with one another. Not unilateral action for a nation's own interest, or for a nation's own power, or even to protect a nation's own future potential national security against some future, possible threat someday. That's not what the spirit of the UN Charter—or the letter of the UN Charter—calls for. Or in Article 1 of the UN Charter, it talks about the self-determination of peoples. Well, this is a very complex question in relation to Vietnam, and yet not as complex as people would make it out. It goes on. People who read the Charter and Article 2, and Article 33, and Article 51, and Article 53 would not have a hard time figuring out that there's something wrong in relation to the UN Charter that the United States is doing in Vietnam. But I think that Dean Rusk assumed that people were not likely to read the Charter, and so he mentioned it happily and confidently.

After showing, in great detail, how Rusk had based his account of alliances, international obligations, failed negotiations, and "democratic" elections in South Vietnam on distortions, deception, and outright lies, Zinn offered this powerful indictment of American exceptionalism:

What's interesting, I think, is that we always thought that in this country we were different . . . It wasn't just Manifest Destiny, and it wasn't just we are born free, or all the other things that people talk about. But we have always really believed that we are not subject to the same human laws or social laws that govern any other people in the world. That we are unique. And that we are exempt and always have been exempt from the stupidity that other countries got involved in—armies fighting, men dying in the mud, and for no good reason. But we never have been exempt, and we are not now, and it's time for us to realize this. It's also true that ever since governments were first formed, and tyranny—which I think is the natural companion of government—began, people have felt the need to gather from time to time in various places, even in school auditoriums, and to declare the rights of conscience against the inhumanity of government. And always in history—and this impresses me—the poets, and the playwrights, and the philosophers and the novelists have been the ones who have cried out against the stupidity of war. Aristophanes, and Tolstoy, and Mark Twain, and Gandhi, and E. E. Cummings, and people like that. The singers, the artists, the musicians spoke out, sang out, always for life against death. And it seems to me they are doing this today. . . . And every day, more and more Americans, in and out of uniform, are declaring their refusal to fight in the war, and more and more citizens are declaring that "we'll support and help them in every way." What it seems to me we are doing, we are in effect declaring our independence from this war. As was said almost 200 years ago when another kind of Declaration of Independence was issued, "a decent respect for the opinions of mankind requires that we should declare the reasons for the separation of ourselves" from the war in Vietnam.

And each of us has the right to state his own reasons for separating himself from the war. And I would like to declare mine. To put it most plainly . . . I'm simply ashamed of the conduct of the American government in Vietnam. Because the government calls itself American, I call myself American, and yet when I read in the newspapers that our Air Force has bombed again and again the residential areas of North Vietnamese cities; or that it has bombed again and again—too often to be an accident—villages that are devoid of military significance; or that it's bombed a hospital for lepers in North Vietnam thirteen times; when I read that we've dropped leaflets on a village, saying "We have bombed your village before, why are you still there? If you don't leave, the B-52s will come over and they will bomb you again." Villages are not bombed by accident; villages are bombed deliberately. I remember Bernard Fall reporting, in one of his last articles before his death, about his trip on an American plane, when they went over a fishing village on the coast in South Vietnam.[30] The fishing village was reported by intelligence as having possibly been a Viet Cong hangout. So they bombed the fishing village. Fishermen lived there, and fishermen's families lived there, but that's war, of course. But this is done again, and again, and again—too often, too much. 50,000. 100,000. Nobody knows how many casualties there are a year. But we know there is an enormous amount of casualties. Of course the other side inflicts casualties. This is always an easy out—"Well, the other side inflicts casualties." But it stands to reason that by the magnitude of our firepower, that when you are flying very high, dropping bombs, very large bombs with huge explosive power, that this is not pinpoint bombing.[31] And it stands to reason that you're going to kill more people than anybody else will kill: in fact, we *admit* this, in fact we are proud of it, because the figures we release all the time show how we have killed five times or ten times as much as anybody else has killed. And this shows that we are winning. Or at least that we're not losing. Or at least that perhaps we're on our way to success. Or at least that in two years we'll be able to de-escalate. Perhaps slowly, gradually, over a period. That's what all of this shows. When I read about the terrible story of Ben Suc, that appeared in the *New Yorker* and which now has been put into a book by Jonathan Schell—I mean, this is storm trooper tactics.[32] This is the picture we used to see of the German soldiers moving into the villages of Lidice in Czechoslovakia, and taking off the women and the children, killing every man they could find, burning the place to the ground. That's what we did to Ben Suc, a village with temples a thousand years old, and huts that had stood for generations, as long as people could remember. And then we levelled the whole thing with bulldozers. And then one of the American officers standing nearby said to somebody who asked "What's going on?"—"Well, these people will be better off this way. You know those old huts they lived in? They weren't too hot. And now we'll put them in nice, clean Quonset huts, tin roofs, and we'll give them candy. Lollipops for the children, toys on Christmas. Have a big campaign in Massachusetts to send toys over for Christmas." This is the kind of thing we do.

This is the first war we've had on television. And when you just watch these scenes on television, you have to feel ashamed. That's the way I feel. It's not that the guys—GIs—are vicious, or terrible or not that they're any different than anybody else, but this is what war is. Young, and well-meaning, and nice guys are put into uniform, and they're given guns, and they're given orders and people in Washington, or in Moscow, or anywhere else, call the tune and somehow the orders come down, and then very nice people end up doing vicious things to other nice people.

Well, somebody has to stop this. Somebody has to extricate themselves from this. I personally want to disassociate myself from these acts. That's not my idea of what America should stand for. I don't think we have the right. I mean, what are our *credentials* for going into another country and destroying it? What are our credentials for saying that "We are going to give you a better society than you had before. We *know* what's better for you. These people are no good for you"? Can we prove by what our actions have produced in other parts of the world—in Korea, in Formosa, in the Philippines, in Thailand, in Latin America, in Saudi Arabia—can we prove by what our actions have produced in these places that we can produce just societies for people by our power, by our wealth? I don't think so.

And what about the American casualties? Now they're up to 15,000–90,000 wounded. And it's painful to think of them. It arouses a kind of anger, because they didn't have to die, and they didn't have to lose arms and legs and come crippled out of the jungles of Vietnam. They were *sent* to Vietnam, under the orders of politicians in Washington and generals in the Pentagon. Very ordinary men, good to their families, jovial at cocktail parties, who have become corrupted by possessing the largest store of wealth and the most terrible collection of instruments of death in world history. These are men who have appointed themselves guardian of every spot on earth against the infidel, Communism. And have declared their determination to save people, everywhere, from Communism, whether these people want to be saved from it or not. And even if they have to kill every one of these people in order to save them. We used to think that fanaticism ruled only in other countries.

Zinn continued by insisting that, contrary to Rusk's assertion that the war in Vietnam was one of North Vietnamese aggression against South Vietnam, the "whole historical and statistical record" showed that "the force that we are fighting against is a southern force." He urged his audience not to be blinded by anticommunism, and to accept that the National Liberation Front, even if led by Communists, might actually in this case be on the side of "national independence" and the rights of the peasant majority in South Vietnam. Near the end of his remarks, Zinn offered these powerful words, which I believe represent the finest example of his thinking about what it means to be a citizen. They should ring loudly in the ears of anyone who tries to tell Americans what kind of history they can and cannot learn:

Just one word about loyalty and patriotism. I don't think we owe loyalty to a government—because that's an anti-democratic notion, that you owe loyalty to a government. I think we owe loyalty to our fellow Americans, who are in danger of being killed by the incompetence of the government. It's a basic principal of American democracy—we forget it easily—that the government is not to be worshipped or obeyed without question. The government is set up to preserve life, liberty, and the pursuit of happiness, and when the government no longer does that, we no longer owe it allegiance. . . . So patriotism isn't blind support of the government, and it's not blind allegiance to the flag. It's support for the people of the country and for the principles that the nation is supposed to stand for. And therefore, patriotism may require opposing the government at certain times. . . . And so I think we owe it to our conscience, and to the people of this country, and to the principles of American democracy, to declare our independence of this war and to resist it, in every way we can, until it comes to an end, and until there's peace in Vietnam. And perhaps then we can begin to rethink our view of the world, recast our thinking. . . . And if we begin thinking perhaps in a new way, then we can address ourselves to the fundamental issues. To life and love and the things that we are here for, I think. Thank you.

The months following Zinn's visit to IU saw a series of national and international events that did little to quell campus turmoil in Bloomington or elsewhere. In late January, the North Vietnamese launched the Tet offensive, undermining Gen. William Westmoreland's assurances that the escalation of the previous year had put the U.S. on the path to victory. At the end of March 1968, an exhausted and dispirited President Johnson stunned the nation with the announcement that he would not seek re-election, thus opening up the field to antiwar Democrats Eugene McCarthy and Robert Kennedy. Four days later, Martin Luther King Jr. was assassinated in Memphis. Beginning in late April, students at Columbia University occupied buildings until they were routed by the police. During these same months in Bloomington, several of the Dow Chemical protestors received fines and short jail sentences. CIA recruiters, scheduled to come to campus in February, declined to do so fearing more protests, while Dow recruiters returned in March, setting off a new round of local campus conflict over the war. The end of April brought a campaign speech in Bloomington by Robert Kennedy (he spoke against the war, but also said he would end student draft deferments) followed by another three-day IU teach-in on the war and a brief student strike. Kennedy won the state's Democratic primary, only to be struck by an assassin's bullet himself in early June. As Mary Ann Wynkoop observes, Howard Zinn became, if only briefly, part of a local movement whose popularity refutes the notion that "student unrest and antiwar protests only happened in big cities or on large university campuses on the coasts." Indeed, "students at Indiana University proved that there was dissent in the very heart of the country."[33]

ALEX LICHTENSTEIN, Professor of History and American Studies at Indiana University, teaches U.S. and South African history. He first read portions of this speech at the "Zinn Read-In" held at Purdue University on November 5, 2013. This article originally appeared in volume 110, June 2014.

NOTES

1. "Convocations," *Arbutus* 75 (1968), 56.

2. When they discovered that Rusk had a scheduled address in Columbus, Indiana, on October 30, the Convocations Committee sent him an invitation on October 5, asking him to speak at the campus on October 31. F. Reed Dickerson to Dean Rusk, October 5, 1967, Box 141 Ru 1966–68, Indiana University President's Office records, 1962–1968, C304, University Archives and Records (UAR), Wells Library, Indiana University.

3. Thomas J. Schoenbaum, *Waging Peace and War: Dean Rusk in the Truman, Kennedy, and Johnson Years* (New York, 1988), 437.

4. Terry Anderson, *The Sixties* (New York, 2004), 99–100; Maurice Isserman and Michael Kazin, *America Divided: The Civil War of the 1960s*, 4th ed. (New York, 2012), 176–78; Norman Mailer, *The Armies of the Night: History as a Novel: Novel as History* (New York, 1968); *The Spectator*, October 23, 1967; Mary Ann Wynkoop, *Dissent in the Heartland: The Sixties at Indiana University* (Bloomington, Ind., 2002), 53–54; Simon Hall, *Rethinking the American Anti-war Movement* (New York, 2012), 28–34; Tom Wells, *The War Within: America's Battle Over Vietnam* (Berkeley, Cal.,1994), 195–203; *Indiana Daily Student*, October 21, 24, 1967, p. 1.

5. "Dean Rusk Welcoming Committee," Eggshell Press collection, C292, UAR. Digital copy available at: http://www.dlib.indiana.edu/omeka/archives/studentlife/archive/files/482d39987b8e0fa c1e53daf7681b0927.jpg.

6. *The Spectator*, October 23, 1967, p. 2.

7. "Dean Rusk Welcoming Committee"; see also the *Logansport Pharos Tribune and Press*, October 30, 1967, p. 2.

8. *The Spectator*, October 23, 1967, p. 16.

9. The further text of Dickerson's letter, however, makes it apparent that Zinn was actually the committee's fourth choice.

10. *Indiana Daily Student*, October 27, 1967, p. 2; F. Reed Dickerson to unspecified "Editor," October 24, 1967, Box 46, Convocations Committee Meetings, 1967–68, Indiana University President's Office records, 1962–1968, C304, UAR.

11. *Indiana Daily Student*, October 31, 1967, p. 1; *Indianapolis Star*, October 31, 1967, p. 19; Wynkoop, *Dissent in the Heartland*, 54–55. Additional documents can be found at: dlib.indiana.edu/omeka/archives/studentlife/exhibits/show/studentdemonstrationsatiu/1967dowchemicalsitin/1967dowchemicalsitinpt2.

12. *Indiana Daily Student*, November 1, 1967, p. 1. One congressional report from the time, however, indicated that by the end of 1965, when the U.S. already had 170,000 troops in Vietnam, the Viet Cong's total force of 230,000 included only 14,000 North Vietnamese regulars who had infiltrated into the South. See *The Vietnam Conflict: The Substance and the Shadow*, report of Sen. Mike Mansfield et al. to the Committee on Foreign Relations, United States Senate, January 6, 1966 (Washington, D.C., 1966), 2–3. Zinn cited this report in his remarks.

13. *Bloomington Tribune*, October 31, 1967, p. 1; *Indiana Daily Student*, November 1, 1967, p. 1.

14. Wells, *The War Within*, 212.

15. *The Spectator*, November 13, 1967, p. 15.

16. *Indiana Daily Student*, November 1, 1967, p. 1; *The Spectator*, October 30, 1967, p. 2; *The Spectator*, October 9, 1967.

17. "Rusk Welcoming Committee"; *Indiana Daily Student*, November 1, 2, 9, 1967; verbatim copies of letters, "Student-Faculty Viet-Nam Controversy," November 8, 1967, Box 160 Students, Indiana University President's Office records, 1962–1968, C304, UAR.

18. Howard Zinn, *You Can't Be Neutral on a Moving Train: A Personal History of Our Times* (Boston, 1994), 107–108; Martin B. Duberman, *Howard Zinn: A Life on the Left* (New York, 2012), 113–14.

19. Zinn, *You Can't Be Neutral*, 96, 100.

20. Howard Zinn, *Vietnam: The Logic of Withdrawal* (Boston, 1967); Zinn, *You Can't Be Neutral*, 110; Duberman, *Howard Zinn*, 125–27, 147–48.

21. *New York Times*, June 11, 1967, p. 310; Zinn, *Logic of Withdrawal*, 115–16.

22. See invitation letters in folder 22, Box 16, Appearances/Speaking Engagements, Howard Zinn papers, Tamiment Library, New York University.

23. Zinn, *You Can't Be Neutral*, 116.

24. Howard Zinn, "Dow Shall Not Kill," *The Spectator*, November 27, 1967, pp. 3–5.

25. "WFIU: Howard Zinn—Convocation Address on the Necessity of Immediate Withdrawal from Vietnam, Indiana University, Bloomington, IN," reels 276–77, box 78, Howard Zinn papers, Tamiment Library.

26. *Indiana Daily Student*, December 1, 1967, p. 1.

27. Editorial note: The transcript has been edited to maintain the character and original flow of Zinn's speech; inaudible, partial, repetitive, and filler words have been excised for clarity. The editors have added punctuation and paragraphing to suggest the natural pauses of the speech and have also standardized capitalization, grammar, and spelling. Analysis by the author, Alex Lichtenstein, is distinguished by the use of italics.

28. *Cleveland Plain Dealer*, March 21, 1967.

29. Actually, in his Canton, Ohio speech, Debs said: "The master class has always declared the wars; the subject class has always fought the battles." See a portion of the text and a reading of the speech at http://zinnedproject.org/materials/eugene-debs-canton-ohio/. I like to think that Zinn reached for the Debs example that evening because he might have observed or been shown a depiction of the great Indiana radical that appears in one of the Thomas Hart Benton murals in the lobby of the IU Auditorium.

30. Fall, who had fought in the French Resistance during World War II and subsequently investigated war crimes for the Nuremberg Trials, had reported on the conflict in Vietnam since the 1950s. In February 1967, while covering the war for *The New Republic*, he was killed by a mine. See *Reporting Vietnam. Part One: American Journalism, 1959–1969* (New York, 1998), 806–07. Zinn did not have his reference quite right—the article appeared in 1965 in *Ramparts* magazine. Bernard Fall, "A Vietnam Album: This Isn't Munich, It's Spain," *Ramparts*, December 1965, 23–29. One can imagine that the title caught Zinn's attention.

31. Here Zinn spoke with autobiographical authority, based on his own experience as a World War II bombardier. "At our bombing altitudes," he later wrote, "we saw no people, heard no screams, saw no blood, no torn limbs. I remember only seeing the canisters light up like matches flaring one by one on the ground below." Zinn, *You Can't be Neutral*, 94.

32. Jonathan Schell, "The Village of Ben Suc," *The New Yorker*, July 15, 1967, pp. 28–93; Schell, *The Village of Ben Suc* (New York, 1967). Schell's lengthy article concluded with these words: "having once decided to destroy it, we were now bent on annihilating every possible indication that the village of Ben Suc had ever existed."

33. Wynkoop, *Dissent in the Heartland*, 62–64.

11

★ ★ ★

The Other Side of Campus

Indiana University's Student Right and the Rise of National Conservatism

JASON S. LANTZER

ON A BRISK SPRING DAY in March 1965, an estimated 300 Indiana University students assembled in Dunn Meadow, the green oasis beside the Indiana Memorial Union where students often relaxed between classes or met to play games. This day was different, however, as these students gathered not to enjoy the atmosphere, but to speak their minds about the war in Vietnam. They carried signs, chanted slogans, and generally behaved, according to the campus newspaper, the *Indiana Daily Student* (*IDS*), in a manner not unlike that of an additional 650 students and locals who had also assembled in the meadow to hear speeches about the civil rights movement in the wake of the recent march on Selma, Alabama.[1]

This convergence of civil rights and Vietnam demonstrations may sound like a typical episode of 1960s campus activism, but it was not. A good half of the students attending the Vietnam rally marched *in support of* the United States' commitment to halting the advance of communism in Southeast Asia. While such a show of support was hardly uncommon, either at IU or at other college campuses nationwide, subsequent studies of 1960s campus activism have tended to inherit from government investigators of the period a tendency to define student protest as the purview of the Left.[2] Though a growing body of recent scholarship has challenged these kinds of assumptions about the period, recent discussion, some of it appearing in the pages of the *Indiana Magazine of History*, has focused almost exclusively on the Left.[3]

Obviously, this focus reveals only part of the story. An investigation of the campus activism of the 1960s and 1970s should consider the full range of student expression evoked by the complexity of those times. Far from exhibiting what Richard Hofstadter deemed the "paranoid style" of many conservative American movements (complete with persecution complex and void of relevant ideas), the campus Right at IU and elsewhere provided a number of students with an alternative and highly attractive worldview, one that both defended and critiqued the status quo.[4] The New Right's conservative ideology, like that of the radical Left, stood at odds with the consensus "me-too-ism" of the 1950s, which joined Democratic and Republican elites in agreement on certain foreign and domestic policy essentials. This study draws on contemporary IU sources and on more recent interviews with several of the era's participants to locate conservative activists in a variety of organizations that interacted with each other and with their liberal rivals to challenge and change campus, national, and international issues.[5] Though often viewed as an enigma by consensus liberals and neglected by commentators, the Right's ideas prompted a generation of activists who would, like their more widely recognized counterparts on the Left, recall their campus experiences as the cornerstone of an effective effort to reshape American politics and culture in the decades ahead.[6]

Arriving in Bloomington in the early 1960s, future student activists of both stripes found a campus environment that many still remember with fondness. They appreciated the intellectual climate, dressing up for class, and being taken seriously as young adults. Competing campus political groups, including the Young Democrats and Young Republicans, reflected the prevailing consensus in national politics. More social clubs than activist organizations, these groups sponsored intellectual discussion and mock debates on national issues.[7]

The tone of such events fit well into an academic environment still governed by rules that modern college students would find hard to imagine. As David Steigerwald has pointed out, universities of the time "exercised the right of *in loco parentis* and regulated the lives of their students, separating the sexes and imposing curfews." The culture of proscription carried over to the students themselves. The student paper, for example, published tips about the "social etiquette" of proper campus attire. Though these rules provoked some chafing, they prompted little change as the vast majority of students did not care enough to organize against them—students attended IU to graduate, not agitate.[8] In a growing campus population throughout the 1960s, the *IDS* estimated that the radical Left had never boasted more than one hundred members. IU was "not a Berkeley" in the heart of the conservative Midwest. The "greenbaggers" were the fringe, and they knew it. As the Young People's Socialist League readily admitted in 1965, they were "well aware that we represent a minority point of view on the IU campus. We often find it depressingly difficult to find a sympathetic audience here in Indiana."[9]

More than any other, the issue of anti-communism brought an end to this complacency. For the group that would come to be known as the New Right, the U.S. needed to stand firmly against the Red menace at home and abroad. Those who organized the New Left, on the other hand, worried about domestic witch-hunts and an activist foreign policy that seemed blind to social justice. What both groups feared—perhaps even more than each other—was a continuation of what they saw as complacency in the face of real problems. The extension of these political antagonisms to the nation's growing involvement in Vietnam—and to the growing likelihood that American youth would be called to military service—lay at the heart of a rising tide of campus political activism.[10]

The leading organization on the campus Right was the Young Americans for Freedom (YAF). Established in September 1960 by a group of conservative thinkers gathered at the home of William F. Buckley, Jr., author of *God and Man at Yale* (1951), YAF was staunchly anti-communist and supportive of the domino theory. The IU chapter of YAF grew under the leadership of Thomas Charles Huston, a native of Logansport, Indiana, who completed his undergraduate work at IU in 1963 and then went on to attend law school in Bloomington. Recognized by historians of the Left and Right as a top-notch conservative thinker, Huston made anti-communism the center of his campus activism, believing that those who protested the war in Vietnam only boosted the morale of the nation's chief enemy. Like his YAF colleagues throughout the nation, Huston felt that activists on the Left underestimated the stakes in Vietnam and wrongly minimized the communist threat.[11]

In this crusade against international communism and its campus defenders, Huston found an ideological ally in Robert Turner. Like many young conservatives, Turner, who was the son of a military officer, first became involved in politics by working for Barry Goldwater's 1964 presidential campaign. A member of the campus Reserve Officers Training Corps (ROTC), Turner took a special interest in Vietnam. Due to his connections to the Intercollegiate Society of Individualists, he became IU chapter president of the Society's Conservative League, which, under the direction of history graduate student Phil Crane, had blossomed into the second largest chapter in the nation (behind only the University of Texas). Like its parent organization, the Conservative League devoted itself to educating college students through the distribution of literature and by holding intellectual debates on current issues. In addition, Turner helped form the League's activist arm, Students for an Orderly Society.

Both groups worked with YAF to advance a conservative agenda, sharing ideas and members.[12]

Following the advice of conservative leaders like Buckley, Huston and Turner distanced themselves from the ultra-conservative John Birch Society (founded in 1958 in Indianapolis) because of its extreme, and at times laughable, conspiracy theories, including one that identified President Eisenhower as an agent of international communism. Nevertheless, the Birchers actively engaged IU's campus community. In early 1966, Birchers who were students at IU formally requested that the Indiana General Assembly investigate "communist and pro communist" groups at the university—specifically the Students for a Democratic Society (SDS, founded nationally in 1962 and at IU in 1965) and IU's new W. E. B. Du Bois Club.[13]

The Bircher request quickly led to a controversy over free speech, drawing reactions from all sides. The openly socialist Du Bois Club contended that its Bloomington chapter was being investigated not only for past communist ties, but also as part of the Johnson administration's effort to block campus debates about the war in Vietnam. IU officials quickly pledged themselves to defending free speech, but attempted to sidestep local confrontation by suggesting that the Federal Bureau of Investigation, rather than the state legislature, investigate the matter. The *IDS* editorial board acknowledged the possibility that the Birchers were correct about the club, but asked that people not be so "close[d] minded" about new campus groups before they could even get under way. This stance brought forth a flurry of student letters throughout the month: Judy Lowery blasted the *IDS* for not giving the Right the same intellectual credit it extended to the Left; Thomas Pickering called on liberals to wake up to the dangers posed by communism.[14]

The decision of the IU chapter of the DuBois Club to sponsor communist speakers—including national Communist Party head Herbert Aptheker—forced IU administrators to decide if the group should be banned. Surprisingly, student activists from the Right and Left did not think so. Turner announced publicly in the *IDS* that, while he believed the Du Bois Club to be a communist organization, he also felt that IU students would not join. Firmly committed to the value of student protest, Turner argued that the government lacked the right to halt the formation of a group, no matter what its ideas were, because ideas could be safely debated. When the university at last suspended the Du Bois Club in September 1966, an estimated five hundred students protested at a rally featuring speakers from the SDS, Young Democrats, and Conservative League—all calling for the club to be reinstated. Though members of the campus Left have argued that the club was destroyed by the machinations of the FBI, Turner maintains that the Du Bois Club folded once it could no longer claim persecution by the Right and oppression by the government.[15]

By 1965, the escalation of the conflict in Vietnam had shifted the focus of many conservatives' fears from domestic to international communism, especially in terms of its threat to the people of South Vietnam. Increasingly, conservatives both spoke and demonstrated in support of the war effort (including, as we have seen, in Dunn Meadow). On campus, Bob Turner helped lead the 450-member Student Committee for Victory in Vietnam, which promoted North Vietnamese liberation from the communists. YAF leader Tom Huston took a special interest in anti-communism in Asia, in part because Red Chinese troops had killed his missionary uncle prior to World War II. With his appointment to the post of national YAF chairman in 1965, Huston brought his zeal to a national arena, arguing that South Vietnam needed to be given the opportunity to function as a free and democratic country. As the war went on, YAF eventually took a public stance against the draft (advocating the creation of an all-volunteer army), but conservatives never abandoned the idea of total victory in Vietnam.[16]

To fight against communism abroad implied contending with its defenders at home. Campus efforts in support of the war were countered by the Committee to End the War in Vietnam, a discussion group that maintained that the war was being fought at the behest of major corporations and that only socialism, by taking companies out of politics once and for all, could bring peace. At IU, these sentiments found expression in the picketing of on-campus job recruiters representing such defense-related companies as Dow Chemical and General Electric, as well as the Central Intelligence Agency. As Huston later recalled in response to such actions, "the gauntlet was down and our job was to support our country and its efforts . . . and to show that the [anti-war] protestors weren't the only people that had an opinion."[17]

During the 1965–1966 school year, campus protests about Vietnam became increasingly common and contentious. When General Maxwell Taylor, the U.S. ambassador to South Vietnam, spoke at IU, he was greeted by two very different groups. One, a "Support Senator Hartke" rally, advanced Indiana Senator Vance Hartke's "extricate don't escalate" strategy towards the war. The other, led by YAF and Students for an Orderly Society, aimed to demonstrate to the general that the "vast majority" of IU students supported him in the war effort. A similar encounter accompanied the campus visit of former Vice President Richard Nixon in October 1965. The following May, when the director of the Selective Service spoke at IU, some 2,000 protestors, both pro and con, clashed in Dunn Meadow, where, separated by the Jordan River, they hurled comments—and eggs—at one another.[18]

Divisions among students over the war found other manifestations as well. In October 1965 the Young Democrats and Young Republicans jointly proposed a campus referendum on American policies in Vietnam. SDS called the war blatant "imperialism" and contended that the United States was responsible for more atrocities than the communists. Senior class president Jim Kittle pushed for the student senate to authorize a "Bleed-In" blood drive on campus to show support for the war effort by benefiting American forces in Vietnam. After what the *IDS* called "the vehement protests of Guy Loftman," a fellow senator and head of the campus SDS chapter, the senate voted a compromise that allowed donors to indicate whether they wanted their blood sent to Vietnam or not. When the drive was over it was clear where the participants stood: of the 1,276 pints collected, nearly 1,000 were earmarked for Southeast Asia.[19]

A little over a year after the Bleed-In debate, Turner announced that he was leaving the IU Conservative League to become state chairman of the National Student Committee for Victory in Vietnam—a move that gave him a larger role in shaping the response to anti-war demonstrators, as well as time to write a book about why the U.S. needed to fight to victory in Vietnam.[20] In April 1967, Turner helped bring together the Students for a Free Society, Young Republicans, and the IU and state YAF organizations into a Victory in Vietnam march, which took place in Indianapolis's Military Park alongside a previously scheduled SDS-sponsored anti-war rally. Turner, holding a pro-war sign, attempted to record some of the anti-war speakers. One of the peace activists told him that he had no right to be there and punched through the speaker of his recorder. Turner later told the *IDS*, "it's unfortunate that the champions of free speech should resort to violence." Anti-war activists protested a pro-war rally held in Bloomington later that same month, and the protest/counter-protest pattern continued for the duration of the conflict.[21]

Increasingly, members of the campus Right looked to new ways of winning support that bypassed the familiar politics of public demonstrations. Into this moment stepped R. Emmett Tyrrell, a swimmer who had come to IU from Chicago in 1961 and stayed on after his graduation to begin graduate work in history. Like other IU conservatives, Tyrrell felt that right-wing voices on campus were either not heard or not taken seriously by the *IDS*. Sparse coverage of many conservative events prompted some to challenge the paper's selectivity. Left-leaning activists, expressing similar dissatisfaction from the opposite end of the political spectrum, had reacted by forming *The Spectator* in 1966. In 1967, working from an old house near Ellettsville nicknamed "The Establishment," Tyrrell founded *The Alternative*—a publication designed to inject some fun into campus politics and to retake the campus from SDS and "return student government to the moderate majority." Tyrrell vowed to critique, in Menckenesque fashion, "the perverse, the brutal, and the slightly goof ball" qualities of the New Left. "Are you tired," he began in the first issue, "are you utterly exhausted by the ineffable politicization of everything in Bloomington from sex to the delinquencies issuing from some neurotic girl's creative gut? Are your ears, are they fatigued by Radio Free Kirkwood's tedious pledges of forthcoming liberation? If this sympathy of the absurd has disturbed your slumber welcome to the cloyed audience of *The Alternative*. For the harshly modulated hokum of IU's pestiferous totalitarians has annoyed us also."[22]

The startup faced problems that gradually lessened over time. The paper's $300 monthly publication cost meant that sales needed to reach 1,200–1,500 copies simply to break even. With no institutional support to fall back on, *The Alternative* struggled, but gradually began to receive encouragement and support. The *IDS* noted that the fledgling paper "has made a definite contribution to the field of student journalism at IU" and praised Tyrrell's staff for their readiness to poke fun at "this sometimes pompous business of journalism." Eventually, the paper received money from the Lilly Foundation, and from the Yale-educated editor of the conservative *Indianapolis News*, M. Stanton Evans, who became the staff's advisor. Because of its anti-communist views, the paper could also count on the support of many older faculty members who believed in the threat posed by communism and whose brand of patriotism irked their younger colleagues. In time, *The Alternative* team started a "Beer and Pizza Marching Society," which drew conservative students from around Indiana, including future Vice President Dan Quayle (then a student at DePauw University in Greencastle), to Indianapolis for dinner and drinks. *The Alternative* eventually provided conservatives with a solid base at IU and allowed them to win monetary support from around the state, thereby enabling them to bring to campus such nationally prominent conservative speakers as *National Review* editor William F. Buckley, Jr.[23]

The creation of *The Alternative* and *The Spectator* marked an escalation of both the rhetoric and the actions of campus partisans. After several groups staged a sit-in at Ballantine Hall demanding the creation of an African American studies department, conservatives responded by occupying the Well House and calling for the creation of an Irish studies department. After a rash of "pieing" incidents at public events nationally by members of the Left, Tyrrell orchestrated a Right-wing emulation with a farcical twist. "Dr. Rudolph Montag," purportedly a Columbia University professor, came to visit IU to speak on the "social problem." As a group of one hundred people watched, a member of the wrestling team stood up, yelled "God damn commie," and threw a pie at the visiting "academic." The IU administration discovered the joke only after it tried to apologize to Columbia officials.[24]

Public antics and debate occasionally gave way to more serious threats. In 1968, for example, an anti-war protester let off a stink bomb in the vicinity of military recruiters visiting the Indiana Memorial Union. Later, a fire broke out in the military section of the library, an act of vandalism for which no one was ever punished. John Von Kannon and John Baden, conservative graduate students at the time, recall receiving death threats when they refused to take part in the various campus boycotts. Looking back, conservative activists recall feeling frustrated by the university administration's mindset at times, but do not recall feeling persecuted. Theirs was simply an uphill battle.[25]

Student activists of the 1960s also found a battleground in campus politics. One thing that is often missing in the discussion of the student movement is the "student" part of the equation. Most members of the student body were students first and activists second, if they were activists at all. Students from all points along the political spectrum could agree on, and work together to promote, a number of causes. Indeed, in students' eyes, campus issues nearly always ranked above the debate over Vietnam, despite the more intense media coverage given the war. The same student senate that supported the Bleed-In, for example, supported ending prescribed visiting hours for women. An even greater number of students, it should be noted, abstained from political debate no matter the issue or level. Well into the 1960s, the vast majority remained apathetic to what was going on in the world around them. They had, it seems, other things to do.[26]

By the mid-1960s the situation on the Bloomington campus was beginning to change. Actual campus political parties were emerging—parties intended to last for longer than a single academic year. Each spring students elected a student body president, vice president, and senators to represent them on campus during the following school year and serve as liaison to the university board of trustees and administrators. The dominant parties at IU were Action, whose support lay in the campus Greek system, and Tryus, which garnered its support mostly in the dormitories. Action won the 1964 election, then swept to another victory the following year after Tryus was hit by academic problems. In 1966

Tryus won the presidency, while Action held the senate. And yet, as important as these elections were to participants, they only prompted about one-third of the student body to vote.[27]

Low voter turnout could be an advantage, however. Left-leaning activists believed that if they could mobilize and extend their base, they could take control of student government. In the spring of 1966, campus SDS chairman Guy Loftman organized the Progressive Reform Party (PRP), which drafted a platform calling for more student control of the university. Together with Robin Hunter, a graduate student from Canada and cofounder of IU's SDS chapter, Loftman was ready to craft a new style of campus politics.[28]

Campus conservatives did not take the Loftman challenge very seriously at first. Action and Tryus, they reasoned, had similar students'-rights platforms. Turner, who doubted if Loftman could hold his own in the campaign, believed that Loftman was really a proxy candidate for Hunter, whom the conservative found to be both "bright and articulate." When Loftman claimed to have Turner's support, the conservative fired off a letter to the *IDS* noting that, while he and Loftman saw eye-to-eye on many issues, the election of the SDS chairman as student body president would do IU more harm than good. But the Loftman bandwagon was rolling. The SDS leader received the tentative endorsement of the *IDS*, which argued that student government was losing "good members" and was in need of some shaking up.[29]

Despite conservative criticism, Loftman won a three-way race by energizing his base and successfully reaching out to the increasing number of students who were moving off campus; Tryus and Action split the remaining votes generated from their usual constituencies. The degree to which Loftman won personal, but not political, support is indicated by the fact that while PRP candidates contested a majority of the thirty-three senate seats they succeeded in capturing only five. Further, with just over 40 percent of students voting in the election, and with fewer than half of all votes cast going to PRP, the *IDS* cautioned that Loftman was not a majority choice for president and would likely find himself caught between the interests of his party and those of the student body.[30]

Loftman's victory was part of a wider trend of New Left campus government electoral conquests at Big 10 schools, including Northwestern, Michigan, Michigan State, and Wisconsin. According to the *IDS*, moderates held office in Illinois, Ohio State, and Minnesota, with Right or CenterRight parties in control of only Purdue and Iowa. Yet this was also a fractious time for the Left and for SDS in particular. Nationally, the group was increasingly torn between those pushing for a more aggressive stance against the war and those who continued to debate ideological issues of socialism and anarchy. The group's subsequent campaign to remove the ROTC from the Bloomington campus met with resistance from university chancellor Herman B Wells, as well as from numerous letter-writers to the *IDS*. And while Loftman argued that he was ready to work with the senate, the SDS asserted that it controlled the PRP's legislative agenda.[31]

The Alternative quickly seized on the PRP's ties to more radical groups like SDS. The paper charged Loftman with acting on the belief that "student government should DO something for the students—whether the students like it or not." "Who," asked Tyrrell and his colleagues, "came to be governed? Did not some come to gain education?" Loftman's opponents grew increasingly harsh in the year to come. *The Alternative* called him "the pink eyed man of destiny," and once remarked that "we did not make guy loftman the butt of ridicule, God did, and as we are but the humble servants of the Lord we must remark on him and the pile of animated garbage festering around him." John Galt accused Loftman of suffering from a "multiple personality disorder," maintaining that the student body president assumed the mantle of leadership only when it served his purposes, that he utilized his title to garner attention while pretending not to, and that he claimed to be a man of the people while constantly seeking more power for himself.[32]

Loftman tried to steer a middle-Left course amidst this partisanship. He made a point of establishing his disapproval of the campus drug culture and stressed his focus on giving students more control "over the decisions which affect their lives," such as rules governing women's hours. Loftman, who hoped to use the quiet summer session to begin implementing his program, quickly found himself facing a roadblock in the person of Rock Winchell. Winchell, a senior from Jasper, fought against the seating of PRP senators who were not actually enrolled for the summer session. His opposition forced a campus referendum, which he won, much to the dismay of Loftman. (Demonstrating that student apathy hardly took the summer off, less than one out of every twelve students on campus bothered to vote in the summer of 1967).[33]

Loftman also spent the summer trying to gain a greater understanding of the university's finances. Based on his study, he decided to take aim at one particular proposed expenditure: the construction of a new basketball arena, to be named Assembly Hall. Despite support from the IU administration, the Student Athletic Board, and the *IDS*, Loftman questioned the wisdom of asking students to pay for a facility that many would never use. In a series of open forums across campus, Winchell and YAF member James Bopp, Jr., began debating Loftman, arguing that a "well rounded atmosphere" was essential to the university experience and that an institution like IU would always have facilities or departments that not every student would use. Mark Watson (the president of IU YAF) and other Loftman opponents also bombarded the *IDS* with letters in support of the project. Today, Bopp recalls the university's decision to proceed with the project as a serious blow to Loftman's presidency.[34]

Campus conservatives worked to make sure that SDS would not be able to repeat its success with PRP in the 1968 elections. Supported by other members of student government, including Jim Durkott and Gary Kovener, Winchell merged the two older parties into a new one, Impact. The leaders of the new party appointed floor and dorm captains and instituted a membership fee, ensuring the party plenty of money to use on campus.[35] Hunter and Loftman minced few words in their critique of the new party. The student body president, perhaps smarting from his Assembly Hall defeat, claimed that Impact had no basis for being and—unlike the PRP—no goals of its own. In the same speech he also took the opportunity to blast women for not working harder to end parietals and to criticize the student body in general for not supporting his policies. Loftman, who tried to interest students in campus governance, had discovered the very real lesson that winning an election did not guarantee the success of a party's agenda once in power.[36]

In the meantime, 600 delegates waged a "chaotic" battle over nominations at Impact's first convention, ultimately settling on two Greek candidates—Alpha Tau Omega's Ted Najam and Phi Kappa Psi's Paul Helmke—as the party's ticket for student body president and vice president, respectively. Neither Najam nor Helmke belonged to YAF or to Tyrrell's circle. Najam in particular was no conservative, and Tyrrell and other members of the Right watched as he drifted further and further left in the months to come, while the *IDS* later commented that he seemed "to have taken on in some part the ideology of PRP." But this was campus politics, and the Right's goal was to beat SDS, not to run an ideologue of its own.[37]

In the campaign that followed, PRP was outmatched at every step. Impact's coffers were so full that it could afford to take out one advertisement after another in the *IDS*. The Right's proxy party focused on the lifestyle differences between their candidates and the "hippies" of PRP. Impact officials said they planned to spend about $800 on the campaign, while PRP had barely a quarter of that sum at its disposal. On election night, Impact garnered 4,666 votes to PRP's 3,703. The *IDS* credited Impact "image" versus PRP's, as well as a strong town vote, for its victory.[38]

The victory would not last long. Over the next year the more conservative Bopp challenged Najam and Helmke for being too liberal. Helmke invited Bopp to run with him in 1969, but the YAF member chose instead to run against

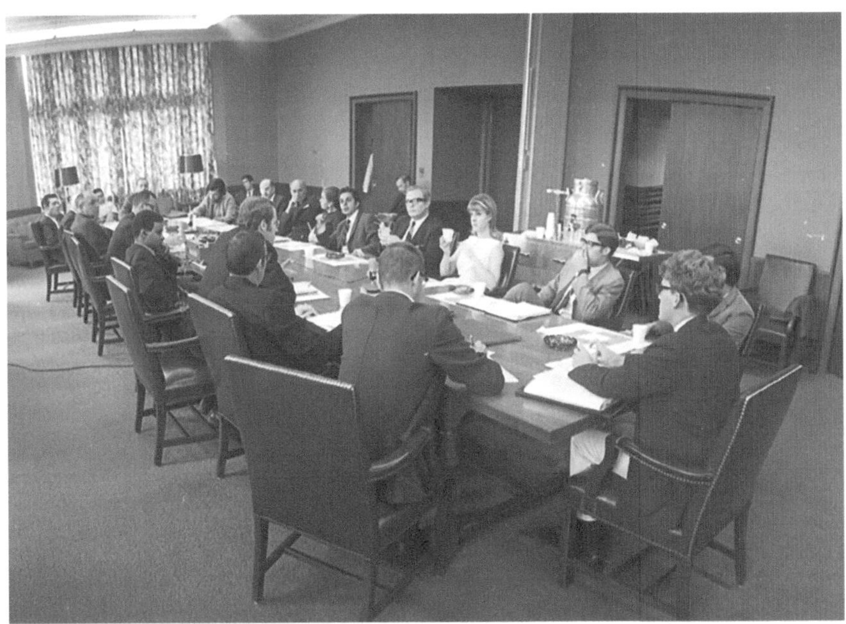

A May 1969 meeting between members of the IU Board of Trustees, administrators, and student leaders after a lock-in protest at Ballantine Hall on the Bloomington campus. Student body president was Paul Helmke, a conservative Republican who would later serve three terms as mayor of Fort Wayne, Indiana. *Courtesy IU News Bureau Photograph Collection, Indiana University Archives.*

him. Helmke then opted to leave the party and run as an independent, taking with him a good chunk of Impact's base. Helmke told the *IDS* that he had grown tired of the dealmaking and compromising of party politics, and that he believed that the majority of the student body preferred a more centrist candidate. It was up to Bopp to try to hold Impact together; he even went door-to-door to drum up support. Despite this effort, the turnout at the 1969 convention was much smaller than the year before, and the morale of the party was low.[39] While Tyrrell viewed Helmke as having drifted leftward, Helmke's tactics and stands on the issues were not far from Bopp's. Meanwhile, the left, too, had splintered, with Loftman throwing his support behind Mel Yancey of the United Student Movement rather than Russell Block of the Revolutionary Students Party. As far as the campus was concerned, Helmke had successfully positioned himself firmly in the Center. The *IDS* endorsed him, as did Najam on the eve of the election. Helmke emerged the clear winner, taking 4,288 votes to Yancey's 2,090. Bopp finished third with 1,516; Impact was finished as a party.[40]

Helmke wanted to use his time as president to seek change without tearing the campus apart. To do so, he willingly borrowed tactics from both the Left and the Right. In the wake of widespread worries over rising student fees, he organized public meetings and even urged students to boycott classes so they could go home and tell their parents about the problem. In Helmke's own subsequent assessment, such "coat and tie" activism proved largely successful. Others agreed. The *IDS* credited Najam's success, as well as Helmke's, to Loftman's radicalism. As mainstream student leaders, they had proven able to exact reforms from an IU administration apprehensive about the prospect of more Loftmans in its future. Later, looking back on his time in office, Najam would credit his and Helmke's victories to the idealism and "activism" of the period—characteristics that, as the 1970s dawned, would diminish considerably.[41]

And yet two years of centrist campus government did little to halt the renewed divisiveness reflected in the 1970 victory of Keith Parker. A field lieutenant of the Black Panthers, Parker told the *IDS* that he believed the world to be divided between "reactionary Pigs" and "progressive People," with only a small minority unaffiliated in the center. When asked specifically about right-wing activists, Parker said that he hoped to sponsor an education weekend that would "expose all their fascist tactics." Despite such rhetoric, only 20 percent of students voted, suggesting that student apathy remained strong.[42]

However, within weeks of his election Parker announced his plans to visit Hanoi, via Moscow, on a student peace mission—a proposal that brought conservative criticism from campus to the state house. Though the student senate was unable or unwilling to condemn the trip, the *IDS* editorial board called Parker "selfish" for putting his own interests above those of the university. State Senator (and future governor) Robert Orr not only condemned the trip but also asked IU students how they could have elected Parker president in the first place. Several members of the Indiana General Assembly spoke of raising IU tuition as a measure both to punish, and to reexert control over, the Bloomington campus. In sum, Parker's trip did little to enhance the campus's reputation among a cohort of Indiana politicians who already tended to group any call for students' rights together with antiwar protest into evidence of an "ominous Left" that threatened America's very existence.[43]

The controversial student body president attempted damage control, speaking to IU students and the Bloomington press upon his return. However, letters to the *IDS* largely ridiculed the trip, asking why Parker spent so much time working on a non-binding peace treaty between American and North

Vietnamese students when real issues awaited his attention back in Bloomington. Parker responded that the war did affect students; to argue that his trip was the sole cause of the legislature's threatened tuition increase was, he contended, to ignore the economic troubles in which the state was already enmired.[44]

The trip controversy proved a boon to the campus Right. Von Kannon exposed the money trail that had funded Parker's trip, tracing it to the national Black Panther Party and surmising that Parker had actually acted as the Party's representative to Hanoi, not simply as a concerned American college student. The funding for the trip had come, more specifically, from Brown County resident Larry Canada, who owned the lot on Kirkwood Avenue that had once been the site of the Black Market and the Panther Party's local headquarters.[45]

Fearful of state intervention, the Board of Trustees moved to rein in student government, voting to end the mandatory $.50 student government fee. In the ensuing debate, Parker shifted discussion from the scandal around his trip towards the trustees' attack on student government, leaving his opponents perplexed. Von Kannan rejoiced at the lifting of the tax, but in his *IDS* column, he also pointed out that the trustees' decision to revoke the fee had taken Parker off the hook for his Vietnam trip.[46]

When Parker's term came to an end, the editors of the *IDS* found little benefit in his time in office. While crediting him with establishing a student legal service, the paper believed that Parker's polarizing presidency had done more harm than good to IU. To his claim to having given future presidents an "alternative" path to follow in office, the *IDS* reported that Parker had only reduced the power of student government by antagonizing state lawmakers, IU administrators, and a good number of students.[47]

To Von Kannan, Parker's departure signaled the end of fun in campus politics. The frontrunners in the 1971 student elections were, as he pointed out, individuals with a long interest in politics, not the amorphous "people" whom Parker had claimed as his power base. All told, there were fourteen presidential tickets; and with only 25 percent of the campus voting, the election required a run-off election that was itself a mess of legal maneuvering, including the elimination and reinstatement of several tickets. The eventual winner was Mary Scifres, the first woman to be elected to the position in the university's history, who promised to make student government more open to the student body.[48]

Scifres maintained a liberal platform but managed to do so in a manner that seemed, to conservatives like Von Kannan, less confrontational than Parker's. The student body president would advocate student support of such causes as Ralph Nader's Public Interest Research Group, the (now voluntary) student government fee, activist Angela Davis's legal defense fund, and abortion rights.

Scifres presented her viewpoint in an *IDS* column that was more informational than directive in tone. Von Kannan, the most public conservative on campus, sometimes used his own *IDS* column to debate Scifres's stance on abortion, the war, and other issues. As the journalistic sparring between the two suggests, sharp divisions remained between Right and Left, but both sides had come to realize how little student government could, in fact, accomplish in one year. By the mid-l970s, the *IDS* found "little evidence of IU's recent turmoil," and campus elections drew less of the attention they had attracted in earlier years.[49]

If campus politics was a game, it was still a game that could prepare a person for serious work. Richard Nixon's election in 1968 provided conservative campus activists with an opportunity to take their cause from the campus to the halls of power. One of the first to make the transition from student activist to political operative was Tom Huston. After graduating from IU's law school (1966), he served first as an Army officer attached to the Defense Intelligence Agency (1967–1969) and then as an associate counsel to President Nixon during a period that saw escalating violence at Kent State, Jackson State, and other college campuses. Nixon responded to the threat by asking Congress for 1,000 additional FBI agents to provide "instant action" in the case of campus turmoil. Huston, from his background as a local, state, and national YAF leader, agreed that "the campus is the battleground of the revolutionary movement." Believing further that groups such as the Black Panthers and the Weathermen (the anarchist spinoff group of SDS), working on-campus and off, were plotting to overthrow the federal government, the president called upon Huston to draft a scheme for domestic intelligence gathering.[50]

The former student activist urged Nixon to utilize YAF to confront campus radicals, but the president was reluctant to do so, perhaps because of his own misgivings about the conservative movement.[51] Ultimately, Huston's proposal—now known as the Huston Plan—called on the White House to centralize all domestic intelligence gathering into a new agency and to authorize the use of wiretaps and other forms of surveillance of suspected subversive groups. To those who contended that the plan infringed on civil liberties, Huston argued that bugging a group to prevent a terrorist act was hardly the same thing as beating a confession out of an innocent person. Nor was he alone in his zeal. In a syndicated column that appeared in the *IDS*, Barry Goldwater had likewise argued that enforcing law and order should not be construed as a repression of civil liberties. Nevertheless, it was fierce opposition from FBI director J. Edgar Hoover (who opposed centralization), rather than from civil rights advocates within the Nixon White House, that eventually defeated the proposal.[52]

Other veterans of the IU Right influenced the evolution of national conservative politics from the Nixon era through the Reagan revolution of the 1980s.[53] By 1974, Nixon's last year in office, R. Emmett Tyrrell's *Alternative* had grown into a regional, campus equivalent to Buckley's *National Review*. That year Tyrrell borrowed from his campus competitors and renamed his publication *The Spectator*; a decade later, feeling that the conservative moment had arrived, he moved his operation (now *The American Spectator*) to Washington, D.C. From his place in the nation's capitol Tyrrell challenged the Clinton administration during the 1990s by highlighting the president's financial scandals and extra-marital affairs. Phil Crane, organizer of IU's Conservative League, also contributed to the Republican ascendancy. Originally elected to fill the congressional seat vacated by Donald Rumsfeld when Rumsfeld signed on as an economic adviser to President Nixon, Crane served the Illinois 8th District from 1969 until his defeat in 2004.

Other former student activists, such as John Baden and John Von Kannon, entered the conservative foundations and think tanks that, in the words of one conservative commentator, "helped to transform the terms of political debate" in the 1980s. Jim Kittle became a successful businessman and now leads the Indiana Republican Party. Robert Turner is now a law professor at the University of Virginia, and James Bopp and Tom Huston practice law in Terre Haute and Indianapolis, respectively. The moderates who allied themselves to the Right also made marks on the political scene: Ted Najam rose from circuit judge to the Indiana Court of Appeals, while Paul Helmke went home to Fort Wayne and served the city as its mayor.[54]

Looking back on their time in Bloomington, these one-time student activists argue that as New Deal-era liberalism collapsed, as the old consensus establishment gave way and the New Left fell apart, they stepped in to fill the breach. While SDS activists had questioned what it meant to be an American, YAF members had prepared their agenda to be implemented via the political process. With other leaders of the New Right, they learned their lessons during the Goldwater campaign, captured the Republican Party, implemented their ideas under Nixon and Reagan, and have now helped to define American politics for forty years.[55] In government, in political discourse, and in academia, the conservatives who came of age at IU in the 1960s have left their mark on the state and nation.

JASON S. LANTZER is assistant director of the University Honors Program, Butler University, Indianapolis. This article originally appeared in volume 101, June 2005.

NOTES

1. *Indiana Daily Student*, March 10, 11, 12, 13, 1965; hereafter cited as *IDS*.

2. "Restless Youth," U.S. Central Intelligence Agency report, September 1968, reproduced in *Declassified Documents Reference System* (Farmington Hills, Mich., 2005).

3. Mary Ann Wynkoop, *Dissent in the Heartland: The Sixties at Indiana University* (Bloomington, Ind., 2002); Martin Ridge, Byrum Carter, Keith S. Parker, Michael J. King, and Mary Ann Wynkoop, "Remembering Indiana University in the 1960s: Perspectives on *Dissent in the Heartland*," *Indiana Magazine of History* 99 (March 2003), 48–58. For treatment of conservative student protest see Kenneth Heineman, *Campus Wars: The Peace Movement at American State Universities in the Vietnam Era* (New York, 1993); David Steigerwald, *The Sixties and the End of Modern America* (New York, 1995), 273, 275; Gregory L. Schneider, *Cadres for Conservatism: Young Americans for Freedom and the Rise of the Contemporary Right* (New York, 1999).

4. Richard Hofstadter, *The Paranoid Style in American Politics and Other Essays* (New York, 1967).

5. Interviewees were selected from the ranks of conservative activists at IU in the 1960s. The process began with names identified by R. Emmett Tyrrell and from reports in the *IDS*, and the referral list lengthened as the interviewing progressed. Not all individuals could be located, nor did every contacted individual respond, notably Thomas Huston and M. Stanton Evans. Notes from the interviews and email exchanges will eventually be deposited in an appropriate archive.

6. James Bopp, Jr., telephone interview with author, May 7, 2004; Robert E Turner, email to author, April 23, 2004; "Forum on American Conservatism," *American Historical Review*, 99 (April 1994), 409–52; Rick Perlstein, *Before the Storm: Barry Goldwater and the Unmaking of the American Consensus* (New York, 2001); John Micklethwait and Adrian Wooldridge, *The Right Nation: Conservative Power in America* (New York, 2004); Steigerwald, *The Sixties and the End of Modern America*, 273–74; Dominick Cavallo, *A Fiction of the Past: The Sixties in American History* (New York, 1999), 3, 6–7. For an example of the consensus establishment attempting to understand the Right, see Daniel Bell, ed., *The Radical Right* (New York, 1963).

7. Turner, email to author, April 23, 2004; *IDS*, October 28, November 2, 4, 1966.

8. Steigerwald, *The Sixties and the End of Modem America*, l; *IDS*, October 15, 1963, February 12, 1966. Bopp, telephone interview with author, May 9, 2003; Paul Helmke, telephone interview with author, April 28, 2004; R. Emmett Tyrrell, Jr., interview with author, April 22, 2003; Wynkoop, *Dissent in the Heartland*, 23–24, 137–41.

9. *IDS*, October 1, 1965, April 15, 1966. Tyrrell interview; Helmke interview; Wynkoop, *Dissent in the Heartland*, 43–44.

10. Tyrrell interview; John Andrew, "Pro-War and Anti-Draft: Young Americans for Freedom and the War in Vietnam," in Marc Jason Gilbert, ed., *The Vietnam War on Campus: Other Voices, More Distant Drums* (Westport, Conn., 2001), 3–5; Todd Gitlin, *The Sixties: Years of Hope, Days of Rage* (New York, 1989), 62–63.

11. Turner, email to author, April 23, 2004; Tyrrell interview; John Von Kannon, email to author, April 28, 2004; *IDS*, September 28, 1963, November 6, 1964, October 22, 1965, January 17, 1967; *Indianapolis Star, June* 1, 1966. On the origins and growth of YAF, see Schneider, *Cadres for Conservatism*, 32; Andrew, "Pro-War and Anti-Draft," 1–2; James T. Patterson, *Grand Expectations: The United States, 1945–1974* (New York, 1996), 455. On Huston see John Robert Greene, *The Limits of Power: The Nixon and Ford Administrations* (Bloomington, Ind., 1992), 34; Wynkoop, *Dissent in the Heartland*, 13–14. YAF's popularity is evidenced by the fact that in 1964 it added 5,400 new members, while SDS possessed a total membership of approximately 1,500. Micklethwait and Wooldridge, *The Right Nation*, 51.

12. Turner, emails to author, April 25, May 23, 2003, April 23, 2004; *IDS*, March 3, 1964, January 6, March 16, April 12, 1966. On ISI see Schneider, *Cadres for Conservatism*, 16–17; Perlstein, *Before the Storm*, 70–75. The group has since renamed itself the Intercollegiate Studies Institute.

13. *IDS*, March 20, 1964, February 2, 1965, February 3, March 2, 1966; "Antiwar and Antidraft Agitation Continues," J. Edgar Hoover to the White House Situation Room, cable, July 26, 1968, *Declassified Documents*; Wynkoop, *Dissent in the Heartland*, 14–18. The *IDS* reported that a similar inquiry in 1964, carried out under the authority of a 1951 Anti-Subversives Act, resulted in the dissolution of the Young Socialist Alliance at IU. *IDS*, February 18, 1964. However, while the topic of anti-communism came up repeatedly in the Indiana Legislature during the late 1940s and early 1950s, and an anti-communist bill was proposed in 1951, the author found no reference to the passage of such an act. *Journal of the House of Representatives of the State of Indiana, 87th Session* (Indianapolis, 1951), 164, 343.

14. *IDS*, February 15, 23, 26, March 8, 11, 1966. The FBI labeled the Du Bois Club a front organization for the Communist Party, and Gitlin later characterized them as being "dominated by the children of Communist and fellow traveler activists." "W.E.B. Du Bois Clubs of America," FBI Report, February 1, 1967, *Declassified Documents*; Gitlin, *The Sixties*, 179.

15. *IDS*, April 29, May 3, 4, 1965, February 8, April 9, September 12, 17, 21, 23, 1966, February 22, 1967; Turner, emails to author, May 23, 2003, April 23, 2004; "W.E.B. Du Bois Clubs," *Declassified Documents*; Wynkoop, *Dissent in the Heartland*, 32–36, 71–73. On collaboration between Right and Left see Andrew, "Pro-War and Anti-Draft," 7.

16. Tyrrell interview; *IDS*, March 11, 13, 1965, October 7, 1967, January 9, 1968. On Huston see Schneider, *Cadres for Conservatism*, 97–98; on YAF's draft stance see Andrew, "Pro-War and Anti-Draft," 8–11; Bopp, telephone interview with author, May 7, 2004.

17. Huston, undated, in Schneider, *Cadres for Conservatism*, 93; Helmke interview; *IDS*, February 17, 22, 1968, March 3, 1970; "Report on Civil Rights and Anti-war Movements," CIA report, December 1968, *Declassified Documents*. YAF appropriated this tactic in 1965 by protesting the Firestone Tire Company's proposed expansion into communist Romania, forcing the manufacturer to withdraw. Thomas C. Mann, telegram, April 17, 1965, *Declassified Documents*.

18. Turner, email to author, May 23, 2003; *IDS*, March 13, October 19, 1965, January 8, February 25, May 3, 1966.

19. *IDS*, October 8, 16, 29, 30, November 4, 6, 1965. During the debate, Kittle and Loftman also clashed over the SDS's on-campus advocacy of draft-dodging.

20. *IDS*, April 6, September 30, 1967. Turner's eventual tome—published two years after U.S. withdrawal—argued that North Vietnam ran the war in the South, thereby countering New Left claims that the war resulted from a U.S.-supported puppet government oppressing the Vietnamese people for imperialistic ends. Turner, *Vietnamese Communism: Its Origins and Development* (Stanford, Calif., 1975); Gitlin, *The Sixties*, 261–82.

21. Turner, in *IDS*, April 11, 1967; Turner, email to author, April 23, 2003; Tyrrell interview; *IDS*, April 6, 11, 15, 1967. For other examples of protest and counter-protest see *IDS*, February 22, 1968, October 8, 16, 1970, April 27, May 11, 1971; Wynkoop, *Dissent in the Heartland*, 40–41.

22. R. Emmett Tyrrell, Jr., *The Conservative Crack-Up* (New York, 1992), 21, 44–68; *The Alternative*, September 1967; Tyrrell interview; *IDS*, March 2, 1966, February 13, 1969; Schneider, *Cadres for Conservatism*, 110–16; Byron York, "The Life and Death of *The American Spectator*," *The Atlantic Monthly* 288 (November 2001), 91–105. On *The Spectator*, published in Bloomington from 1966–1970, see Wynkoop, *Dissent in the Heartland*, 155–63.

23. *IDS*, January 12, 1968; Tyrrell interview; *IDS*, December 3, 1964, January 11, 12, February 8, October 12, 16, 17, 18, 1968; Tyrrell, *The Conservative Crack-Up*, 57–58, 64–65, 232–33; Pro-Schneider, *Cadres for Conservatism*, 115; Steigerwald, *The Sixties and the End of Modem America*, 276. In many ways, Buckley served as the ultimate role model for Tyrrell: a student rebel who had gone on to found a successful conservative magazine.

24. Von Kannon interview; *The Alternative*, November–December 1967. Later, Bloomington antiwar activists used a bakery missile on Clark Kerr, the former president of the University of California, when he spoke at the campus in 1969. Wynkoop, *Dissent in the Heartland*, 94–96.

25. John Baden, email to author, May 14, 2003; Bopp, telephone interview with author, May 7, 2004; Turner, email to author, April 23, 2004; Von Kannon interview; Von Kannon email; *IDS*, October 11, 17, 1968; Wynkoop, *Dissent in the Heartland*, 45; Heineman, *Campus Wars*, 3–5.

26. *IDS*, February 23, 1964, February 22, March 16, April 15, 1966; Wynkoop, *Dissent in the Heartland*, 22. On the lack of anti-war protest at another Indiana campus see Anthony o. Edmonds and Joel Shrock, "Fighting the War in the Heart of the Country: Anti-War Protest at Ball State University," in Gilbert, ed., *The Vietnam War on Campus*, 142–48.

27. Bopp, telephone interview with author, May 7, 2004; Helmke interview; *IDS*, October 1, 9, 1964, February 26, April 9, 1965, April 22, 1966.

28. *IDS*, October 5, 1965, March 16, 18, 21, 22, 1967; Wynkoop, *Dissent in the Heartland*, 23–30. Loftman entered JU as a Republican and joined a fraternity, but after visiting Europe he became a socialist and dedicated himself to New Left causes on the Bloomington campus. *Indianapolis News*, August 28, 1967.

29. Turner, emails to author, April 23, May 23, 2003, April 23, 2004; Helmke interview; *IDS*, March 31, 1965, April 12, 13, October 7, 1967, March 22, 1968.

30. Bopp, telephone interview with author, May 7, 2004; Helmke interview; *IDS*, April 14, 15, 1967; *Arbutus*, 75 (1968), 58–59.

31. *IDS*, April 20, 25, May 10, 1967, January 4, October 4, 29, 31, November 1, 1968, September 29, October 2, 15, 1970; Wynkoop, *Dissent in the Heartland*, 30–31, 69–70.

32. *The Alternative*, September 1967, October–November 1967, January–February 1968, April–May 1968; Galt in *IDS*, September 20, 1967.

33. *Indianapolis News*, August 28, 1967. *Bloomington Herald-Telephone*, April 20, 1967; *IDS*, July 7, 13, 14, 20, 22, 25, 27, 28, August 3, 1967.

34. Bopp, telephone interviews with author, May 9, 2003, May 7, 2004. *IDS*, July 18, 21, August 1, September 12, 13, 16, 19, 20, 21, 22, 23, 1967; *Indianapolis News*, August 28, 1967.

35. Bopp, telephone interview with author, May 9, 2003; Von Kannon interview; *IDS*, September 23, 26, 27, 28, 1967. Impact has been contrastingly characterized as both a "student conservative party" and as an apolitical student party. Schneider, *Cadres for Conservatism*, 115; Wynkoop, *Dissent in the Heartland*, 61.

36. *IDS*, September 26, 30, 1967, February 16, 1968.

37. *IDS*, October 3, 1968. Helmke interview; Tyrrell interview; *IDS*, March 5, 9, 20, 21, April 2, October 3, 1968; *Arbutus*, 76 (1969), 80–81; Wynkoop, *Dissent in the Heartland*, 64–67. Loftman supported the PRP nomination of Mark Oring,

who hinted that if elected he might shut down student government in order to force a showdown with the administration. *IDS*, March 14, 15, 1968.

38. *IDS*, April 3, 4, 5, 1968; Bopp, telephone interview with author, May 7, 2004; Helmke interview.

39. Bopp, telephone interview with author, May 9, 2003; Helmke interview; Tyrrell interview; *IDS*, March 20, 21, 22, 26, 27, April 8, 9, 1969, March 6, 1970.

40. Helmke interview; *IDS*, October 10, 1968, April 15, 16, 17, 19, 1969.

41. Helmke interview; *IDS*, April 15, 1969, April 10, 1972.

42. *IDS*, October 1, 28, 1970; *The Alternative*, May–June 1970; Tyrrell interview. For Wynkoop's account of Parker's presidency see *Dissent in the Heartland*, 102–108.

43. *IDS*, November 17, 18, 20, December 1, 2, 4, 7, 8, 9, 18, 1970; Helmke interview; Wynkoop, *Dissent in the Heartland*, 79.

44. *IDS*, January 5, 6, 7, 13, 1971; *Bloomington Herald-Telephone*, January 6, 7, 1971.

45. *IDS*, December 11, 1970. The Black Market was firebombed on December 26, 1968, allegedly by the local Ku Klux Klan, and the space is now home to People's Park. Wynkoop, *Dissent in the Heartland*, 128–31, 168–70, 176–78. Canada had drawn attention previously by taking out a full page in the *IDS* for an "Appeal to Reason" on Vietnam, which was blasted by the *IDS*, September 20, 23, 1967.

46. *IDS*, February 4, 9, 16, 1971.

47. *IDS*, May 28, 1971.

48. *IDS*, February 18, 26, May 13, 1971. See also ibid., April 24, May 5, 12, 15, 19, 20, 26, 1971.

49. *IDS*, April 10, 1972. See also ibid., October 14, 21, November 11, 19, 30, 1971, February 7, 14, April 13, 19, 1972; Wlady Pleszczynski, email to author, April 30, 2003.

50. Huston, in *Indianapolis Star*, June 3, September 23, 1973. For example, at a teach-in at IU in 1970, students were told that it was up to them to "stop the government" if the government would not stop the war in Vietnam. *IDS*, October 27, 1970.

51. Schneider, *Cadres for Conservatism*, 121, 149.

52. *IDS*, April 12, 1966, October 7, 9, November 5, 1970; *Indianapolis Star*, June 1, 1966, June 3, 1973. On the Huston Plan see Stephen E. Ambrose, *Nixon: The Triumph of a Politician, 1962–1972* (New York, 1989), 264–65, 362, 367–69; Greene, *Limits of Power*, 133; Joan Hoff, *Nixon Reconsidered* (New York, 1994), 20, 228, 277, 283–93; Steigerwald, *The Sixties and the End of Modem America*, 292–93; Ted Morgan, *Reds: McCarthyism in Twentieth-Century America* (New York, 2003), 586–94. Huston told the Star that he believed that Nixon's refusal to stand up to Hoover and implement the plan helped lead to the formation of the Plumbers

and to Watergate. That the Huston Plan became public knowledge at the height of Watergate did not help Huston's case or Nixon's reputation. Huston's complete testimony before Congress about the Plan can be found at http://www.aarclibrary.org/publib/church/reports/vol2/html/ChurchV2_0001a.htm.

53. That Reagan cultivated a closer relationship with the campus Right than did Nixon and Goldwater may help explain the increased prominence of former campus activists in the 1980s. Lou Cannon, *Governor Reagan: His Rise to Power* (New York, 2003), 271–96. YAF members commonly date their relationship with Reagan to a letter he wrote to YAF national chairman Ron Docksai requesting YAF support for Nixon's 1972 reelection campaign. Kiron K. Skinner, Annelise Anderson, and Martin Anderson, eds., *Reagan: A Life in Letters* (New York, 2003), 174–75.

54. Gregg Easterbrook, "Ideas Move Nations: How Conservative Think Tanks Have Helped to Transform the Terms of Political Debate," *The Atlantic Monthly* 257 (January 1986), 66–80. Baden is founder and chairman of the Foundation for Research on Economics and the Environment in Bozeman, Montana; Von Kannon is vice president and treasurer of the Heritage Foundation in Washington, D.C.

55. Pleszczynski email; Tyrrell interview; Von Kannon interview; *The Alternative*, May–June 1970; Steigerwald, *The Sixties and the End of Modem America*, 5; Mary C. Brennan, *Turning Right in the Sixties: The Conservative Capture of the GOP* (Chapel Hill, N.C., 1995); Schneider, *Cadres for Conservatism*, 1, 161–82; Cavallo, *A Fiction of the Past*, 60, 216; York, "The Life and Death of *The American Spectator*." Gitlin concluded that he and his fellow New Left activists largely failed to keep their part of the student activist movement going beyond the 1960s. Gitlin, *The Sixties*, 434–36; Gitlin, *The Whole World* is *Watching: Mass Media in the Making & Unmaking of the New Left* (Los Angeles, 1980).

Dawn Bakken is Associate Editor of the *Indiana Magazine of History,* a scholarly journal of state and midwestern history. She is author of *On This Day in Indianapolis History.*